Modern Critical Interpretations

James Joyce's
Ulysses

Modern Critical Interpretations

The Oresteia
Beowulf
The General Prologue to
   The Canterbury Tales
The Pardoner's Tale
The Knight's Tale
The Divine Comedy
Exodus
Genesis
The Gospels
The Iliad
The Book of Job
Volpone
Doctor Faustus
The Revelation of St.
   John the Divine
The Song of Songs
Oedipus Rex
The Aeneid
The Duchess of Malfi
Antony and Cleopatra
As You Like It
Coriolanus
Hamlet
Henry IV, Part I
Henry IV, Part II
Henry V
Julius Caesar
King Lear
Macbeth
Measure for Measure
The Merchant of Venice
A Midsummer Night's
   Dream
Much Ado About
   Nothing
Othello
Richard II
Richard III
The Sonnets
Taming of the Shrew
The Tempest
Twelfth Night
The Winter's Tale
Emma
Mansfield Park
Pride and Prejudice
The Life of Samuel
   Johnson
Moll Flanders
Robinson Crusoe
Tom Jones
The Beggar's Opera
Gray's Elegy
Paradise Lost
The Rape of the Lock
Tristram Shandy
Gulliver's Travels

Evelina
The Marriage of Heaven
   and Hell
Songs of Innocence and
   Experience
Jane Eyre
Wuthering Heights
Don Juan
The Rime of the Ancient
   Mariner
Bleak House
David Copperfield
Hard Times
A Tale of Two Cities
Middlemarch
The Mill on the Floss
Jude the Obscure
The Mayor of
   Casterbridge
The Return of the Native
Tess of the D'Urbervilles
The Odes of Keats
Frankenstein
Vanity Fair
Barchester Towers
The Prelude
The Red Badge of
   Courage
The Scarlet Letter
The Ambassadors
Daisy Miller, The Turn
   of the Screw, and
   Other Tales
The Portrait of a Lady
Billy Budd, Benito Cer-
   eno, Bartleby the Scriv-
   ener, and Other Tales
Moby-Dick
The Tales of Poe
Walden
Adventures of
   Huckleberry Finn
The Life of Frederick
   Douglass
Heart of Darkness
Lord Jim
Nostromo
A Passage to India
Dubliners
A Portrait of the Artist as
   a Young Man
Ulysses
Kim
The Rainbow
Sons and Lovers
Women in Love
1984
Major Barbara

Man and Superman
Pygmalion
St. Joan
The Playboy of the
   Western World
The Importance of Being
   Earnest
Mrs. Dalloway
To the Lighthouse
My Antonia
An American Tragedy
Murder in the Cathedral
The Waste Land
Absalom, Absalom!
Light in August
Sanctuary
The Sound and the Fury
The Great Gatsby
A Farewell to Arms
The Sun Also Rises
Arrowsmith
Lolita
The Iceman Cometh
Long Day's Journey Into
   Night
The Grapes of Wrath
Miss Lonelyhearts
The Glass Menagerie
A Streetcar Named
   Desire
Their Eyes Were
   Watching God
Native Son
Waiting for Godot
Herzog
All My Sons
Death of a Salesman
Gravity's Rainbow
All the King's Men
The Left Hand of
   Darkness
The Brothers Karamazov
Crime and Punishment
Madame Bovary
The Interpretation of
   Dreams
The Castle
The Metamorphosis
The Trial
Man's Fate
The Magic Mountain
Montaigne's Essays
Remembrance of Things
   Past
The Red and the Black
Anna Karenina
War and Peace

These and other titles in preparation

Modern Critical Interpretations

James Joyce's
Ulysses

Edited and with an introduction by
Harold Bloom
Sterling Professor of the Humanities
Yale University

Chelsea House Publishers
NEW YORK ◇ PHILADELPHIA

Printed and bound in the United States of America

10   9   8   7   6   5   4   3

∞ The paper used in this publication meets the minimum
requirements of the American National Standard for
Permanence of Paper for Printed Library Materials,
Z39.48–1984.

Library of Congress Cataloging-in-Publication Data
James Joyce's Ulysses.
    (Modern critical interpretations)
    Includes index.
    Summary: Critical essays published during the last twenty-
five years on Joyce's celebrated novel "Ulysses."
    1. Joyce, James, 1882–1941. Ulysses. [1. Joyce, James,
1882–1941. Ulysses. 2. English literature—Irish authors
History and criticism]   I. Bloom, Harold.   II. Series.
PR6019.09U6582   1987   823'.912   87-5830
ISBN 1–55546–021–6

Contents

Editor's Note / vii

Introduction / 1
    HAROLD BLOOM

The Backgrounds of *Ulysses* / 7
    RICHARD ELLMANN

Doing Things in Style: An Interpretation of "The Oxen of the Sun" in James Joyce's *Ulysses* / 25
    WOLFGANG ISER

Ithaca / 39
    A. WALTON LITZ

The Autonomous Monologue / 57
    DORRIT COHN

The Aesthetic of Delay / 69
    HUGH KENNER

A Clown's Inquest into Paternity: Fathers, Dead or Alive, in *Ulysses* / 81
    JEAN-MICHEL RABATÉ

Righting *Ulysses* / 99
    FRITZ SENN

Bloom's Metaphors and the Language of Flowers / 123
    RAMÓN SALDÍVAR

Nature and Culture in the "Sirens" Episode of Joyce's *Ulysses* / 133
    CHERYL HERR

Chronology / 145

Contributors / 151

Bibliography / 153

Acknowledgments / 159

Index / 161

Editor's Note

This book gathers together a representative selection of what I judge to be the best criticism of Joyce's *Ulysses* that has been published during the past quarter-century. The critical essays are reprinted here in the chronological order of their original publication. I am grateful to Charles Ford, Henry Finder, and Chantal McCoy for their assistance in editing this volume.

My introduction is a Bloomian excursus upon the Jewishness of the other Bloom and upon Joyce's agon with Shakespeare. Richard Ellmann, Joyce's definitive biographer, sketches the literary and the Dublin backgrounds of *Ulysses,* after which Wolfgang Iser interprets the reader's share in "The Oxen of the Sun" episode.

In the essay by A. Walton Litz, the "Ithaca" episode receives a thorough investigation. Dorrit Cohn studies the "Penelope" section as an autonomous monologue, while Hugh Kenner analyzes a crucial moment in the novel as an instance of Joyce's "aesthetics of delay."

A Lacanian reading of the metaphor of fatherhood in *Ulysses* is attempted by Jean-Michel Rabaté, and another instance of a contemporary mode of interpretation is offered by Fritz Senn, who studies some of the roles of language itself in the novel. The same concern informs Ramón Saldívar's exegesis of Bloom's metaphors.

In this book's final essay, Cheryl Herr considers the "Sirens" episode, and finds in it an aggressive gathering of cultural topoi, conventions that "fabricate both art and life."

Introduction

It is an odd sensation to begin writing an introduction to a volume of Joyce criticism on June 16, 1985, particularly if one's name is Bloom. Poldy is, as Joyce intended, the most *complete* figure in modern fiction, if not indeed in all Western fiction, and so it is appropriate that he have a saint's day in the literary calendar: Bloomsday. He is, thankfully, no saint, but a mild, gentle sinner; in short, a good man. So good a man is he that even the critic Hugh Kenner, who in his earlier commentary saw Poldy as an instance of modern depravity, an Eliotic Jew as it were, in 1980 could call Joyce's hero "fit to live in Ireland without malice, without violence, without hate." How many are fit to live, in fact or fiction, in Ireland or America, without malice, without violence, without hate? Kenner, no sentimentalist, now finds in Poldy what the reader must find: a better person than oneself.

Richard Ellmann, Joyce's biographer, shrewdly says of Poldy that "he is not afraid that he will compromise his selfhood." Currently fashionable criticism, calling itself "Post-Structuralist Joyce," oddly assimilates Joyce to Barthes, Lacan, Derrida; producing a Poldy without a self, another floating signifier. But Joyce's Poldy, as Ellmann insists, is heroic and imaginative; his mimetic force allies him to the Wife of Bath, Falstaff and Sancho Panza, and like them his presence is overwhelming. Joyce's precursors were Dante and Shakespeare, and Poldy has a comprehensiveness and immediacy worthy of his ancestry. It is good to remember that, after Dante and Shakespeare, Joyce cared most for Wordsworth and Shelley among the poets. Wordsworth's heroic naturalism and Shelley's visionary skepticism find their way into Poldy also.

How Jewish is Poldy? Here I must dissent a touch from Ellmann, who says that when Poldy confronts the Citizen, he states an ethical view "more Christian than Judaic." Poldy has been unbelieving Jew, Protestant and

Catholic, but his ethical affirmations are normative Jewish, as Joyce seems to have known better than Ellmann does. When Poldy gazes upon existence, he finds it good. The commonplace needs no hallowing for Poldy. Frank Budgen, taking the hint from Joyce, emphasizes how much older Poldy seems than all the other inhabitants of Joyce's visionary Dublin. We do not think of Poldy as being thirty-eight, prematurely middle-aged, but rather as living in what the Hebrew Bible called *olam:* time without boundaries. Presumably, that is partly why Joyce chose to make his Ulysses Jewish rather than Greek. Unlike a modern Greek, Poldy is in surprising continuity with a lineage of which he has little overt knowledge. How different would the book have been if Joyce had centered on a Greek living in Dublin? The aura of exile would not be there. Joyce, the Dubliner in exile, tasting his own stoic version of a Dantesque bitterness, found in Poldy as wandering Jew what now seems his inevitable surrogate. Poldy, not Stephen, is Joyce's true image.

Yet Poldy is certainly more like Homer's Ulysses than like the Yahwist's Jacob. We see Poldy surviving the Cyclops, but not wrestling with one among the Elohim in order to win a new name for himself. Truly Jewgreek, Poldy has forsworn the Covenant, even if he cannot escape from having been chosen. Joyce, too, has abandoned the Church, but cannot escape the intellectual discipline of the Jesuits. Poldy's sense of election is a little more mysterious, or perhaps it is Joyce's sense of his hero's election that is the true mystery of the book. At the end of the Cyclops episode, Joyce evidently felt the necessity of distancing himself from Poldy, if only because literary irony fails when confronted by the heroic pathos of a creation that defies even Joyce's control.

> —Are you talking about the new Jerusalem? says the citizen.
> —I'm talking about injustice, says Bloom.
> —Right, says John Wyse. Stand up to it then with force like men.

But that is of course not Poldy's way. No interpolated sarcasm, however dramatically wrought, is able to modify the dignity of Poldy's rejoinder:

> —But it's no use, says he. Force, hatred, history, all that. That's not life for men and women, insult and hatred. And everybody knows that it's the very opposite of that that is really life.
> —What, says Alf.
> —Love, says Bloom. I mean the opposite of hatred.

Twelve delirious pages of hyperbole and phantasmagoria follow, detailing the forced exit of the noble Poldy from the pub, and ending in a grand send-up indeed:

> When, lo, there came about them all a great brightness and they beheld the chariot wherein He stood ascend to heaven. And they beheld Him in the chariot, clothed upon in the glory of the brightness, having raiment as of the sun, fair as the moon and terrible that for awe they durst not look upon Him. And there came a voice out of heaven, calling: *Elijah! Elijah!* And he answered with a main cry: *Abba! Adonai!* And they beheld Him even Him, ben Bloom Elijah, amid clouds of angels ascend to the glory of the brightness at an angle of forty-five degrees over Donohoe's in Little Green Street like a shot off a shovel.

It is all in the juxtaposition of "ben Bloom Elijah" and "like a shot off a shovel," at once a majestic deflation and a complex apotropaic gesture on Joyce's own part. Like Falstaff and Sancho Panza, Poldy runs off with the book, and Joyce's strenuous ironies, dwarfing the wit of nearly all other authors, essentially are so many reaction-formations against his love for (and identity with) his extraordinary hero. Homer's Ulysses may be as complete as Poldy, but you wouldn't want to be in one boat with him (you would drown, he would survive). Poldy would comfort you in every sorrow, even as he empathizes so movingly with the pangs of women in childbirth.

Joyce was not Flaubert, who at once was Madame Bovary and yet was wholly detached from her, at least in aesthetic stance. But how do you maintain a fixed stance toward Poldy? Falstaff is the monarch of wit, and Sancho Panza the Pope of innocent cunning. Poldy's strength, as Joyce evidently intended, is in his completeness. "The complete man" is necessarily a trope, but for what? On one side, for range of affect, like Tennyson's Ulysses, Poldy is a part of all that he has met. His curiosity, his susceptibility, his compassion, his potential interest—these are infinite. On another side, for cognitive activity, Poldy, unlike Stephen, is certainly not brilliant, and yet he has a never-resting mind, as Ulysses must have. He can be said to have a Shakespearean mind, though he resembles no one in Shakespeare (a comparison of Poldy and Shylock is instructive). Poldy is neither Hamlet nor Falstaff, but perhaps he is Shakespeare, or Shakespeare reborn as James Joyce, even as Stephen is the younger Dante reincarnated as Joyce. We can think of Poldy as Horatio to Stephen's Hamlet, since Horatio represents us, the audience, and we represent Shakespeare. Poldy is our representative, and it is Joyce's greatest triumph that increasingly we represent him, as we always have and will represent Shakespeare.

Post-Structuralist Joyce never wearies of reminding us that Poldy is a trope, but it is truer to say that we are tropes for Poldy, who as a super-mimesis of essential nature is beyond us. I may never recover from a walk through a German park with a dear friend who is the most distinguished of post-structuralists. When I remarked to him, in my innocent cunning, that Poldy was the most lovable person in Western fiction, I provoked him to the annoyed response that Poldy was not a person, but only language, and that Joyce, unlike myself, knew this very well. Joyce knew very well that Poldy was more than a person, but only in the sense that Poldy was a humane and humanized God, a God who had become truly a bereft father, anguishing for his lost Rudy. Poldy is not a person only if God is not a person, and the God of the Jews, for all his transcendental sublimities, is also very much a person and a personality, as befits his immanent sublimities. Surely the uniqueness of Yahweh, among all the rival godlings, is that Yahweh is complete. Yahweh is the complete God, even as Poldy is the complete man, and God, after all, like Poldy, is Jewish.

II

French post-structuralism is of course only a belated modernism, since everything from abroad is absorbed so slowly in xenophobic Paris. French Hegel, French Freud, French Joyce are all after the event, as it were, just as French romanticism was a rather delayed phenomenon. French Joyce is about as close to the text of *Ulysses* and *Finnegans Wake* as Lacan is to the text of *Three Essays on the Theory of Sexuality* or Derrida to Hegel and Heidegger. Nor should they be, since cultural belatedness or Alexandrianism demands the remedy of misprision, or creative misreading. To say that "meaning" keeps its distance from Poldy is both to forget that Poldy is the Messiah (though which Messiah is not clear) and that one name (Kabbalistic) for Yahweh is "language." The difference between Joyce and French Joyce is that Joyce tropes God as language and the belated Parisians (and their agents) trope the Demiurge as language, which is to say that Joyce, heroic naturalist, was not a Gnostic and Lacan was (perhaps unknowingly).

As a knowing Gnostic, I lament the loss of Joycean heroic naturalism and of Poldy's natural heroism. Let them deconstruct Don Quixote; the results will be as sorrowful. Literary criticism is a mode which teaches us not only to read Poldy as Sancho Panza and Stephen as the Don, but more amiably takes us back to Cervantes, to read Sancho as Poldy. By a Borgesian blessing in the art of mistaken attribution, we then will learn to read not only *Hamlet* and the *Inferno* as written by Joyce, but *Don Quixote* as well, with the divine Sancho as an Irish Jew!

Joyce necessarily is closer to Shakespeare than to Cervantes, and Joyce's obsession with *Hamlet* is crucial in *Ulysses*. His famous reading of Hamlet, as expounded by Stephen, can be regarded as a subtle coming-to-terms with Shakespeare as his most imposing literary father in the English language. Ellmann, certainly the most reliable of all Joyce scholars, insisted that Joyce "exhibits none of that anxiety of influence which has been attributed to modern writers . . . If Joyce had any anxiety, it was over not incorporating influences enough." This matter is perhaps more dialectical than Ellmann realized. Not Dante, but Shakespeare is Joyce's Virgil, as Ellmann also notes, and just as Dante's poetic voice matures even as Virgil fades out of the *Commedia,* so Shakespeare had to fade out of *Ulysses* even as Joyce's voice matured.

In Stephen's theory, Shakespeare is the dead king, rather than the young Hamlet, who becomes the type of the Romantic artist, Stephen himself. Shakespeare, like the ghost, has been betrayed, except than Anne Hathaway went Gertrude one better, and cuckolded the Bard with both his brothers. This sexual defeat has been intensified by Shakespeare's loss of the dark lady of the sonnets, and to his best friend, a kind of third brother. Shakespeare's revenge is to resurrect his own dead son, Hamnet, who enters the play as Prince Hamlet, with the purpose of vindicating his father's honor. Such a resurrected son appears to be free of the Oedipal ambivalences, and in Joyce's view does not lust after Gertrude or feel any jealousy, however repressed, for the dead father. So Stephen and Poldy, as two aspects of Shakespeare/Joyce, during the "Circe" episode gaze into a mirror and behold a transformed Shakespeare, beardless and frozen-faced ("rigid in facial paralysis"). I do not interpret this either as the view that Poldy and Stephen "amount only to a paralytic travesty of a Shakespeare" (W. M. Schutte) or that "Joyce warns us that he is working with near-identities, not perfect ones" (Ellmann). Rather, I take it as a sign of influence-anxiety, as the precursor Shakespeare mocking the ephebe Joyce: "Be like me, but you presume in attempting to be too much like me. You are merely a beardless version, rigid in facial paralysis, lacking my potency and my ease of countenance."

The obscene Buck Mulligan, Joyce's black beast, weakly misreads *Hamlet* as masturbation and Poldy as a pederast. Joyce himself, through Stephen, strongly misreads *Hamlet* as the cuckold's revenge, a play presumably likelier to have been written by Poldy than by Stephen. In a stronger misreading still, I would suggest that Joyce rewrites *Hamlet* so as to destroy the element in the play that most menaces him, which is the very different, uncannily disinterested Hamlet of act 5. Stephen quotes the subtle Sabellian heresy that the Father was Himself His Own Son. But what we may call the even subtler Shakespearean heresy (which is also Freudian) holds rather that the Son was Himself His Own Father. This is the Hamlet of act 5, who refers to his dead father only once, and then only as the king. Joyce's Hamlet has no Oedipus complex. Shakespeare's Hamlet may have had one, but it passes away in the interval between acts 4 and 5.

Stephen as the Prince does not convince me; Poldy as the ghost of the dead king, and so as Shakespeare/Joyce, is rather more troublesome. One wishes the ghost could be exorcised, leaving us with the fine trinity of Shakespeare/Poldy/Joyce, with Poldy as the transitional figure reconciling forerunner and latecomer, a sort of Messiah perhaps. Shakespeare is the original Testament or old aesthetic Law, while Joyce is the belated Testament or new aesthetic dispensation. Poldy is the inter-Testamentary figure, apocryphal and apocalyptic, and yet overwhelmingly a representation of life in the here and now. Joyce went on to write *Finnegans Wake*, the only legitimate rival to Proust's vast novel in the Western literature of our time. More than the difficulties, both real and imaginary, of the *Wake* have kept Joyce's common readers centered upon *Ulysses*. Earwicker is a giant hieroglyph; Poldy is a person, complete and loving, self-reliant, larger and more evocative even than his book.

The Backgrounds of *Ulysses*

Richard Ellmann

Then, pious Eneas, conformant to the fulminant firman which enjoins on the tremylose terrain that, when the call comes, he shall produce nichthemerically from his unheavenly body a no uncertain quantity of obscene matter not protected by copriright in the United Stars of Ourania or bedeed and bedood and bedang and bedung to him, with this double dye, brought to blood heat, gallic acid on iron ore, through the bowels of his misery, flashly, faithly, nastily, appropriately, this Esuan Menschavik and the first till last alshemist wrote over every square inch of the only foolscap available, his own body, till by its corrosive sublimation one continuous present tense integument slowly unfolded all marryvoising mood-moulded cyclewheeling history (thereby, he said, reflecting from his own individual person life unlivable, transaccidented through the slow fires of consciousness into a dividual chaos, perilous, potent, common to allflesh, human only, mortal) but with each word that would not pass away the squidself which he had squirtcreened from the crystalline world waned chagreenold and doriangrayer in its dudhud. This exists that isits after having been said we know.

Finnegans Wake

Joyce had been preparing himself to write *Ulysses* since 1907. It grew steadily more ambitious in scope and method, and represented a sudden outflinging of all he had learned as a writer up to 1914. Its use of many styles was an extension of the method of *A Portrait of the Artist,* where the style, at first naive, became romantic and then dramatic to suit Stephen's ontogeny. Now Joyce hit upon the more radical device of the undependable narrator with a style adjusted to him. He used this in several episodes of *Ulysses,* for example in "Cyclops," where the narrator is so obviously hostile to Bloom as to stir up sympathy for him, in "Nausicaa," where the narrator's gush-iness is interrupted and counteracted by Bloom's matter-of-fact reporting, and in "Eumaeus," where the narrator writes in a style that is constabular. The variety of these devices made T. S. Eliot speak of the "anti-style" of *Ulysses,* but Joyce does not seem to oppose style so much as withdraw it to a deeper level. His ebullient hand shows through its concealments.

The most famous of the devices of *Ulysses,* the internal monologue, was also the result of earlier experiments. Joyce had been moving rapidly towards a conception of personality new to the novel. Unlike Henry James, who worked by analysis of great trends in moral life, he had begun to evolve in *Dubliners* and *A Portrait* a synthetic method, the construction of character by odds and ends, by minutiae. He did not allow his characters the sudden, tense climaxes towards which James ushered the people of his books, and preferred instead to subdue their dramas. His protagonists moved in the world and reacted to it, but their basic anxieties and exaltations seemed to move with slight reference to their environment. They were so islanded, in fact, that Joyce's development of the interior monologue to enable his readers to enter the mind of a character without the chaperonage of the author, seems a discovery he might have been expected to make.

He had observed approaches to the interior monologue in Dujardin, George Moore, Tolstoy, even his brother's journal. He had toyed with Freud's theories of verbal association; his notes to *Exiles* first list a group of words: "Blister-amber-silver-oranges-apples-sugarstick-hair-sponge-cake-ivy-roses-ribbon," and then proceed to gloss them: "The blister re-minds her of the burning of her hand as a girl. She sees her own amber hair and her mother's silver hair." The notion of dispensing with the gloss and slightly elaborating the key words, as if a multitude of small bells were ringing in the mind, was close at hand. Joyce's first interior monologue was inserted at the end of *A Portrait of the Artist,* where however he makes it seem less extraordinary by having Stephen write it in a journal. It had a dramatic justification there in that Stephen could no longer communicate with anyone in Ireland but himself. But it was also a way of relaxing by sentence fragments and seemingly casual connections among thoughts the more formal style of most of the narrative:

> *March 21, morning.* Thought this in bed last night but was too lazy and free to add it. Free, yes. The exhausted loins are those of Elizabeth and Zacchary. Then he is the precursor. Item: he eats chiefly belly bacon and dried figs. Read locusts and wild honey. Also, when thinking of him, saw always a stern severed

head or death mask as if outlined on a grey curtain or veronica. Decollation they call it in the fold. Puzzled for the moment by saint John at the Latin gate. What do I see? A decollated precursor trying to pick the lock. . . .

March 22. In company with Lynch, followed a sizable hospital nurse. Lynch's idea. Dislike it. Two lean hungry greyhounds walking after a heifer.

March 23. Have not seen her since that night. Unwell? Sits at the fire perhaps with mamma's shawl on her shoulders. But not peevish. A nice bowl of gruel? Won't you now?

Having gone so far, Joyce in *Ulysses* boldly eliminated the journal, and let thoughts hop, step, jump, and glide without the self-consciousness of a journal to account for their agitation.

Another formative element in *Ulysses,* the counterpoint of myth and fact, was begun when Joyce first evolved the name and character of Stephen Dedalus, when he allowed the imagery of Calvary to play over the last scene in "The Dead," when he parodied Dante's division into three parts in "Grace." In his notes to *Exiles* Joyce constantly compares his characters to Biblical ones: Robert Hand is the elder brother in the parable of the Prodigal Son; Bertha's state at one point is "like that of Jesus in the garden of olives," and she is also like Isolde, her "sister-in-love." And Richard and Robert are Sacher-Masoch and Sade. In *Ulysses* Joyce uses not only the Homeric and post-Homeric legend, but a variety of other identifications: Stephen is not only Daedalus but Icarus, Hamlet, Shakespeare, Lucifer. Asked why he entitled his book *Ulysses,* Joyce replied, "It is my system of working." The principal task in the book was to find a pagan hero whom he could set loose in a Catholic city, to make Ulysses a Dubliner. Stephen Dedalus could not take this role, for he was Joyce's immature *persona;* as a mature *persona* Joyce chose Leopold Bloom. Stephen and Bloom came from opposite ends of his mind and life, but there were necessarily many resemblances, which Joyce emphasized and justified by making the older man like a father to Stephen.

This counterpoint, which Joyce from the first intended, enabled him to secure the same repetition with variations that he had obtained in *A Portrait.* In the earlier book he had conceived of the whole work as a matrix in which elements of Stephen's being might form and reform; in *Ulysses* he plays Stephen's youthful point of view against Bloom's mature point of view, often confronting them with the same places and ideas. So the two traverse at different times the same parts of Dublin, or think of like things at the same moment. They repeat each other, and then the events are recapitulated on a deeper level in the "Circe" episode, and again, in wider contexts, in the last two episodes, "Ithaca" and "Penelope." [There is also a repetition of incidents from *A Portrait*, often with parodic changes. Stephen's vision of the girl at the seashore, with its stages of excitement carefully delineated, is parodied in "Nausicaa" by Bloom's orgasmic but equally detached contemplation of Gerty MacDowell. In the same way, Stephen's announcement, while walking with Cranly in *A Portrait*, that he is leaving the Church in favor of art, is parodied by Bloom's announcement to his friends Mastiansky and Citron that he is giving up religion for Darwinism.] The enclosing framework in *Ulysses* is in part the body, which supplies an organ to preside over each episode, but it is also the day, which interacts with the minds of the characters, certain hours encouraging certain moods. In the end the whole day seems to terminate in Molly Bloom's nocturnal mind; life returns to its source.

Joyce did not have his book all in mind at the beginning. He urged a friend later not to plan everything ahead, for, he said, "In the writing the good things will come." He knew his modern Ulysses must go through Dublin in a series of episodes like those of the Odyssey. An early plan, communicated to his brother on June 16, 1915, envisaged twenty-two episodes; a later one, announced to Miss Weaver on May 18, 1918, reduced them to seventeen. The eventual number was eighteen. The narrative coalesced excitingly: the Cyclops as a nationalist, Circe as madam of a brothel, were principal connections with Homer, and soon there were more subtle relationships as well. The Trojan horse, for example, is scarcely mentioned in Homer, but Joyce remembered that Dante made it the reason for Ulysses' being in hell. He turned this Odyssean adventure into Bloom's misadventure in volunteering an unconscious tip about the prospects of a dark horse in the races. (Bloom is himself transformed into a horse in the "Circe" episode.) Joyce's high spirits made him see many parallels of this kind: in the "Cyclops" episode, as Stuart Gilbert notices, the cigar Bloom keeps brandishing in front of the citizen is like the spear Ulysses uses to blind the Cyclops; the post-Homeric legend tells how Ulysses stole the statue of Pallas Athena, and in Joyce's book Bloom takes an erotic, profane look at the goddesses in the National Museum. The many light-hearted cross-references of this kind have lent support to the idea that *Ulysses* is a great joke on Homer, but jokes are not necessarily so simple, and these have a double aim. The first aim is the mock-heroic, the mighty spear juxtaposed with the two-penny cigar. The second, a more subtle one, is what might be called the ennoblement of the mock-heroic. This demonstrates that the world of cigars is devoid of heroism only to those who don't understand that Ulysses' spear was merely a sharpened stick, as homely an instrument in its way, and that Bloom can demonstrate the qualities of man by word of mouth as effectively as Ulysses by thrust of spear.

Joyce's version of the epic story is a pacifist version. He developed an aspect of the Greek epic which Homer had emphasized less exclusively, namely, that Ulysses was the only good *mind* among the Greek warriors. The brawny men, Achilles and Ajax and the rest, relied on their physical strength, while Ulysses was brighter, a man never at a loss. But of course Homer represents Ulysses as a good warrior, too. Joyce makes his modern Ulysses a man who is not physically a fighter, but whose mind is unsubduable. The victories of Bloom are mental, in spite of the pervasive physicality of Joyce's book. This kind of victory is not Homeric, though Homer gestures towards it; it is compatible with Christianity, but it is not Christian either, for Bloom is a member of a secular world. Homer's Ulysses has been made less athletic, but he retains the primary qualities of prudence, intelligence, sensitivity, and good will. Consequently Joyce, as might be expected, found the murder of the suitors at the end of the Odyssey to be too bloody as well as too grand. The only bloodletting at the end of *Ulysses* is menstrual. Joyce has Bloom defeat his rival, Blazes Boylan, in Molly Bloom's mind by being the first and the last in her thoughts as she falls off to sleep. In the same way Joyce enabled Richard Rowan in *Exiles* to defeat Robert Hand in Bertha's mind.

Another aspect of his hero Joyce borrowed as much from Dante as from Homer. In Dante Ulysses makes a voyage which Homer does not mention, a voyage which expresses his splendid lust for knowledge. In canto 26 of the *Inferno,* Ulysses says: "Neither fondness for my son nor reverence for my aged father, nor the due love that should have cheered Penelope, could conquer in me the ardor that I had to gain experience of the world, and of human vice and worth." This longing for experience, for the whole of life, is related to that of Stephen crying at the end of *A Portrait,* "Welcome, O life," but Bloom is able, with the persistent, ruminative curiosity which is his middle class correlative for Ulysses' lust, to cover even more of life and the world in his thoughts than Stephen is. He does so, too, without the element of ruthlessness that Dante, modifying Homer's picture of a less hasty hero, criticizes in Ulysses, and which is also prominent in the Stephen of *A Portrait.*

The relationship of Bloom and Ulysses has sometimes been thought to be more tenuous than this: Ezra Pound, for example, insists that the purpose of using the Odyssey is merely structural, to give solidity to a relatively plotless work. But for Joyce the counterpoint was important because it revealed something about Bloom, about Homer, and about existence. For Bloom *is* Ulysses in an important sense. He is by no means a Babbitt. Our contemporary notion of the average man, *l'homme moyen sensuel,* is a notion conditioned by Sinclair Lewis and not by Joyce. It is not a notion which is congenial in Ireland. Irishmen are gifted with more eccentricities than Americans and Englishmen. To be average in Ireland is to be eccentric. Joyce knew this, and moreover he believed that every human soul was unique. Bloom is unusual in his tastes in food, in his sexual conduct, in most of his interests. A critic has complained that Bloom has no normal tastes, but Joyce would undoubtedly reply that no one has. The range of Bloom's peculiarities is not greater than that of other men.

At the same time, Bloom maintains his rare individuality. His responses to experience are like other people's, but they are wider and cleverer. Like Ulysses, though without his acknowledged fame, he is a worthy man. Joyce does not exalt him, but he makes him special. Aldous Huxley says that Joyce used to insist upon a "thirteenth-century" etymology for the Greek form of Ulysses' name, Odysseus; he said it was a combination of *Outis*—nobody, and *Zeus*—god. The etymology is merely fanciful, but it is a controlled fancy which helps to reinforce Joyce's picture of the modern Ulysses. For Bloom is a nobody—an advertisement canvasser who, apart from his family, has virtually no effect upon the life around him—yet there is god in him. By god Joyce does not intend Christianity; although Bloom has been generously baptized into both the Protestant Church and the Catholic Church, he is obviously not a Christian. Nor is he concerned with the conception of a personal god. The divine part of Bloom is simply his humanity—his assumption of a bond between himself and other created beings. What Gabriel Conroy has to learn so painfully at the end of "The Dead," that we all—dead and living—belong to the same community, is accepted by Bloom from the start, and painlessly. The very name Bloom is chosen to support this view of Bloom's double nature. Bloom is, like Wallace Stevens's Rosenbloom, an ordinary Jewish name, but the name also means flower, and Bloom is as integral as a flower. Lenehan in the book comments about him, "He's not one of your common or garden . . . he's a cultured allround man, Bloom is." He achieves this distinction in part by not belonging in a narrow sense, by ignoring the limits of national life; he is not so much an Irishman as a man.

The desire Joyce has that Bloom be respected encourages him to give Bloom the power that he has himself, to infuse common things with uncommonness. Bloom's monologue is a continuous poetry, full of phrases of extraordinary intensity. In the first chapter in which he appears, his mind wanders to thoughts of the East; he imagines himself walking by mosques and bazaars, and says to himself, "A mother watches from her doorway. She calls her children home in their dark language." Passing Larry O'Rourke's public house, he says, "There he is, sure enough, my bold Larry, leaning against the sugarbin in his shirtsleeves watching the aproned curate swab up with mop and bucket." Or, when he considers the cattle-market where he once worked, he says to himself, "Those mornings in the cattlemarket the beasts lowing in their pens, branded sheep, flop and fall of dung, the breeders in hobnailed boots trudging through the litter, slapping a palm on a ripemeated hindquarter, there's a prime one, unpeeled switches in their hands." Or when he thinks of modern Palestine: "A barren land, bare waste. Volcanic lake, the dead sea: no fish, weedless, sunk deep in the earth. No wind could lift those waves, grey metal, poisonous foggy water. Brimstone they called it raining down: the cities of the plain: Sodom, Gomorrah, Edom. All dead names. A dead sea in a dead land, grey and old. Old now. It bore the oldest, the first race. A bent hag crossed from Cassidy's clutching a naggin bottle by the neck. The oldest people. Wandered far away over all the earth, captivity to captivity, multiplying, dying, being born everywhere."

It might be supposed that this is Joyce talking for Bloom, and not Bloom's way of thinking at all, that just as the scullions in Shakespeare speak like poets, so does everyone in Joyce. But this is not so. Stephen and Molly, it is true, have their own particular forms of eloquence, although Molly's is limited in scope and Stephen's is hyperconscious; Bloom's surpasses theirs. But there are other examples of interior monologue in *Ulysses* which show none of this disparity between conversation and inward thought. In the "Wandering Rocks" episode, Father Conmee is on his way to the Artane orphanage to arrange to have one of Dignam's children admitted there, and Joyce writes: "The Superior, the Very Reverend John Conmee S.J. reset his smooth watch in his interior pocket as he came down the presbytery steps. Five to three. Just nice time to walk to Artane. What was that boy's name? Dignam, yes. *Vere dignum et iustum est.* Brother Swan was the person to see. Mr. Cunningham's letter. Yes. Oblige him, if possible. Good practical catholic: useful at mission time."

And here is another example, of the Dignam boy himself: "Master Dignam walked along Nassau street, shifted the porksteaks to his other hand. His collar sprang up again and he tugged it down. The blooming stud was too small for the buttonhole of the shirt, blooming end to it. He met schoolboys with satchels. I'm not going tomorrow either, stay away till Monday. He met other schoolboys. Do they notice I'm in mourning? Uncle Barney said he'd get it into the paper tonight. Then they'll all see it in the paper and read my name printed and pa's name." Bloom differs from lesser Dubliners in that his internal poetry is continual, even in the most unpromising situations. It is one of the primary indications of the value Joyce attaches to him.

The verisimilitude in *Ulysses* is so compelling that Joyce has been derided as more mimic than creator, which charge, being untrue, is the greatest praise of all. After his death, when the British Broadcasting Corporation was preparing a long program about him, its representatives went to Dublin and approached Dr. Richard Best to ask him to participate in a radio interview. "What makes you come to me?" he asked truculently. "What makes you think *I* have any connection with this man Joyce?" "But you can't deny your connection," said the men of the BBC, "After all, you're a character in *Ulysses*." Best drew himself up and retorted, "I am not a character in fiction. I am a living being." The incident is a useful warning. Even with a *roman à clef*, which *Ulysses* largely is, no key quite fits. Art lavishes on one man another's hair, or voice, or bearing, with shocking disrespect for individual identity. Like Stephen in the "Circe" episode, art *shatters* light through the world, destroying and creating at once. So, when Dubliners asked each other in trepidation after the book appeared, "Are you in it?" or "Am I in it?" the answer was hard to give. A voice sounded familiar for an instant, a name seemed to belong to a friend, then both receded into a new being. For instance, the name of Mrs. Purefoy, whose labor pains end in the "Oxen of the Sun" episode with the birth of a boy, comes appropriately enough from Dr. R. Damon Purefoy, in 1904 Dublin's leading obstetrician. As *Finnegans Wake* insists, "The traits featuring the chiaroscuro coalesce, their contrarieties eliminated, in one stable somebody." Even the personages who retain their actual names, like Dr. Best himself, are often altered; so Best is depicted as saying ceaselessly, "Don't you know?" not because this was one of his expressions, which it was not, but because it seemed to Joyce the sort of expression that the fictional Best should use.

Still Joyce made Stephen Dedalus emphasize in *Ulysses* that the artist and his life are not distinct. Stephen fabricates Shakespeare's personal development from the evidence of his work. *Venus and Adonis* demonstrates for him that Shakespeare was seduced by Anne Hathaway, like Venus, an older woman; the gloomy *Richard III* and *King Lear* testify that Anne betrayed her husband with his two brothers-in-law Richard and Edmund, whose names Shakespeare accordingly attributes to the villains of those plays; the late plays show by their lightened feelings that the birth of a granddaughter had reconciled Shakespeare to his lot.

This theory, which according to friends Joyce took more seriously than Stephen (Stephen says he does not believe his own theory, but means that it is a parable of the relation of art to life, rather than a biography susceptible of verification), suggests that *Ulysses* divulges more than an impersonal and detached picture of Dublin life; it hints at what is, in fact, true: that nothing has been admitted into the book which is not in some way personal and attached. In *Finnegans Wake* Joyce goes so far as to say of Shem the Penman that, like a spider, he produced "from his unheavenly body a no uncertain quantity of obscene matter" and "with this double dye . . . wrote over every square inch of the only foolscap available, his own body." Instead of being creation's androgynous god, the artist, Joyce now says, is its squid. Of course Joyce was both.

The daughters of memory, whom William Blake chased from his door, received regular employment from Joyce, although he speaks of them disrespectfully. His work is "history fabled," not only in *A Portrait* but in *Ulysses* as well. He was never a creator *ex nihilo;* he recomposed what he remembered, and he remembered most of what he had seen or had heard other people remember. The latter category was, in a city given over to anecdote, a large one. For the main body of his work Joyce relied chiefly upon his early life in Dublin and the later visits he had made there. Certain comic material was ready at hand, and, in thinking back upon his native city, he prepared his great convocation of the city's eccentrics. There was Professor Maginni, the dark, middle-aged dancing master of North Great George's Street. Everyone knew his costume of tailcoat and dark grey trousers, silk hat, immaculate high collar with wings, gardenia in buttonhole, spats on mincing feet, and a silver-mounted, silk umbrella in hand. There were also Mrs. M'Guinness the queenly pawnbroker, and the five Hely's sandwichmen, each bearing a letter of the name; there was "Endymion" Farrell, who carried two swords, a fishing rod, and an umbrella, who wore a red rose in his buttonhole, and had upon his head a small bowler hat with large holes for ventilation; from a brewer's family in Dundalk, he was said to have fallen into a vat and never recovered. Then there was the one-legged beggar known as "The Blackbird," who used to sing and to curse under his breath if he got nothing for it.

Less known than these, but familiar to Joyce or his family, was a cluster of other characters. When Molly Bloom objects to the singing of Kathleen Kearney, the name is a modification of that of Olive Kennedy, who appeared on a concert program with Joyce in 1902. Other names brought up by

Molly had a similar basis in fact; Tom Devin's two sons were friends of the Joyces, and Connie Connolly was the sister of his Belvedere classmates Albrecht and Vincent Connolly. Even the dog Garryowen was not made up of stray barks and bites, but belonged to the father of Joyce's Aunt Josephine Murray, whom Gerty McDowell accurately identifies as "Grandpapa Giltrap." To find some of his characters Joyce went among the dead, the best example being Pisser Duff, whose name he delicately altered to Pisser Burke. Duff looked harmless, but was a violent man who hung around the markets, brushing down horses while their owners drank at pubs. He was beaten to death by the police in Gardiner Street about 1892, but Joyce evoked him to be a friend of the equally vicious narrator of the "Cyclops" episode. One of the most curious composites is Lenehan, the parasite who speaks French. The name is borrowed from Matt Lenehan, a reporter on the *Irish Times,* but the personality Joyce took from a friend of his father named Michael Hart, who was dead by about 1900. Mick Hart, because of his habit of speaking French, was called Monsart (that is, Monsieur Hart). He worked, as Joyce implies, for a racing paper called *Sport,* and always attended the races in flashy attire. "Lenehan" makes his first appearance in Joyce's work in "Two Gallants," when he is depicted accurately as longing to marry a rich girl. For this purpose Hart paid court for a time to the daughter of Joseph Nagle, one of the three brothers who kept a big public house in Earl Street; but nothing came of it. He knew a great deal about racing and was fond of writing doggerel; his greatest day was that, still recalled by Dubliners, when he "tipped the double" in verse; that is, he predicted the winners of both the Lincolnshire Handicap and the Grand National Steeplechase.

Not long after this triumph he went downhill, and spent his later days in "knocking around on the hard." He continued to write verse; Joyce gives one of his successful productions, a limerick, in the "Aeolus" episode. Yet, as if to belie his reincarnation *Ulysses,* Joyce includes Michael Hart in a list of Bloom's friends who are now dead.

Joyce's surface naturalism in *Ulysses* has many intricate supports, and one of the most interesting is the blurred margin. He introduces much material which he does not intend to explain, so that his book, like life, gives the impression of having many threads that one cannot follow. For example, on the way to the funeral, the mourners catch sight of Reuben J. Dodd, and Mr. Dedalus says, "The devil break the hasp of your back." This reaction seems a little excessive unless we know that Dodd had lent money to Joyce's father, and that the subsequent exactions were the efficient cause of Mr. Dedalus's irritation. In the "Circe" episode Mulligan says,

"Mulligan meets the afflicted mother," a remark based upon a story current in Dublin that Gogarty, returning home late one night during his medical course, staggered up the steps of his home on Rutland Square, reciting a station of the Cross at each step until, as he reached the top of the stairs and his worried mother opened the door, he concluded, "Gogarty meets the afflicted mother." Stephen's allusions to "The Tinahely twelve" and "Cranly's eleven true Wicklowmen to free their sireland" refer to a remark that J. F. Byrne had made to George Clancy; they agreed that twelve men with resolution could save Ireland, and Byrne said that he thought he could find twelve such men in Wicklow. With numerous truncated references of this sort Joyce edged his book.

The "Circe" episode offers an extended instance of Joyce's merging observations and reading into a new form. There was, to begin with, the necessity of finding an adequate setting. Following a long series of Homeric commentators who have moralized Circe's den as a place of temptation where the bestial aspects of men emerge, Joyce decided on the redlight district of Dublin for his scene. The word "Nighttown" he had picked up from Dublin journalists, who always spoke of the late shift as "Nighttown." Joyce used it instead of the customary word for the brothel area, "Monto," so called from Montgomery Street. Monto was labeled about 1885 by the Encyclopedia Britannica as the worst slum in Europe. It was concentrated chiefly in Mecklenburg Street, which became Tyrone Street and is now a dreary Railway Street, the name having been changed twice as part of an effort, vain until recently, to change its character. The street is made up of eighteenth-century houses; while some of these had by 1900 decayed into tenements, others, the "flash houses," were kept up beautifully by women who appeared in full evening dress before their select clientele.

Horse Show week in August was especially grand in Monto. The British officers arrived in numbers for the event, and the Monto ladies sent their cards at once to the officers' mess. The ladies drove to the races in pony traps, and afterwards a procession of innumberable cabs followed them back to Monto. The Boer War also proved a great boon to their business. In 1902 the Irish Battalion of Yeomanry returned from South Africa, and a dull-witted society paper published an anonymous poem sentimentally celebrating the heroes' return, in which however the first letter of each line formed the acrostic sentence, "Whores will be busy." This poem, which was quickly comprehended, killed the paper. It was correctly attributed to Gogarty, then a medical student.

Joyce's knowledge of Monto was of course as complete as his knowledge of the *Evening Telegraph,* which he used in the "Aeolus" episode. He does not have Bloom and Stephen patronize the lower numbers of Mecklenburg Street, near Mabbot Lane, since these were usually patronized by English "tommies"; these houses were full of religious pictures, behind which the ladies kept "coshes," pieces of lead pipe, to prevent trouble. Joyce asked one of his visitors in the thirties to secure a complete list of the names and addresses on Mecklenburg Street, and seems to have retained his interest in them. A lady appropriately named Mrs. Lawless lived at No. 4; her neighbour, at No. 5, was Mrs. Hayes, a grandmotherly type. But at the upper end of the street were the principal houses. Bloom, searching for Stephen at Mrs. Cohen's (No. 82), knocks first by mistake at No. 85, but is told that this is Mrs. Mack's house. Actually Mrs. Mack kept two houses, No. 85 and No. 90, and was so well known that the whole area was sometimes called "Macktown."

As for Mrs. Cohen, she was older than Mrs. Mack, and by 1904 had either retired or died, but Joyce restored her in business because her name suited the Jewish themes in the book. Her girls were probably modelled on contemporary prostitutes. Florry Talbot, for instance, was probably Fleury Crawford. The description of another girl, Kitty Ricketts, suggests Becky Cooper, probably the best known among Dublin prostitutes from the beginning of the century until the twenties. Joyce was probably familiar also with Lady Betty and May Oblong (Mrs. Roberts); he reserved the latter's name for Finnegans Wake, where all Dublin is d'Oblong.

Yet the deeper problem of "Circe" was to relate Bloom and Stephen on the unconscious level, to justify the father-son theme that Joyce had made central in his book. He does so chiefly in terms of one trait which the two men share, their essentially inactive roles. Joyce is quite earnest about this. He has shown Bloom throughout as the decent man who, in his pacific way, combats narrowmindedness, the product of fear and cruelty, which Stephen combatted in A Portrait and still combats. Once it is understood that Joyce sympathizes with Bloom and Stephen in their resistance in terms of mind rather than body, an aspect of the library episode becomes less baffling. Stephen Dedalus asserts there that Shakespeare was not Hamlet but Hamlet's father. Since Stephen in so many ways resembles Hamlet, and since he obviously thinks of himself as like Shakespeare, this identification may seem capricious. But it fits Joyce's notion both of the artistic temperament and of the desirable man. Joyce, Stephen, and Bloom share the philosophy of passivity in act, energy in thought, and tenacity in conviction. Hamlet, on the other hand, is the hero of a revenge-play; however unwittingly and fumblingly, he sheds a great deal of blood. Joyce does not encourage this view of the artist, and so he relates Shakespeare to the suffering father, the victim, rather than to the avenging son. The artist endures evil—he doesn't inflict it. If he revenges himself, it is psychically only, by a play or a novel. "I detest action," says Stephen to the soldiers. Because he takes this position, he belongs, in the extended metaphor which underlies all *Ulysses,* to the family of Bloom, who tells the Citizen, "It's no use. . . . Force, hatred, history, all that. That's not life for men and women, insult and hatred." They are son and father mentally, if not physically, and both of them argue that what is physical is incidental.

The kinship of Stephen and Bloom, on the surface so unlikely, is established with great adroitness. Joyce makes use of two sources to aid him, both literary; the first is Leopold von Sacher-Masoch, the second is William Blake. In the worst light Bloom's passivity in the face of Boylan's advances to Molly, and his rejection of force in the "Cyclops" episode, seem part of a willing submission comparable to that of Sacher-Masoch. In the best light they are Blake's rejection of the corporeal.

While writing the "Circe" episode Joyce drew heavily upon Sacher-Masoch's book, *Venus im Pelz.* Much of the material about flagellation is derived from it. *Venus in Furs* tells of a young man named Severin who so abases himself before his mistress, a wealthy woman named Wanda, and so encourages her cruelty toward him, that she becomes increasingly tyrannical, makes him a servile go-between, and then, in a rapturous finale, turns him over to her most recent lover for a whipping. There are many similarities to "Circe." The society ladies who appear to Bloom, Mrs. Yelverton Barry (a name modified from that of a suspected transvestist) and Mrs. Bellingham (an actual name) are as fond of wearing furs as Wanda. Mrs. Bellingham recounts accusingly of Bloom, "He addressed me in several handwritings with fulsome compliments as a Venus in furs and alleged profound pity for my frostbound coachman Balmer while in the same breath he expressed himself as envious of his earflaps and fleecy sheepskins and of his fortunate proximity to my person, when standing behind my chair wearing my livery and the armorial bearings of the Bellingham escutcheon garnished sable, a buck's head couped or." The hero of *Venus in Furs* wears his lady's livery, has to follow her at ten paces, and suffers luscious indignities comparable to those of Balmer.

Like Severin too, Bloom is depicted as welcoming his being birched, as even requesting this privilege. Wanda, reluctant at first to yield to her lover's strange importunities, is gradually attracted by them: "You have corrupted my imagination and inflamed my blood," she tells him; "Dangerous potentialities were slumbering in me, but you were the first to awaken them." Mrs. Mervyn Talboys puts it more ludicrously in *Ulysses,*

"You have lashed the dormant tigress in my nature into fury." Severin asks to be allowed to put on his mistress's shoes, and is kicked for performing the task too slowly. Bloom is similarly set to lacing the shoes of Bella Cohen, and fears she will kick him for his ineptitude. The more fearful and hateful Bella is, the more Bloom admires her; so Bella, like Wanda, puts her foot on Bloom's neck. The willing slavery of Severin to Wanda, which is sealed by an agreement she makes him sign, is echoed in Bloom's promise never to disobey Bella, and in her announcement to him, "What you longed for has come to pass. Henceforth you are unmanned and mine in earnest, a thing under the yoke."

The degradation of Bloom continues. Like Severin he is forced to usher in Bella's new lover, Blazes Boylan. A scene in *Venus in Furs,* in which Severin attends Wanda at her bath, is reflected in an equivalent scene in *Ulysses.* And the climax of Sacher-Masoch's book, when Wanda, pretending affection, coyly persuades Severin to let her bind him against a pillar, and then turns him over to her new lover for a merciless flogging, is echoed in Bella's pretense of affection which facilitates her pulling Bloom's hair. Even the references to the marble statuette that Bloom takes home in the rain, and to the nymph, "beautiful immortal," whose "classic curves" are pictured above his bed, are paralleled in the "stone-cold and pure" plaster cast of Venus to which Severin prays in *Venus in Furs.*

Closely as he followed his source, Joyce made two major modifications. First, his version of Sacher-Masoch is a vaudeville version; and second, Bloom's masochistic fantasies occur in his unconscious mind; he berates himself, and makes himself worse than he is, because he is *conscious* of having allowed too much in reality. Then masochism is modified by Blakeism. Several references are made to Blake in the "Circe" episode, the most important at its end. There Stephen falls out with two soldiers, who accuse him of attacking the king because of his declaration, "But in here it is I must kill the priest and the king." Joyce has in mind here an incident that occurred during Blake's stay at Felpham, when he put two soldiers out of his garden in spite of their protests that as soldiers of the king they should not be handled so. He replied to them, or was alleged to have replied, "Damn the king," was therefore haled up for treason, and barely got off. (In *Finnegans Wake* the two soldiers become three, and have an equally unpleasant role to play.) Stephen does not put the soldiers to flight; rather, to parody Blake as well, they knock *him* down, but not before he has stated his contention that the authorities, religious and secular, must be defeated in spiritual rather than corporeal warfare. This is Blake's central conception of the conquest of tyranny by imagination.

Having displayed the body's defeat and the spirit's victory in both their ridiculous and noble aspects, Joyce brings about the mental purgation of Bloom and Stephen at the end of the episode. They are purged in a surprising way, for so reserved a book, that is, by love. The theme of family love, the love of parent for child and of child for parent, runs covertly throughout *Ulysses*. Molly Bloom's thoughts return to the lambswool sweater she knitted for her son Rudy, who died when he was only eleven days old. The hyperborean Stephen, who claims to have denied his family, almost yields to affection when he comes upon his sister reading Chardenal's French primer, and remorse over his treatment of his mother accounts for his vision of her at the end of "Circe." But Bloom emerges even more decisively from the Circean sty with his vision of Rudy as he might be now:

> Against the dark wall a figure appears slowly, a fairy boy of eleven, a changeling, kidnapped, dressed in an Eton suit with glass shoes and a little bronze helmet, holding a book in his hand. He reads from right to left inaudibly, smiling, kissing the page.
>
> BLOOM
> (Wonderstruck, calls inaudibly.) Rudy!
> RUDY
> (Gazes unseeing into Bloom's eyes and goes on reading, kissing, smiling. He has a delicate mauve face. On his suit he has diamond and ruby buttons. In his free left hand he holds a slim ivory cane with a violet bowknot. A white lambkin peeps out of his waistcoat pocket.)

Tenderness is not contrary to Joyce's temperament. This is the vision of a fond father, colored as such visions are; and the sentimental coloring is offset by the bizarre attire and the detachment of the child, both of which establish a sense of distance and estrangement from Bloom. The relation of Bloom and Rudy, as of Molly and Rudy, is profoundly moving; so is the relation of Bloom to his own father, who committed suicide by taking aconite poison. Joyce deliberately says nothing about its emotional quality, but he has Bloom at one point recall a few snatches from the letter found at his father's bedside: "To my dear son Leopold. Tomorrow will be a week that I received . . . it is no use Leopold to be . . . with your dear mother . . . That is not more to stand . . . to her . . . all for me is out . . . be kind to Athos, Leopold . . . my dear son . . . always . . . of me . . . das Herz . . . Gott . . . dein." Paternity is a more powerful motif in the book than sexual love.

The phrase, "Be kind to Athos," refers to Bloom's father's dog—and kindness to animals, who are so much like children, and can repay affection only with affection, is another of those quite ordinary and undistinguished aspects of human nature that Joyce underlines. Even the Citizen, like Homer's Cyclops, is good to Garryowen. The kindness of Bloom on June 16, 1904, begins with animals and ends with human beings. So he feeds his cat in the morning, then some sea gulls, and in the "Circe" episode a dog. He remembers his dead son and dead father, he is also concerned about his living daughter, and he never forgets his wife for a moment. He helps a blind man cross a street. He contributes very generously—beyond his means—to the fund for the children of his friend Dignam who has just died; and, when he begins to see Stephen as a sort of son, he follows him, tries to stop his drinking, prevents his being robbed, risks arrest to defend him from the police, feeds him too, and takes him home in what Joyce calls, half-humorously, "orthodox Samaritan fashion." Stephen will not stay the night with Bloom—the barrier between man and man breaks down only occasionally and usually only a little, and the barrier quickly reforms— but in the temporary union of the two Joyce affirms his perception of community.

The relation of Bloom and Stephen confirms Joyce's point of view in another way: Bloom's common sense joins Stephen's acute intelligence; Stephen Dedalus, the Greek-Christian-Irishman, joins Bloom Ulysses, the Greek-Jewish-Irishman; the cultures seem to unite against horsepower and brutality in favor of brainpower and decency. The two men are contrasted in the book with those who are strong: Stephen can't swim while Mulligan swims beautifully; Bloom is only a walker, while the Citizen is the holder of the shotput record for all Ireland; and Bloom is a cuckold while Blazes Boylan is the loud-mouthed adulterer; but we spend most of the book inside Bloom's consciousness, and never enter Boylan's, as if coarseness had no consciousness. It is true that Mulligan is clever as well as strong, but it is a cleverness that goes with brutality. Stephen and Bloom, the mental men, are ranged against Mulligan and Boylan, the burly men, and Joyce's partisanship is clear.

The scheme of value of *Ulysses* comes closer to explicit expression in the "Circe" episode than it does anywhere else. It is buttressed by another passage in the "Ithaca" episode. When Bloom and Stephen are walking home to 7 Eccles Street from the cabman's shelter, they discuss a great many things, and Joyce notes, with some understatement, that their views were on certain points divergent. "Stephen," he writes, "dissented openly from Bloom's view on the importance of dietary and civic selfhelp while

Bloom dissented tacitly from Stephen's views on the eternal affirmation of the spirit of man in literature." While the loftiness of Stephen's statement is mocked, that literature embodies the eternal affirmation of the spirit of man is not a crotchet of Stephen but a principle of Joyce, maintained by all his books. It is no accident that the whole of *Ulysses* should end with a mighty "yes."

Doing Things in Style: An Interpretation of "The Oxen of the Sun" in James Joyce's *Ulysses*

Wolfgang Iser

Shortly after Joyce's *Ulysses* was published in 1922, T. S. Eliot saw in the multifarious allusions to the literature of the past the fabric indispensable to the literature of the future. "In using the myth, in manipulating a continuous parallel between contemporaneity and antiquity, Mr. Joyce is pursuing a method which others must pursue after him. They will not be imitators, any more than the scientist who uses the discoveries of an Einstein in pursuing his own, independent, further investigations. It is simply a way of controlling, of ordering, of giving a shape and a significance to the immense panorama of futility and anarchy which is contemporary history" ("Ulysses, Order and Myth"). If the Homeric myth in *Ulysses* is to be regarded as a means of giving shape to a world of futility and anarchy, then clearly a link must be established between past and present that will enable the myth to exercise its "ordering" function. The nature of this link is something that has caused many a headache to Joyce critics down through the years. Is the Homeric epic to be viewed as an "objective correlative"— as defined by Eliot in his "Hamlet" essay—that enables us to grasp the modern situation in the first place? Or does the literary parallel reveal a structural principle that moulds the modern world just as it did the ancient? These two lines of thought represent the two basic approaches to the function of the Homeric parallel. According to both, the apparent chaos of the "Welt-Alltag" (World Weekday) of June 16, 1904, is related to the sequence of adventures in the *Odyssey,* and through this connection is to bring to life

From *The Implied Reader: Patterns of Communication in Prose Fiction from Bunyan to Beckett.* © 1974 by the Johns Hopkins University Press.

in the reader's mind the outlines of an order which is to be read into the events of that day. This view has gained currency through the fact that in the modern world we are denied direct insight into the meaning of events, so that the Homeric parallel appears to offer a way of projecting a hidden meaning onto the chaos of everyday life. But herein lies the inherent weakness of this approach, for it says nothing about the way in which myth and the present day can be brought together.

If Homer's epic contains the meaning, and Joyce's novel contains only a confusing plethora of appearances interspersed with allusions to Homer, such a view must lead ultimately to a Platonizing interpretation of the modern novel. The *Odyssey* will then act as the ideal, while Bloom's wanderings are nothing but the copy of a homecoming which for Ulysses means completion, but for Bloom entails just one more grind in the ceaseless monotony of everyday life. Whenever interpretation is dominated by the idea of an analogy, one is bound to be dogged by the consequences inherent in the old conception of the *analogia entis*.

There is, however, another possible interpretation of the Homeric parallel to *Ulysses,* and Joyce himself offered certain indications of this. He called the *Odyssey* "the most beautiful, all-embracing theme" in all world literature. Going into details, he suggests that Ulysses embodies the most vivid conglomeration of all human activities, so that for him the Homeric hero becomes an archetype for humanity. Some Joyce scholars have tried to couple this statement with the idea that the modern novel is an attempt to renew Homeric archetypes. And so the concept of literary permanence comes to the fore whenever the critic concerned makes a fetish of the "unbroken tradition" of Western literature. But such a naive view of permanence demands a blind eye for all the differences between Joyce's novel and Homer's epic. Even though the permanence interpretation of *Ulysses* does not insist that Bloom is nothing but a return of Ulysses, it does insist that he *is* a Ulysses in modern dress. Such a metaphor, however, obscures rather than illuminates the intention of Joyce's novel. Indeed both "schools of thought"—that of analogy and that of permanence—even though they are backed up by some of Joyce's own statements, by existing parallels, and by the actual grouping of the episodes in the novel, shed light only on starting-points and not on intentions.

A hint as to the intention might be found in the oft quoted conclusion of Joyce's *A Portrait of the Artist as a Young Man:* "Welcome, O life! I go to encounter for the millionth time the reality of experience and to forge in the smithy of my soul the uncreated conscience of my race." This corresponds to what we have come to expect in modern times of our novel-writers. Ernst Kreuder, in his treatise on the *Unanswerable,* has described it as follows: "We expect the novelist, by virtue of his imagination, his inventive energy, his story-telling art, and his creative vision, to take us out of an exhaustively explained world of facts and into the inexplicable. . . . The aim of the epic poet can be called a paradoxical one: the completion of the unbounded. The leading of the reader up to the indecipherableness of an existence that flows without end." In the light of such an expectation, the Homeric parallel takes on a very precise function. If the novel is to uncover a new dimension of human existence, this can only present itself to the conscious mind of the reader against a background made recognizable by allusions and references which will thus provide a sufficient amount of familiarity. But the "uncreated conscience," which the novel is to formulate, cannot be the return of something already known—in other words, it must not coincide purely and simply with the Homeric parallel. Harry Levin [in *James Joyce: A Critical Introduction*] has rightly pointed out that the links between Joyce and Homer are parallels "that never meet." While the Homeric allusions incorporate into the text a familiar literary repertoire, the parallels alluded to seem rather to diverge than to converge. Here we have the conditions for a rich interplay that goes far beyond the lines of interpretation laid down by the analogy or permanence theories. Indeed there arises a certain tension out of the very fact that there is no clearly formulated connection between the archaic past and the everyday present, so that the reader himself is left to motivate the parallelism indicated as it were by filling in the gaps between the lines.

This process only comes to the fore if one in fact abandons the idea of the parallels and instead takes the modern world and the Homeric world as figure and ground—the background acting as a sort of fixed vantage point from which one can discern the chaotic movements of the present. By means of the allusions, Bloom's and Stephen's experiences are constantly set off against this background, which brings home to the reader the great gulf between Joyce's characters and those of Homer. If Bloom is, so to speak, viewed through Ulysses, and Stephen through Telemachus, the reader who knows his Homer will realize what is missing in these two modern men. Thus greater emphasis is thrown on those features which do not coincide with Homer, and in this way the individuality is given its visible outline. Individuality is therefore constituted as the reverse side of what is suggested by the Homeric allusions; being conditioned by the very nonfulfillment of the expectations arising from these allusions. Joyce's characters begin to take on a life of their own the moment we, the readers, begin to react to them, and our reactions consist of an attempt to grasp and hold fast to their individuality—a process that would be quite unnecessary if they were immediately recognizable types representing an immediately recognizable frame of reference. Here the reader is compelled to try and find the frame of reference for himself, and the more intensively he searches, the more inescapably he becomes entangled in the modern situation, which is not explained for him but is offered to him as a personal experience.

The Homeric repertoire is not, however, only a background enabling us to grasp the theme of modern everyday life. The interaction can also be two-way, with Ulysses occasionally being viewed through the perspective of Bloom. This is significant in the light of the fact that for Joyce, Homer's hero epitomized humanity. How, then, could he lack something which Bloom has simply by not being identical with Ulysses? Obviously because humanity never coincides completely with any of its historical manifestations—it is a potential which is realized differently at different times. Even if Ulysses is an ideal manifestation, this only becomes apparent through the Bloom perspective, which mirrors not just the ideality of Ulysses but also—and much more significantly—the fact that humanity, whatever its outward circumstances, can only be apprehended as individual manifestations arising out of reactions to historical situations. And so the Homeric myth itself takes on another dimension against the foreground-turned-background of the "Welt-Alltag"—a dimension aptly described by S. L. Goldberg [in *The Classical Temper: A Study of James Joyce's* Ulysses] as follows: "Once divorced from their origin in implicit, pious belief—and that is the only condition under which we now know the myths of Greece and, for most of us, the myths of Christianity as well—their meanings are perpetually created in our experience, are the colouring they take on from the material into which we project them. The myth is like a potentiality of meaning awaiting actualization in the world we recognize as real, in a specific 'now and here.' "

II

The actualization of this potential is not left to the discretion of the individual reader. On the contrary, the manner in which he perceives and conceives events will be guided by the stylistic technique with which they are represented. In *Ulysses* the function of style is so important that a whole chapter is devoted to it. For Joyce, style as the technique of communication was of prime significance. When Stanislaus wanted to discuss fascism with his brother, Joyce remarked laconically: "Don't talk to me about politics. I'm only interested in style." The chapter entitled "The Oxen of the Sun" sheds a good deal of light on this obsession, although Joyce critics generally have tended to look on it with a certain amount of embarrassment, regarding the linguistic experiments as an obvious digression from the novel's apparent subject matter—everyday life in Dublin. The most acceptable explanation for this widespread unease is given by Goldberg, though he too has certain qualms about this chapter:

> The "symbolic" scheme so violently obtruded into these chapters from "Wandering Rocks" to "Oxen of the Sun" attempts much the same effect as the Homeric parallel, but without its foundation and enactment in the characters' own lives and in the reader's belief in the abiding poetic truth of the original myth. The trouble with these chapters in short is that their order is not "aesthetic" enough. Perhaps this is the necessary price for the attempt Joyce makes to shift our attention from the represented reality to the shaping activity of the artist. Given the strategic need to bring himself, as artist, into the action of his book, Joyce could hardly use the old tactic of direct authorial commentary. That would draw attention to him, but not as a dramatis persona and certainly not as an unmoved mover suggested within yet beyond the action. What he did, however, is in its way very like intruded authorial comment.

If Joyce's "failure" lies in the fact that here he discloses his technique instead of continuing the dramatization of individual attitudes, by unraveling this technique we should be able to gain a good deal of insight into its function within the novel's overall framework of presentation. Here we might bear in mind Ezra Pound's pronouncement: "I believe in technique as the test of a man's sincerity."

The subject of this chapter is Bloom's visit to a maternity hospital. There he and his friends wait for Mrs. Purefoy's confinement. The conversation is mainly about love, procreation, and birth. The linguistic presentation of these themes takes place on different, contrasting levels of style. The chapter begins with an enigmatic invocation, and this is followed by an equally cryptic succession of long and tortuous sentences, which seem to lose their meaning as they progress. Immediately after these comes the sequence of historical styles that takes up the whole of the chapter. The subjects of love, procreation, and birth are dealt with in all the characteristic styles of English literature, from alliterative prose right through to pidgin English. "The Oxen of the Sun" starts with three sentences, each of which is repeated three times. An impression of some sort of magic arises out of these triads. The sentences are: "DESHIL HOLLES EAMUS. Send us, bright one, light one, Horhorn, quickening and wombfruit." And finally the Dada-sounding "Hoopsa, boyaboy, hoopsa." These three sentences, deciphered, convey the following: Bloom feels an urge to go to Holles Street, where Dr. Horne's maternity hospital is situated. There is an invocation to the art of Dr. Horne to help the fruit of the womb to come into the world. And finally we have the threefold delight of the midwife as she holds the newborn babe in her hands. These banal contents leap to life through the use of Latin words, Latin-sounding turns of phrase, a rhythmic beat, and an incantatory evocativeness. But they also take on a peculiar sort of tension, for the simplicity of the content and the complexity of the presentation seems out of all proportion. Are linguistic montages and magic incantations necessary to make us aware of ordinary, everyday events? This question, right at the beginning of the chapter, is symptomatic of the whole, and indeed here we have a technique which Joyce uses frequently in *Ulysses:* individual chapters begin with a sort of codified theme which is then orchestrated by the narrative process. The invocation then gives way to a completely different style. With long-drawn-out, mainly unpunctuated sentences, an attempt is made to describe the nature and significance of a maternity hospital. But it is only after very careful study that the reader begins to discern this intention. The lack of punctuation excludes any logical linguistic pattern, and behind this there obviously lies the fear of making any concrete statement about the object to be described. Joyce himself gives voice to this fear: "For who is there who anything of some significance has apprehended but is conscious that that exterior splendour may be the surface of a downward-tending lutulent reality." His awareness of the danger that he will capture only the surface view of things, makes him approach the object as it were from all linguistic sides, in order to avoid a perspective foreshortening of it. And so the long appositions are not set out as such, and dependent clauses are left unmarked, for divisions of this kind would involve premature definition of the object concerned. At the same time, however, the language makes wide use of specialized vocabulary and precise nuances of meaning, and this gives rise to the impression that the institution is to be described with the utmost exactitude, although in fact it tends to become more and more blurred. Through this effort to depict the object from as many sides as possible, the maternity hospital seems almost to become something living and moving. And this is a stylistic feature typical not only of the chapter in question, but also of important sections of the whole novel: language is used not to fix an object, but to summon it to the imagination. The multiplication of perspectives will blur the outline, but through it the object will begin to grow, and this growth would be stunted if one were to try and define, since definition involves restriction to a chosen viewpoint which, in turn, involves a stylization of the reality perceived. It is therefore scarcely surprising that practically every chapter of *Ulysses* is written in a different style, in order—as Broch puts it—to transfer "the object from one stylistic illumination to another," (*Dichten und Erkennen*) for only in this way is "the highest degree of reality" to be achieved. The constant change of perspective modifies the definition inherent in each stylistic variant, and so reveals the object as something continually expanding. In this way, even the most commonplace things seem potentially illimitable.

From the invocation that opens this chapter, we may conclude that only a cryptic form of language can succeed in making statements about even the simplest of things. The relation between language and object becomes a mystery, and the tension arising from this is extended by the next stylistic form which, as it were, sets the object in motion through its changing nuances of observation. Thus the basis is laid for the subsequent array of styles emanating from the history of English literature. If one bears in mind the fact that the two different levels of style at the start of the chapter seek only to set us on the road to the maternity hospital and to evoke the nature of such institutions, whereas now we are to be confronted with the great themes of love, procreation, and birth, one might expect the gap between language and object to reach unbridgeable proportions. If the simple themes at the beginning were difficult to deal with linguistically, surely these much broader subjects will totally exceed the capacity of language. And yet, surprisingly, this is not so. Although he may be confused at first, the reader actually needs only a basic knowledge of English literature in order to understand completely all that is going on. Without doubt, Stuart Gilbert's commentary offers some very useful guidelines on this, but critics have never really accepted the parallelism he suggests between the sequence of period styles and the development of the embryo, or the many other references and cross-symbols he worked out as a ground plan for *Ulysses*. Goldberg ends his critique of Gilbert's book with the question: "But if Mr. Gilbert's way of interpreting it [i.e., *Ulysses*] is generally felt to be wrong, what is the right way, and why?" As far as "The Oxen of the Sun" is concerned, a provisional answer must be: because Gilbert's equation of the individual styles with embryonic development is too rigid—not unlike the analogy theory that always seeks to establish precise equivalents in *Ulysses* and the *Odyssey*. Gilbert overlooks the latent comedy that runs through the imitations and shows up the degree of deformation brought about by each individual style.

We can gain a closer insight into the nature of the historical sequence of styles by having a look at a few examples: first, in imitation of old English poetry, we are given an alliterative prose impression of Dr. Horne's maternity hospital. A mainly substantival style captures the outside of things and sets them side by side *en bloc* and unconnected. It seems as if the articles of equipment described are simply there for their own sake, although the alliteration does hint at certain unformulated connections. The function of the individual items remains hidden from perception, so that they take on an element of incomprehensibility which transforms their practical value into some secret sort of reference. The style itself brings about an effect of contrast, insofar as this austere, alliterative prose follows on directly from the attempt, through extreme nuances of language, to describe the nature and importance of a maternity hospital. The consequences of the next style are quite different: events in the maternity hospital are recounted in the form of a late medieval travel book. Everything seems somehow to be tinged with excitement. The surface description of things is conditioned by the need to understand the new in terms of the familiar. However, this technique gets into severe difficulties when the traveler is confronted by a tin of sardines in olive oil. The resultant comedy derives from the incongruity between a style rigidly seeking to define the object in its own gallant terms, and the mundane object itself. The determinant pressure exerted by this style is so great that the advertising agent Leopold Bloom suddenly becomes the medieval "traveller Leopold." Then the language changes again: the characters waiting in the hall of the maternity hospital converse in the style of Sir Thomas Malory. Once again the unifying tendency of the style affects the very identity of the characters. The medieval traveler Leopold of a moment ago now becomes "Sir Leopold." The highly stylized discussion concerns traditional moral problems connected with birth (e.g., whether a wife should be allowed to die for her baby), and then suddenly Stephen raises the subject of contraception. Now neologisms creep into the conversation as signs of human independence, defining man's interference with the God-given order of things. Here it becomes evident that the style shaped by the ideal of Christian knighthood is no longer capable of coping with the multifarious problems under discussion—namely, of love and procreation. Nevertheless, the attempt is made to use the system of references inherent in the ideal of the Christian knight in order to work out an idea of love that cannot be fitted into this system. This incongruity between style and object is apparent all through the series of imitations from one century to another. After a love passage in the language of the Arcadian shepherds, there arises an inner indignation against the trend of the conversation, and this is expressed in the form of a Bunyan allegory.

The spiritual conflict transforms the maternity hospital and its trappings into "the land of Phenomenon," with an unreal outer world giving way to the reality of the inner. The hidden thoughts and feelings of the people concerned are externalized as allegorical characters that enact the ensuing conflict. But here, too, the relation between object and style becomes absurdly unbalanced, as the lusts of the characters are suddenly allegorized, bringing about an extraordinary sort of psychomachia. In medieval literature, allegory personified the Christian moral code. The personification of sexual urges, carried to extremes by Joyce, destroys the whole principle of the form as it had been used up to and including Bunyan.

As a sort of relief from all this personified "inwardness," there now follows a minute description of the external events of the evening, in the diction of Samuel Pepys. The most insignificant trifles are so lovingly observed that they seem over life-size, and every detail becomes a whole world in itself. After this, the central subject of the chapter enters into the realm of Utopian projects, conveyed in the style of the moral weeklies. In pseudoscientific detail the characters discuss various practical methods of controlling with mechanical perfection all the processes of intimacy. This latent Utopianism is conveyed through a number of tales which are intended to establish the illusion that these special cases actually happened in the lives of particular people. Through these stories, the reader is meant to accept as perfectly natural the life planned for him on a "national fertilising farm." In order to bring about this acceptance, the style imitates the narrative form of the moral weeklies, which were designed to create intimate contact with the public. But here the style sets out projects which destroy all intimacy; again we have total incongruity.

The stylistic idiosyncrasies of the great eighteenth-century novelists offer plenty of variations on the love theme through the individualization of speech, while the nineteenth-century parodies nearly all hypostatize the moods and emotions associated with love. All these overblown treatments of the subject show an extremely one-sided view, for each style reveals a latent ideology, constantly reducing the reality to the scope of individual principles. In the language of Landor, the unseemly side of love is again glossed over, this time through the respectability of mythological characters. There is a similar sweet innocence to be found in the homely Dickensian passage that follows a little later. Love is peace and domestic bliss. But in between, there is a detailed section on sex determination and infant mortality that is couched in the scientific terminology of hygiene and biology, with the apparent claim of being able to define these phenomena within the theory of scientific positivism. Again, the relation between subject and treatment is grotesque, and the overall parody is enhanced here by the actual sequence of the styles. Next we come to theological interpretations in the style of Ruskin, Carlyle, and Newman, setting the world of appearances against its metaphysical background—though here, too, we have different definitions of love and the world under perception. After this series of rich and varied styles, the language at the end of the chapter seems to explode into a chaos of possibilities, and in this confused linguistic hodgepodge meaning finally seems to go by the board; it fades away in the elusiveness of language.

III

From these briefly sketched examples we may draw certain conclusions which together will give us a degree of insight into the Joycean technique of style. Although the various consequences are very closely connected with one another, we shall gain a clearer understanding of them by first examining them separately. To begin with, this stylistic historical tour of English literature is designed to grasp a particular subject through language. Each individual style projects a clearly recognizable idea of love, procreation, or birth. Joyce's style imitations therefore fulfill the demands summarized by John Middleton Murry as follows: "Style is a quality of language which communicates precisely emotions or thoughts, or a system of emotions or thoughts, peculiar to the author. . . . Style is perfect when the communication of the thought or emotion is exactly accomplished; its position in the scale of absolute greatness, however, will depend upon the comprehensiveness of the system of emotions and thoughts to which the reference is perceptible" (*The Problem of Style*). The styles imitated by Joyce are dominated by such thoughts or thought systems, and the predetermined, predetermining nature of all style is demonstrated quite unmistakably through the individual variations. The judgments inherent in each style create a uniform picture of the subject presented, choosing those elements of the given reality that correspond to the frame of reference essential to all observation. The particular point of view, then, determines which individual phenomena out of all those present are, or are not to be presented. And this, for Joyce, is the whole problem of style. Presentability or non-presentability is not a quality inherent to any observable reality, but has to be imposed on that reality by the observer. This involves a latent deformation of the object perceived, which in extreme cases is degraded to the level of a mere illustration of some given meaning. If now we go back to the beginning of the chapter, we notice not only the counterpoint that exists between the introduction and the subsequent historical sequence of styles but also the richly contrasting tensions between the different types of presentation. At the start it seemed that banal objects could only be captured by a cryptic language, while the next passage showed that as language approached, reality seemed rather to withdraw than to come closer. The account was split up into a bewildering number of facets, with language attempting to comprehend the subject matter from every conceivable angle. To do this, it had to be freed from the normative restrictions of grammar and syntax, for only then could it sow all the nuances in the imagination of the reader. The account could contain no judgment, because otherwise it would not be presenting the object itself but the frame of reference in which the object was viewed. And it is such frames of references that are in fact presented by the ensuing series of imitations. Joyce's aim, however, was not solely to show up the limitations of all styles through the systems of thought underlying them but also to evoke those aspects of an object that are kept concealed by the perspective mode of observation. Hence the fact that virtually every chapter of *Ulysses* is written in a different style. Herein lies a basic difference between Joyce and all other modern writers. Joyce wanted to bring out, if not actually to overcome, the inadequacy of style as regards the presentation of reality, by constant changes of style, for only by showing up the relativity of each form could he expose the intangibility and expansibility of observable reality. And so in "The Oxen of the Sun" we have the themes of love, procreation, and birth discussed in a series of historically sequent styles which each convey a single, one-sided viewpoint.

This leads us to the second conclusion to be drawn from the examples given. If style reproduces only aspects of reality and not—in contrast to its implicit claims—reality itself, then it must be failing in its intention. This idea is worked up through the element of parody in the stylistic impersonations. Joyce caricatures the formal restrictions of each style, so that Leopold Bloom, the main character in the novel, finds himself taking on a corresponding variety of identities. The resultant distortion is one that the reader can scarcely ignore, since he already knows a good deal about Bloom's character from the preceding chapters. We find the same distortion in the treatment of the main theme of the chapter, for it is not love itself that is presented, but only the way in which Malory, Bunyan, Addison, and the other writers understood it. Indeed one has the impression that the different views presented by the different styles exclude rather than supplement one another. With each author, the theme takes on a different shape, but each treatment seems to assume that it is offering *the* reality.

And so there emerges a latent naiveté underlying every style. One might perhaps wonder which of the views comes closest to the truth, but it is patently obvious that every one of the authors has cut reality to the shape of a particular meaning not inherent in that reality. By parodying the styles, Joyce has exposed their essentially manipulative character. The reader gradually becomes conscious of the fact that style fails to achieve its ends, in that it does not capture reality but imposes upon it an historically preconditioned form. The parody through which this process is set in motion contains a polemic element attacking this intrinsic tendency of style to edit observed realities. If now we think back to the invocation with which Joyce ended *A Portrait,* we must expect his meeting with reality to aim at an extension of experience beyond the frontiers of the already familiar. And for a presentation of this, there must, paradoxically, be total freedom from the restrictions of any one consistently sustained mode of presentation.

This brings us to our third conclusion. With his historical panoply of individual and period styles, Joyce exposes the characteristic quality of style—namely, that it imposes form on an essentially formless reality. Thus in the various views of love that are presented, the decisive influence is the historical conditions which shaped the understanding of the subject during the period concerned. Clearly, then, the theme itself is so multifarious that it can encompass every possible historical reflection of it, and the more clearly defined the judgment, the more historically conditioned is the style. Out of the series of parodies, then, emerges the fact that not only are the styles one-sided but they are also conditioned by sets of values that will change from period to period. In other words, the same subject (in this case, love) will take on a different form when viewed under different conditions or at different times. Which style can best capture the reality of the subject? The answer, clearly, is none, for all styles are relative to the historical conditions that shape them.

This brings us to a fourth and last conclusion: if the factors that shape a style are essentially historical, the resultant definition of the object to be described can only be a pragmatic one, since it depends on ever-changing historical conditions. But the pragmatic nature of style can only be exposed through some sort of comparative survey—in this case, the historical sequence—since none of the authors Joyce parodies would have regarded their own form of presentation as a merely pragmatic view of the subjects they were dealing with. Now if style can only accomplish a pragmatic definition, its function in illuminating observed reality must be figurative, or metaphorical, for the limited system of references that forms it is applied to the unlimited reality it is attempting to convey. This is the only way, of course, in which style can build up a uniform picture. But if style can only capture objects in a metaphorical manner, it must be counted simply as one of those rhetorical devices of which Lessing once said: "that they never stick strictly to the truth; that at one moment they say too much, and at another too little." Joyce's chronological exhibition of styles shows clearly that they are all metaphorical and can only offer a preconditioned, one-sided view of their subject matter. The intrinsic aim of style is to capture a phenomenon as accurately as possible, but being only a metaphor, it cannot help but miss out a whole range of aspects of that phenomenon. Roman Ingarden, in describing the views that come to light through the style of a work of art, has said: "The views that we have during our experiences of one and the same thing change in different ways, and much that in an earlier view emerged only in the form of an unrealized quality will, in a later view, be present and transformed into a realized quality. But present in every view of an object are both realized and unrealized qualities, and it is intrinsically impossible ever to make the unrealized qualities disappear" (*The Literary Work of Art*). Joyce's parodies seek to change "unrealized qualities" into "realized," and with this process he shows us how the phenomenon itself begins to expand—for every definition excludes aspects which must themselves then be defined.

If we take up Goldberg's view of "The Oxen of the Sun" as the author's commentary on his novel, we may reasonably extend our findings to the use of style throughout the whole book. While the theme of this one chapter is love, the theme of *Ulysses* itself is everyday human life, and the stylistic presentation of this varies from chapter to chapter, because it can never be grasped as a whole by any one individual style. Only by constantly varying the angle of approach is it possible to convey the potential range of the "real-life" world, but in literature the "approach" is what gives rise to the style. By constantly changing the style, Joyce not only conveys the preconditioned, one-sided nature of each approach but also seems to set both object and observer in motion, thus accumulating an assembly of mobile views that show the essential expansiveness of reality. In this sense, "The Oxen of the Sun" epitomizes the technique of the whole novel. The sequence of styles brings out the one-sidedness of each and the constant expansion of the subject. One aspect after another appears within the mirror of style, but "hey, presto, the mirror is breathed on" and that seemingly all-important facet "recedes, shrivels, to a tiny speck within the mist." What Joyce says in this chapter about sins or evil memories is true also of these hidden aspects of reality, and in "The Oxen of the Sun," as throughout the novel, this insight is constantly developed: they are "hidden away by man in the darkest places of the heart but they abide there and wait. He may suffer their memory to grow dim, let them be as though they had not been and all but persuade himself that they were not or at least were otherwise. Yet a chance word will call them forth suddenly and they will rise up to confront him in the most various circumstances.''

Ithaca

A. Walton Litz

If *Ulysses* is a crucial testing ground for theories of the novel, as it seems to have become, then the "Ithaca" episode must be a *locus classicus* for every critic interested in the traditions of English and European fiction. Here the extremes of Joyce's art, and of fiction in general, are found in radical form: the tension between symbolism and realism, what Arnold Goldman has called the "myth/fact paradox," gives the episode its essential life (*The Joyce Paradox*). Joyce once told Frank Budgen that "Ithaca" was his "favourite episode," the "ugly duckling of the book," and his frequent references to the episode in his letters reveal a personal and artistic involvement seldom matched in his work on the other chapters. He was acutely aware that "Ithaca" culminated his risky "scorched earth" policy of constantly altering the novel's styles and narrative methods, so that "the progress of the book is in fact like the progress of some sandblast," each successive episode leaving behind it "a burnt up field." He also knew that the reader who had mastered the "initial style" of the earliest episodes, that subtle blending of interior monologue and distanced description derived from *A Portrait of the Artist,* would prefer it "much as the wanderer did who longed for the rock of Ithaca."

These defensive remarks were made in mid-1919, when Joyce felt compelled to justify the "musical" techniques of "Sirens," and they clearly reflect his anxiety at that moment in the composition of *Ulysses* when the

From *James Joyce's* Ulysses: *Critical Essays,* edited by Clive Hart and David Hayman. © 1974 by the Regents of the University of California. The University of California Press, 1974.

life of the novel began to gravitate from external drama to the internal reality of the various styles and artifices. This clearcut shift in artistic aims midway through Joyce's work on *Ulysses* was somewhat masked by the final revisions, when he recast many of the earlier episodes in forms that satisfied his later sense of the novel's design; but he attached so much importance to this transitional moment in the making of the novel that he once thought of writing an "*Entr'acte*" to celebrate the mid-point in the narrative, and on a chart of the episodes sent to John Quinn in September 1920 the first nine episodes (through "Scylla and Charybdis") are clearly separated from the last nine (beginning with "Wandering Rocks"). Just as the structural centre of *Ulysses* represents a turning point in the motions of Bloom and Stephen, the beginning of their tentative progress toward each other, so it announces a fundamental change in the novel's aesthetic ground-base. From "Wandering Rocks" and "Sirens" onward, the "reality" to be processed into art is both the imitated human action and the rich artistic world already created in the earlier and plainer episodes. Technique tends more and more to become subject matter, and by the time we reach "Ithaca" the form of the episode is as much the substance as the actual interchanges between Bloom and Stephen.

So both the action and the stylistic development of *Ulysses* reach a climax in "Ithaca," which Joyce considered "in reality the end as 'Penelope' has no beginning, middle or end." Although he had a general sense of the novel's ending from the start of his work on it, and could refer easily to the "Nostos" (the last three episodes) during the process of composition, Joyce evidently had no clear notion of the local form of "Ithaca" until 1919–20; yet long before any part of the episode reached paper he had unconsciously rehearsed the role "Ithaca" was to play in a continuing debate on the aims of English and European fiction. It has often been noted that the two lectures Joyce gave at the Università Popolare of Trieste in 1912 established the twin frontiers of his art and looked forward to *Ulysses*. He chose as his subjects Defoe and Blake, treating them as the ultimate masters of painstaking realism and the universal symbolism of spiritual "corre-spondences." But it has not been noted that the tags Joyce chose for his lectures, *verismo* and *idealismo,* were technical terms in a contemporary critical debate on the validity of the "realistic" novel. What Joyce did in his lectures was to liberate the terms from literary controversy and use them to describe two complementary methods for universalizing experience. One way toward completeness, as the editors of the Blake lecture remark, is through the overwhelming accretion of encyclopaedic detail: Robinson Cru-soe is an archetypal figure—Joyce speaks of him as such—because we know him, like Bloom, in all the petty but revealing details of ordinary life. Commenting on Defoe's *The Storm,* Joyce noted that the "method is simplicity itself."

> The book opens with an inquiry into the causes of winds, then recapitulates the famous storms in human story, and finally the narrative, like a great snake, begins to crawl slowly through a tangle of letters and reports. . . . The modern reader does a good deal of groaning before he reaches the conclusion, but in the end the object of the chronicler has been achieved. By dint of repetitions, contradictions, details, figures, noises, the storm has come alive, the ruin is visible.

This is the technique of much of "Ithaca," an accumulation of details which has no inherent "aesthetic" limits but relies on the epic impact of overmastering fact. One can see the method in action in the growth of the notorious question-and-answer on the universal significance of water, where the exchange in the basic manuscript

> What in water did Bloom, carrying water, returning to the range, admire?
> Its universality: its equality and constancy to its nature in seeking its own level: its vastness in the ocean of Mercator's projector: its secrecy in springs, exemplified by the well by the hole in the wall at Ashtown gate: its healing virtues: its properties for cleansing, quenching thirst and fire, nourishing plant life: its strength in rigid hydrants: its docility in working millwheels, electric power stations, bleachworks, tanneries, scutchmills: its utility in canals, rivers, if navigable; its fauna and flora: its noxiousness in marshes, pestilential fens, faded flowers, stagnant pools in the waning moon.

finally took this form:

> What in water did Bloom, waterlover, drawer of water, watercarrier returning to the range, admire?
> Its universality: its democratic equality and constancy to its nature in seeking its own level: its vastness in the ocean of Mercator's projection: its umplumbed profundity in the Sundam trench of the Pacific exceeding 8,000 fathoms: the restlessness of its waves and surface particles visiting in turn all points of its seaboard: the independence of its units: the variability of states

of sea: its hydrostatic quiescence in calm: its hydrokinetic turgidity in neap and spring tides: its subsidence after devastation: its sterility in the circumpolar icecaps, arctic and antarctic: its climatic and commercial significance: its proponderance of 3 to 1 over the dry land of the globe: its indisputable hegemony extending in square leagues over all the region below the subequatorial tropic of Capricorn: the multisecular stability of its primeval basin: its luteofulvous bed: its capacity to dissolve and hold in solution all soluble substances including millions of tons of the most precious metals: its slow erosions of peninsulas and downwardtending promontories: its alluvial deposits: its weight and volume and density: its imperturbability in lagoons and highland tarns: its gradation of colours in the torrid and temperate and frigid zones: its vehicular ramifications in continental lakecontained streams and confluent oceanflowing rivers with their tributaries and transoceanic currents: gulfstream, north and south equatorial courses: its violence in seaquakes, waterspouts, artesian wells, eruptions, torrents, eddies, freshets, spates, groundswells, watersheds, waterpartings, geysers, cataracts, whirlpools, maelstroms, inundations, deluges, cloudbursts: its vast circumterrestrial ahorizontal curve: its secrecy in springs, and latent humidity, revealed by rhabdomantic or hygrometric instruments and exemplified by the hole in the wall at Ashtown gate, saturation of air, distillation of dew: the simplicity of its composition, two constituent parts of hydrogen with one constituent part of oxygen: its healing virtues: its buoyancy in the waters of the Dead Sea: its persevering penetrativeness in runnels, gullies, inadequate dams, leaks on shipboard: its properties for cleansing, quenching thirst and fire, nourishing vegetation: its infallibility as paradigm and paragon: its metamorphoses as vapour, mist, cloud, rain, sleet, snow, hail: its strength in rigid hydrants: its variety of forms in loughs and bays and gulfs and bights and guts and lagoons and atolls and archipelagos and sounds and fjords and minches and tidal estuaries and arms of sea: its solidity in glaciers, icebergs, icefloes: its docility in working hydraulic millwheels, turbines, dynamos, electric power stations, bleachworks, tanneries, scutchmills: its utility in canals, rivers, if navigable, floating and graving docks: its potentiality derivable from harnessed tides or watercourses falling from level to level: its submarine fauna and flora (anacoustic, photophobe)

numerically, if not literally, the inhabitants of the globe: its
ubiquity as constituting 90% of the human body: the noxiousness
of its effluvia in lacustrine marshes, pestilential fens, faded flow-
erwater, stagnant pools in the waning moon.

Here the initial passage was enlarged five-fold as it passed through successive
typescripts and proofs, while the subject changed from the normal associations of Bloom's inquisitive mind to a conflation of that mind and the
novel's "epic" aims. Like Defoe's encyclopaedic treatment of the storm,
Joyce's catalogue finally convinces "by dint of repetitions, contradictions,
details, figures," until it ultimately becomes the expression of some omniscient mind meditating on the universal virtues of water.

But if the Defoe lecture is filled with Joyce's admiration for a writer
who, through accumulated data, can turn fact into myth or archetype, the
lecture on Blake reveals his deep affinity with the visionary artist who can
divine the universe in a blade of grass, who through symbolic correspondences can make "each moment shorter than a pulse-beat . . . equivalent
in its duration to six thousand years" and can fly "from the infinitely small
to the infinitely large, from a drop of blood to the universe of stars." Here
the debt to Yeats's interpretations of Blake is obvious, and the theory of
the epiphany is not far in the background. Like Whitman, Joyce possessed
a talent which was both centripetal and centrifugal, tending toward both
the symbolic moment and the scrupulous accumulation of "fact": and these
complementary impulses give "Ithaca" its form and dynamism.

In speaking of the extremes of Joyce's art, it would be pointless to
moderate or ignore their obsessive qualities. Both the symbolism and realism of "Ithaca" have dimensions which are essentially private and disproportionate. Joyce's famous verification of Bloom's entrance into No. 7
Eccles street is a notorious example of a regard for "realism" that goes far
beyond the normal compact between author and reader:

Is it possible (Joyce wrote to his aunt Josephine) for an ordinary
person to climb over the area railings of no 7 Eccles street, either
from the path or the steps, lower himself down from the lowest
part or the railings till his feet are within 2 feet or 3 of the ground
and drop unhurt. I saw it done myself but by a man of rather
athletic build. I require this information in detail in order to
determine the wording of a paragraph.

In the same way, many of the leading symbols in "Ithaca" (such as urination)
seem to have had more significance for the author than for the reader. Like

Henry James's *The Sacred Fount,* the "Ithaca" episode relies so heavily on the author's obsessive techniques and themes that they approach self-parody; and although "Ithaca" is richly comic in its general intent there are times when Joyce, like James, seems unaware of the grotesque effects he is creating. In a sense, "fact" and the private symbol became substitutes for all those conventional supports of society and art and religion that Joyce had rejected.

These "obsessive" qualities in "Ithaca" really lie beyond the reach of conventional criticism, in the realm of psychoanalytic biography or some study of the creative process; they are reminders that most authors need more sanctions and correspondences than they can share with their audience (it is interesting that T. S. Eliot, in his 1956 lecture on "The Frontiers of Criticism," used J. Livingston Lowes's *Road to Xanadu* and Joyce's *Finnegans Wake* to define the "frontiers"). But we should not let Joyce's personal obsessions obscure one central fact: that *Ulysses* is a cross-roads in the history of prose fiction because it both exaggerates and harmonizes certain major tendencies that had marked the novel from its earliest appearances. Emerging in the seventeenth and eighteenth centuries from a convergence of myth (fables, "Romance," moral tales) and fact (journals, diaries, "news"), English fiction has always had a paradoxical relation to reality, as the fruitless attempts to separate "Romance" from "Novel" testify. If *Ulysses* is to be considered as a novel, rather than an "anatomy" or some other hybrid form, it must be because the work is true to the fundamental paradox of the genre even while every aspect of the genre is being tested by parody and burlesque.

Perhaps it is a reluctance to accept this essential ambivalence of both the novel-form and *Ulysses* which lies behind the attempts of so many readers to press *Ulysses*—and especially the "Ithaca" chapter—into some easy equation of "either/or." Either Joyce's method is a satire on the naturalistic writer's preoccupation with detail, or it is a humourless exercise in the manner of classic naturalism. Either it is *reductio ad absurdum* of naive nineteenth-century faith in science, or a serious application of scientific theories to human psychology. "Ithaca" is either a final celebration of Bloom's heroic qualities as Everyman, or a cold revelation of his essential pettiness. Just as the typical reader of *A Portrait of the Artist* finds it difficult to accept the delicate balance of sympathy and irony that marks the novel's close, so the average reader of *Ulysses* seems compelled to indulge in the worst kind of critical bookkeeping, totting up Joyce's ironies and human touches as if some simple formula were really available. But the genius of Joyce and of *Ulysses* lies in the indisputable fact that the form is both epic and ironic, Bloom both heroic and commonplace. The bed of Ulysses is, in its secret construction, known only to Ulysses and Penelope, while the secret of Bloom's bed is a Dublin joke; but when Bloom dismisses Molly's suitors one by one his reason and equanimity are, as Joyce intended, equal in power to the great bow that only Ulysses could draw. At first Joyce had thought of the slaughter of the suitors as "un-Ulyssean," a bloody act of violence that could not be translated into modern Dublin or reconciled with Bloom's humanism; but finally he came to see that Bloom's equanimity of mind was in its way a comparable achievement. In his attempt "to transpose the myth *sub specie temporis nostri*" Joyce realized that the contrasts between the classical world and the modern world would inevitably be ironic on the level of *fact,* leading only to mock-heroic effects where the disparities in setting and action tend to debase the contemporary experience; but he also knew that on the level of symbol, where the fundamentals of human psychology are revealed, Bloom would prove a worthy counterpart to the hero of Homer's epic. Any reading of *Ulysses* that aims at doing justice to Joyce's complex vision must be composed of constant adjustments and accommodations between myth and fact, and it is in "Ithaca" that these adjustments are most difficult to make.

Joyce began work on "Ithaca" early in 1921, after completing the drafts of "Eumaeus," and was still revising the episode on proof in late January 1922, only a few days before the novel's publication ("Penelope" was actually finished before "Ithaca" so that Valery Larbaud could read it while preparing for his famous séance on December 7, 1921). Thus Joyce could write "Ithaca" with every detail of the novel's plan and action firmly in mind, and it is not surprising that the episode fits into the general scheme of *Ulysses* with absolute precision. In the first stages of his work on "Ithaca" Joyce went through the usual process of grouping his raw materials on successive notesheets, listing the themes and motifs and tags of dialogue which were to be transformed into the episode's characteristic styles. As one might expect, the notesheets are filled with the cosmic equivalents (such as "$JC = 3 \sqrt{God}$") which Joyce referred to in his well-known letter to Frank Budgen:

> I am writing *Ithaca* in the form of a mathematical catechism. All events are resolved into their cosmic, physical, psychical etc. equivalents, e.g. Bloom jumping down the area, drawing water from the tap, the micturition in the garden, the cone of incense, lighted candle and statue so that not only will the reader know everything and know it in the baldest coldest way, but Bloom and Stephen thereby become heavenly bodies, wanderers like the stars at which they gaze.

But mixed with these "cosmic, physical, psychical etc. equivalents" on the notesheets are the terse phrases in Bloom's natural idiom which trigger the cosmic correspondences. For example, an elaborate attempt to relate Stephen and Bloom to Molly in terms of vectors and tangents is prompted by the colloquial "fly off at a tangent," while a natural phenomenon jotted down in Bloom's staccatto speech ("See star by day from bottom of gully") is transformed in the text into pseudo-scientific jargon: "of the infinite lattiginous scintillating uncondensed milky way, discernible by daylight by an observer placed at the lower end of a cylindrical vertical shaft 5000 ft deep sunk from the surface towards the centre of the earth." The notesheets provide overwhelming evidence that the "dry rock pages of *Ithaca*" are supersaturated with Bloom's humanity, a humanity that is enhanced if anything by the impersonality of the prose. As any viewer of the recent film will remember, "Ithaca" yielded scenes of far more warmth and feeling than those provided by such "dramatic" episodes as "Hades" and "Nausicaa." Once again, in the contrast between the apparent coldness of the episode's form and its actual human effects, we are confronted with a paradox to be solved.

It will be best to approach the problems of "Ithaca" in three stages: (1) an analysis of the catechistical form; (2) a scanning of the episode's scenic progression; and (3) an assessment of the general effect of "Ithaca" on our experience of the novel. The question-and-answer form is dictated in part by the "schoolroom" nature of "Ithaca"; in Joyce's *schema* for the novel the episode is an impersonal counterpart to the personal catechism pursued by Stephen in "Nestor." It is customary to think of "Ithaca" as deriving from the form of the Christian catechism and Joyce's early Jesuit training, but the parallels with the catechistical methods of the nineteenth-century schoolroom are equally convincing. Two recent critics have proposed that the form of "Ithaca" is directly indebted to Richmal Mangnall's *Historical and Miscellaneous Questions,* a textbook of encyclopaedic knowledge which went through over a hundred editions during the nineteenth-century and was still in use in Joyce's day. Stephen refers to the book in *A Portrait,* and Robert Graves used it in 1901 at the age of six, although his father thought it out of date. Mangnall's *Questions* is a compendium of undifferentiated "practical" knowledge, cast in the form of a familiar catechism. Questions that any child might ask are phrased in simple form, while a voice of hectoring authority responds with a surfeit of information and misinformation.

What are comets?
Luminous and opaque bodies, whose motions are in different

directions, and the orbits they describe very extensive; they have long translucent tails of light turned from the sun: the great swiftness of their motion in the neighbourhood of the sun, is the reason they appear to us for such a short time: and the great length of time they are in appearing again is occasioned by the extent and eccentricity of their orbits or paths in the heavens.

How many comets are supposed to belong to our solar system: Twenty-one; but we only know.

There can be no doubt that Mangnall's *Questions* was a primary source for Joyce's "mathematico-astronomico-physico-mechanico-geometrico-chemico sublimation of Bloom and Stephen. To the modern adult reader it is filled with unconscious humour and grotesque distortions, but to the young Joyce it must have shimmered with the poetic magic of unfamiliar names and mysterious words (such as gnomon and simony). In Stephen's day-dream of vindication by the rector he associates himself with "the great men whose names were in Richmal Magnall's [*sic*] Questions." The form of Mangnall's *Questions* would have been easily assimilated into the authoritarian structure of Jesuit education, and it is clear from Joyce's early Paris notebook (1903) that he found the catechism a congenial vehicle for his own ideas.

Question: Why are not excrements, children, and lice works of art?
Answer: Excrements, children, and lice are human products—human dispositions of sensible matter. The process by which they are produced is natural and nonartistic; their end is not an aesthetic end: therefore they are not works of art.

As Lynch comments later in *A Portrait,* such a question has "the true scholastic stink," and Joyce himself was certainly aware of the pomposity latent in the form. We may hazard the guess that he chose to cast the most bizarre examples of his aesthetic in catechistical form as a defensive acknowledgment of their potential absurdity. In sum, the catechism must have struck Joyce as a natural and even inevitable form for the climactic episode of *Ulysses* because it was associated with some of his most profound early experiences, and had proved to be a vehicle for precise intellectual argument which simultaneously allowed scope for exaggeration and self-parody.

The greatest danger inherent in the catechistical form would seem to be monotony. The effectiveness of the catechism in the classroom depends upon a sameness in form and rhythm which—as Wordsworth said of poetic meter—opens the memory and fixes the mind in a receptive mood. But such an effect, useful as it might be for the pedagogue, would be disastrous for the novelist, and Joyce kept the technique flexible in "Ithaca" by constant shifts in tone, rhetoric, and quality of subject matter. When we think of the "style" of "Ithaca" we usually think of those set pieces where Bloom's thoughts and actions are cast in the self-confident language of Victorian science, but in fact many of the answers are simple and direct:

> What did Bloom see on the range?
> On the right (smaller) hob a blue enamelled saucepan: on the left (larger) hob a black iron kettle.
> What did Bloom do at the range?
> He removed the saucepan to the left hob, rose and carried the iron kettle to the sink in order to tap the current by turning the faucet to let it flow.

These plain questions-and-answers are then followed by two elaborate exchanges on Dublin's water supply and the universal qualities of water. The effect is to retard our sense of the action while still rendering it in sharp detail: it is as if we were viewing Bloom and Stephen from a great height, against a vast backdrop of general human action and knowledge, while at the same time standing next to them and observing every local detail. It is this "parallax" achieved by the macrocosmic-microcosmic point-of-view which gives the episode, like Hardy's *Dynasts,* the grandeur and sweep that Joyce certainly intended.

Arnold Goldman remarks that "the vein of 'Ithaca' has been re-opened in recent French novels. There the entire novel may be in the style of Joyce's chapter, the programmatic intention of the artist being to circumvent the metaphysical antinomy of subject and object by treating everything as an object." But surely this is just the opposite of Joyce's intention and achievement. Bloom and Stephen do indeed "become heavenly bodies, wanderers like the stars at which they gaze," but at the same time their subjective lives penetrate every detail of objective description. Alain Robbe-Grillet's famous description of the *nouveau roman* stands at the opposite pole from Joyce's method.

> Instead of this universe of "signification" (psychological, social, functional), we must try, then, to construct a world both more solid and more immediate. Let it be first of all by their *presence* that objects and gestures establish themselves, and let this presence continue to prevail over whatever explanatory the-

ory that may try to enclose them in a system of references, whether emotional, sociological, Freudian or metaphysical.

In this future universe of the novel, gestures and objects will be *there* before *something;* and they will still be there afterwards, hard, unalterable, eternally present, mocking their own "meaning," that meaning which vainly tries to reduce them to the role of precarious tools, of a temporary and shameful fabric woven exclusively—and deliberately—by the superior human truth expressed in it, only to cast out this awkward auxiliary into immediate oblivion and darkness.

Henceforth, on the contrary, objects will gradually lose their instability and their secrets, will renounce their pseudo-mystery, that suspect interiority which Roland Barthes has called "the romantic heart of things." No longer will objects be merely the vague reflection of the hero's vague soul, the image of his torments, the shadow of his desires. Or rather, if objects still afford a momentary prop to human passions, they will do so only provisionally, and will accept the tyranny of significations only in appearance—derisively, one might say—the better to show how alien they remain to man.

(*For a New Novel: Essays on Fiction*)

The relationship between objects and personality in Joyce's writing would seem to be much more complex than in Robbe-Grillet's. While "Ithaca" does "resolve" its human figures into their objective counterparts, at the same time the objective universe is suffused with their personalities. Take the following question-and-answer:

By what reflections did he, a conscious reactor against the void incertitude, justify to himself his sentiments?

The preordained frangibility of the hymen, the presupposed intangibility of the thing in itself: the incongruity and disproportion between the selfprolonging tension of the thing proposed to be done and the self abbreviating relaxation of the thing done: the fallaciously inferred debility of the female, the muscularity of the male: the variations of ethical codes: the natural grammatical transition by inversion involving no alteration of sense of an aorist preterite proposition (parsed as masculine subject, monosyllabic onomatopoeic transitive verb with direct feminine object) from the active voice into its correlative aorist preterite proposition (parsed as feminine subject, auxiliary verb and quasi-

> monosyllabic onomatopoeic past participle with complementary
> masculine agent) in the passive voice: the continued product of
> seminators by generation: the continual production of semen by
> distillation: the futility of triumph or protest or vindication: the
> inanity of extolled virtue: the lethargy of nescient matter: the
> apathy of the stars.

Here the typical movement from microcosm to macrocosm, from the "frangibility" of the individual hymen to the "apathy of the stars," is a reflection of Bloom's thought as he strives for equanimity by sinking his own anxieties in the processes of nature. In spite of their pseudo-scientific presentation the "objects" in this passage are as personal and "interior" as those in the closing of "The Dead." In "Ithaca" Joyce did not renounce his interest in "the romantic heart of things," but simply found new means for expressing it.

As Joyce's work on "Ithaca" neared an end in the autumn of 1921 he told his correspondents that he was putting the episode "in order." His methods of gathering material had been ideally suited to the making of "Ithaca," each question-and-answer developing around a phrase or idea and then being fitted into the general design. Clearly he conceived of "Ithaca" as a series of scenes or tableaux, not unlike the narrative divisions in "Circe," and on the early typescripts he blocked out these scenes under the titles "street," "kitchen," "garden," "parlour," "bedroom." We may consider the "narrative" development of "Ithaca" under these headings, since each scene builds to a revealing climax which forwards our understanding of both Bloom and Stephen.

The scene in the street begins with Bloom and Stephen moving in parallel but separate courses. The tone is relaxed, the conversation easy and desultory. Both Stephen and Bloom are "keyless," the victims of usurpers, poised between thought and action: "To enter or not to enter. To knock or not to knock." But whereas Stephen has fallen under the spell of Hamlet's melancholy and indecision, Bloom—like his Homeric namesake, or the active Hamlet—devises a "stratagem," and his acrobatic entrance into No. 7 Eccles street is described in ponderous language which simultaneously satirizes the triviality of the event (in its cosmic context) while emphasizing its importance in the context of Bloom's own life.

> Did he fall?
> By his body's known weight of eleven stone and four pounds
> in avoirdupois measure, as certified by the graduated machine
> for periodical selfweighing in the premises of Francis Froedman,

pharmaceutical chemist of 19 Frederick street, north, on the last feast of the Ascension, to wit, the twelfth day of May of the bissextile year one thousand nine hundred and four of the christian era (jewish era five thousand six hundred and sixtyfour, mohammedan era one thousand three hundred and twentytwo), golden number 5, epact 13, solar cycle 9, dominical letters C B, Roman indication 2, Julian period 6617, MXMIV.

The entire "street" scene establishes Bloom as the focus of our interest, and throws the balance of the narrative toward his competence and resourcefulness. In this episode, by contrast with "Nestor," Stephen will be more learner than teacher.

Events in the "kitchen" scene explore the sympathetic bonds between Stephen and Bloom, as well as their points of difference, culminating in the "exodus" from kitchen to garden which brings their relationship into focus through a symbolic tableau not unlike that at the end of "Circe."

In what order of precedence, with what attendant ceremony was the exodus from the house of bondage to the wilderness of inhabitation effected?

Lighted Candle in Stick borne by
BLOOM.
Diaconal Hat on Ashplant borne by
STEPHEN

With what intonation *secreto* of what commemorative psalm?
The 113th, *modus peregrinus: In exitu Israël de Egypto: domus Jacob de populo barbaro.*

What did each do at the door of egress?
Bloom set the candlestick on the floor. Stephen put the hat on his head.

For what creature was the door of egress a door of ingress?
For a cat.

What spectacle confronted them when they, first the host, then the guest, emerged silently, doubly dark, from obscurity by a passage from the rere of the house into the penumbra of the garden?
The heaventree of stars hung with humid nightblue fruit.

Our reading of the symbolic references woven into this scene will determine in large measure our ultimate attitude toward the "union" of Stephen and Bloom. The echoes from Dante are insistent, and have often been noted.

The opening line from the 113th Psalm, "When Israel went out of Egypt," is twice used by Dante as a text to illustrate his fourfold method of allegory (in the *Letter to Can Grande* and the *Convivio*), and it has been suggested that Joyce is covertly instructing us to read "Ithaca" as a "polysemous" work, which it certainly is: the literal and the allegorical are never more obvious than in this passage, where each literal detail is packed with ceremonial significance. But an elaborate application of Dante's four "levels" would seem more problematic, and the tag from the 113th Psalm is best interpreted as a traditional reference to the resurrection which appears at a crucial turning-point in the *Commedia*.

As Dante and Virgil emerge from Hell at the end of the *Inferno* they are once more able to see the stars (the word upon which each part of the *Commedia* ends), just as Stephen and Bloom emerge from the house to confront "The heaventree of stars hung with humid nightblue fruit." A little later, in the first Canto of the *Purgatorio*, Cato questions: "Who hath guided you? or who was a lamp unto you issuing forth from the deep night that ever maketh black the infernal vale" (*Purgatorio*, 1, 43-45). Similarly, the omniscient voice in "Ithaca" asks:

> What visible luminous sign attracted Bloom's, who attracted Stephen's gaze?
> In the second storey (rere) of his (Bloom's) house the light of a paraffin oil lamp with oblique shade projected on a screen of roller blind supplied by Frank O'Hara, window blind, curtain pole and revolving shutter manufacturer, 16 Aungier street.

In the next Canto of the *Purgatorio* Dante and Virgil encounter the souls about to enter Purgatory, singing the ancient hymn of redemption, "*In exitu Israel de Aegypto*" (*Purgatorio*, 2, 46), the same hymn Stephen chants as he and Bloom leave the kitchen.

The symbolic implications of these accumulated references are overwhelming: the meeting of Stephen and Bloom has provided a release from bondage, a release noted through a traditional combination of Hebrew and Christian imagery. The only question is whether we take these implications as a vehicle for irony, an irony based on the disparity between the trivial and allegorical levels, or as a complex statement of psychological potentialities. The critical problem is exactly the same as that produced by the Homeric parallels, and the same solution suggests itself. On the literal level, bounded by the twenty hours of the novel's action, Stephen and Bloom are mock-heroic figures; but on the figurative level they take on heroic and creative possibilities. Having confined himself to a realistic time-scheme which made impossible the actual dramatization of that dynamic growth of personality so characteristic of the conventional novel, Joyce vested this element in his symbolic structures. To paraphrase Santayana, *Ulysses* is mock-heroic in immediacy, but heroic in perspective, and Joyce's delicate balancing of attitudes is nowhere more evident than in this climactic scene. No critical formula of "either/or" can do it justice. Instead, we must think of Joyce's use of myth in the light of Eliot's "Tradition and the Individual Talent": a vital interchange between past and present which humanizes the past while it enlarges the present.

As Bloom and Stephen stand in the garden before parting, beneath the lamp of Molly which has been Bloom's guide throughout the day, they urinate together, "their sides contiguous, their organs of micturition reciprocally rendered invisible by manual circumposition, their gazes, first Bloom's, then Stephen's, elevated to the projected luminous and semi-luminous shadow." This is the moment of symbolic union, and the fact that it is richly comic in the manner of Sterne does not detract from its ultimate seriousness. Joyce's identification of micturition with creativity is well known, and although W. Y. Tindall may be overly ingenious in making the identification a major theme in [his edition of] *Chamber Music* (where it is of more interest to the psychoanalyst than the literary critic), the explicit association of urination with creativity in *Finnegans Wake* makes a similar interpretation of this scene in "Ithaca" more than probable. As Clive Hart has pointed out, the theme of micturition as creation and transubstantiation is established early in *Ulysses* by the Ballad of Joking Jesus, and there can be no doubt that Joyce intended the garden scene in "Ithaca" to foreshadow a new departure for both Bloom and Stephen (*Structure and Motif in* Finnegans Wake). On the literal level they remain divided, each absorbed in his own thoughts; but the "celestial sign" that they both observe—"a star precipitated . . . towards the zodiacal sign of Leo"—reminds us that Stephen's daylong pilgrimage has led toward this encounter with the humane and inquisitive Bloom, whose personality supplies the qualities lacking in his own sterile spirit.

When Bloom and Stephen say farewell the literal narrative leaves them separate once again, with their futures adumbrated but not dramatized, and Bloom turns from the chill of "proximate dawn" to re-enter the house. Having touched the ultimate reaches of symbol and myth, the episode returns to the level of "objects" and "things"; and Bloom's exploration of the parlour is told in a manner and style that would have delighted Defoe. The catalogues of this section—the furnishings of the room, the contents of the bookshelves, the budget for June 16, 1904—bring the reader back to the irreducible reality of Bloom's life and prepare the way for the next access of myth and symbol at the end of the "parlour" scene. As Bloom's thoughts drift toward travel and escape he is transformed into Everyman and Noman, Elpenor and Ulysses, into a wandering comet whose orbit traces the extremes of his real and potential existences.

> Would the departed never nowhere nohow reappear?
> Ever he would wander, selfcompelled, to the extreme limit of his cometary orbit, beyond the fixed stars and variable suns and telescopic planets, astronomical waifs and strays, to the extreme boundary of space, passing from land to land, among peoples, amid events. Somewhere imperceptibly he would hear and somehow reluctantly, suncompelled, obey the summons of recall. Whence, disappearing from the constellation of the Northern Crown he would somehow reappear reborn above delta in the constellation of Cassiopeia and after incalculable eons of peregrination return an estranged avenger, a wreaker of justice on malefactors, a dark crusader, a sleeper awakened, with financial resources (by supposition) surpassing those of Rothschild or of the silver king.

We know from both the Library episode and an earlier section of "Ithaca" that a nova in Cassiopeia (whose form is a capital "W") announced the birth of William Shakespeare, while "a star (2nd magnitude) of similar origin but lesser brilliancy" had appeared in the Northern Crown to mark the birth of Leopold Bloom. In this passage Bloom disappears in his own personality only to reappear as his mythic counterpart, a Hamlet or Ulysses freed of anxiety and intent upon his mission of revenge. Such transformations become more and more common as the "parlour" scene wears to a close, and Bloom gradually takes on all the ritual and ceremonial significances of the day that has passed. In fact, one might say that "Ithaca" progresses by a rhythmic alternation between mythic or "epiphanic" moments and longer stretches of "realism" which validate these moments.

Once in the "bedroom" Bloom stretches out on the bed, which still bears the evidence of Boylan's recent occupancy, and meditates on the "series originating in and repeated to infinity" of Molly's lovers. Robert M. Adams has pointed out the bizarre elements in Bloom's catalogue, but at this stage in the episode the criteria of "realism" seem curiously irrelevant (*Surface and Symbol: The Consistency of James Joyce's* Ulysses). "Ithaca" closes on the highest plane of mythopoetic intensity, as Joyce's intentions—so often stated in the letters—are fully realized. The episode has developed through a measured oscillation between the literal and allegorical levels, until at the end the balance is thrown finally and irrevocably to the side of symbolism. The sequence of Bloom's thought—"Envy, jealousy, abnegation, equanimity"—sums up the process, as Molly and Bloom are transformed from individual human beings into types and archetypes. It is possible, of course, to see this process as "something of an evasion," but only if the life of *Ulysses* is viewed as more surface than symbol. It was Joyce's unique gift that he could turn the substance of ordinary life into something like myth, not only through the use of "parallels" and allusions but through direct transformation: and the ending of "Ithaca," like that of "Anna Livia Plurabelle," would seem to vindicate his method. Most of *Ulysses* can be understood by the same methods one applies to *The Waste Land*, where the manipulation of a continuous parallel between contemporaneity and antiquity "places" the contemporary action, but the ending of "Ithaca" consists of metamorphosis rather than juxtaposition. As in the conclusion to "Circe," the model is the transformation scene of a typical pantomime (perhaps the pantomime of *Sindbad the Sailor*), and we must believe that Molly has merged into her archetype, Gea-Tellus, while Leopold Bloom has become the archetype of all human possibility, "the manchild in the womb." The ironies of the novel still operate on the literal level—Molly is unfulfilled, Bloom unsatisfied—but these are of lesser importance beside the primaeval realities which close the episode. The final questions ("When? Where?") reflect the novel's traditional concerns with time and space, but the answers are a rebuke to such concerns.

> When?
> Going to a dark bed there was a square round Sinbad the
> Sailor roc's auk's egg in the night of the bed of all the auks of
> the rocs of Darkinbad the Brightdayler.
> Where?

In sleep the limits of the rational mind fall away, and Bloom's desire to solve the problem of "the quadrature of the circle" is satisfied. At the end of "Ithaca," which is the end of *Ulysses* as novel and fable, Bloom subsides into the mythic world of the giant roc, where light is born out of darkness, and into the womb of infinite possibilities. "La réponse à la dernière demande est un point," Joyce instructed the printer on his typescript, and that point contains a double meaning. As a full-stop it marks the conclusion of Bloom's day, the terminus of the novel's literal action, but as a spatial object it represents Bloom's total retreat into the womb of time, from which he shall emerge the next day with all the fresh potentialities of Everyman. Like the Viconian *ricorso*, the final moment of "Ithaca" is both an end and a beginning.

"Ithaca" provides the capstone to our total experience of *Ulysses*. If the novel ended with this episode our view of the major characters and their motives would remain substantially the same, although our sense of reality would be somewhat different. "Penelope" is indeed the "indispensable countersign to Bloom's passport to eternity," as Joyce once called it, since it substantiates the novel's promise of cyclic renewal; but without it we would still have a completed world to savour and interpret. On Joyce's *schema* for the novel, "Penelope" alone is assigned no specific time; its materials (Bed, Flesh, Earth) are essentially timeless. Although its themes are cunningly orchestrated, the random organization being merely illusion, "Penelope" does not contribute to the sequence of styles which is one of our chief interests in *Ulysses*. Instead, the novel subsides into an appearance of naturalness, and our final impression is that of a voice, curious, lively, undiscriminating.

"Ithaca," by contrast, has the appearance of extreme artifice, and has often been taken as the final triumph of Joyce the baroque elaborator over Joyce the "novelist." But such a view rests on the all-too-common assumption that the "novelistic" elements in *Ulysses* must be those of the traditional nineteenth-century novel—the revelation of character through setting, plot, and observed consciousness—and that the devices and correspondences that mark the later chapters must be evaluated as either essential or auxiliary to the novelistic effects. Such a view was put forward in my own earlier work, *The Art of James Joyce,* where many of the artifices found in the last chapters are assigned to the play-instinct or to Joyce's personal need for order while gathering his materials. I still believe that the more recondite correspondences in *Ulysses* were more important to Joyce during the process of composition than they can ever be to us during the process of reading and interpreting, but I have long since abandoned the notion—always a reductive one—that the novelistic elements in *Ulysses* can be separated from the *schema* and claimed as the true line of the work's meaning. What Joyce accomplished in writing *Ulysses* was to shatter the form of the well-made novel and expose its multifarious origins (allegory, "Romance," history, gossip, "news"), and then to reconstitute these materials in a variety of experimental forms. The result is a work of art which renders the bourgeois world in all its detail and potentiality, uniting fact and myth in a classic portrayal of Everyman as dispossessed hero. In its radical form "Ithaca" bypasses the familiar conventions of nineteenth-century fiction and shows us another way in which the novelist's passion for omniscience can be achieved without violating our sense of individual and local reality.

The Autonomous Monologue

Dorrit Cohn

"Penelope" as Paradigm

Within the limited corpus of autonomous interior monologues the "Penelope" section of *Ulysses* may be regarded as a *locus classicus,* the most famous and the most perfectly executed specimen of its species. Given its position within the broader context of Joyce's novel, however, the question must be raised whether it is at all legitimate to consider "Penelope" as an example of an autonomous fictional form. Would it even be comprehensible to a reader unfamiliar with the preceding sections of the novel? A difficult question to answer empirically, since it would be very nearly impossible to find an experimental subject untainted by at least a hearsay acquaintance with Joyce's work. This much seems certain: Joyce's task of making the "plot" of an interior monologue text comprehensible to the reader despite the strict implicitness of reference demanded by the logic of the form was greatly eased by placing it at the end of his novel rather than at its beginning. The fact, moreover, that we know so much of what Molly knows before we hear her silent voice enhances our enjoyment of it by myriad cross-references to the rest of the novel. Even more important, the fact that we know much that Molly does *not* know (for example, the entire truth about Bloom's erotic experiences on Bloomsday) injects an element of dramatic irony into our reading experience that would be lost if "Penelope" were read as a separate novella.

Nonetheless, more than any of the other chapters of *Ulysses,* and more than ordinary narrative units within other novels, "Penelope" stands apart from its context, as a self-generated, self-supported, and self-enclosed fictional text. Joyce himself stressed its extramural status when he commented on the ending of *Ulysses:* "It [the "Ithaca" chapter] is in reality the end as 'Penelope' has no beginning, middle or end." The spherical image he used to describe "Penelope" in a well-known letter to Frank Budgen further underlines its self-enclosure: "It begins and ends with the female *Yes.* It turns like the huge earthball slowly surely and evenly round and round spinning." Joyce's two self-exegetical schemas add yet another element that sets "Penelope" apart: in contrast to the numbered hours that clock all the other episodes, the "Time" marked for the ultimate episode is infinity (∞) in one schema, "Hour none" in the other. But surely the most important sign of "Penelope" 's formal independence is its form itself: the only moment of the novel where a figural voice totally obliterates the authorial narrative voice throughout an entire chapter. No matter how closely the content of Molly's mind may duplicate, supplement, and inform the fictional world of *Ulysses* as a whole, the single-minded and single-voiced form of "Penelope" justifies its consideration as an independent text, a model for that singular narrative genre entirely constituted by a fictional character's thoughts.

One of the most striking structural peculiarities of an autonomous monologue, classically illustrated by "Penelope," is the stricture it imposes on the manipulation of the time dimension. Before we discuss this point, a brief glance at the overall temporal sequence of Molly's thoughts will dispel a critical commonplace. Critics have tended to take Joyce's mythical image of the spinning earthball (in the letter cited above) so literally that they have overstressed the eternal return of the same in "Penelope," while neglecting its sequential unrolling in time. Yet the circularity of Molly's arguments (including the identity of its first and last words) is decisively counteracted by elements that underline its temporal sequence. Prime among these is the fact that her monologue contains a central happening: the inception of her menses; on this account alone it seems to me impossible to maintain [as does Diane Tolomeo in "The Final Octagon of *Ulysses*"] that breaking into ["Penelope"] at any point does not upset the order or sequence. This event is more than incidental; it alters the direction of Molly's thoughts, clearly dividing them into a before and after: whereas her thoughts of Boylan and others concerning the immediate and distant past dominate before, Boylan almost disappears and all memories diminish after. They are replaced by thoughts of the future, largely in the form of scenarios for seducing Stephen and for reseducing Bloom. Molly, in other words, enters a "new moon" in the course of her monologue—a decidedly temporal event, no matter how eternal its mythological overtones. It is an event, moreover, that strongly ties Molly to biological time, the time of a biological organism on its way from birth to death. If we can talk of the circular shape of Molly's monologue at all, then only in the modified sense of the coils of a spiral whose direction (upward or downward?) is left ambiguous, but whose linear advance along the coordinate of time is never left in doubt.

This advance, even if we disregard the evolution of Molly's thoughts, is built into the very technique Joyce chose to express them: for a continuous interior monologue is based on an absolute correspondence between time and text, narrated time and time of narration. The single mark for the passage of time here is the sequence of words on the page. Whereas in ordinary narration time is a flexible medium that can be, at will, speeded up (by summary), retarded (by description or digression), advanced (by anticipation), or reversed (by retrospect), an autonomous monologue—in the absence of a manipulating narrator—advances time solely by the artic- ulation of thoughts, and advances it evenly along a one-way path until words come to a halt on the page. Note, however, that this chronographic progress is associated only with the successive moments of verbalization itself, and not with their content: it remains unaffected by the achronological montage of events that prevails in a monologist's mind, notoriously in Molly's helter-skelter references to different moments of the past and the future.

This even-paced unrolling of time in an autonomous monologue is analogous to the temporal structure of a dramatic scene (or the uninterrupted rendition of dialogue in a narrative scene). The dramaturgic concept of unity of time, in the strictest neoclassical sense of identifying time of action with time of performance, could be applied here, except that the terms of the identity would have to be modified. For if monologue time flows evenly, there is no telling how fast it flows—unless the monologist explicitly clocks himself. Molly's sense of time being what it is ("I never know the time,") the exact length of her insomnia cannot be known. But since it starts sometime after two and ends sometime before daybreak (four o'clock on a June day at Dublin's latitude?) Molly probably thinks faster than most readers read her thoughts, and certainly faster than anyone can recite them. The time of "Penelope" would thus correspond to the common view that thoughts move faster than speech.

The relentless continuity of Molly's text, reinforced as it is by the omission of punctuation, makes its division into eight paragraphs (or "sen- tences," as Joyce called them) stand out the more distinctly: even these brief interruptions in the print inevitably convey moments of silence, time passing without words. These instant pauses appear like a drawing of mental breath before a new phase of mental discourse; or, to use the analogy with drama again, a curtain quickly drawn closed and reopened between the acts of a play in which absolute unity of time prevails. The very fact that paragraphing calls for an interpretation of this kind in "Penelope" shows that paginal blanks, regardless of their size, tend to carry much more than routine significance in interior monologue texts: they convey not only passage of time, but interruption of thought. For this reason lapse into sleep is the most convincing ending for a text of this sort, just as waking out of sleep is its most logical beginning. Molly's monologue, of course, ends in this optimal fashion, but its beginning does not coincide with her awakening. Instead, "Penelope" begins in the only alternate way available to an autonomous monologue, namely *in medias res,* or, better, *in mediam mentem,* casting the reader without warning into the privacy of a mind talking to itself about its own immediate business: "Yes because he never did a thing like that before as ask to get his breakfast in bed with a couple of eggs since the *City Arms* hotel when he used to." This beginning is obviously meant to give the impression of being "no beginning" ("'Penelope' has no beginning, middle or end"), not even a syntactical beginning. Both "Yes" and "because" (not to mention "he") refer to a clause antecedent to the text's inception, which the reader can only gradually reconstruct from clues that will eventually appear in the text. Not until one reaches the words at the very bottom of the first page ("yes he came somewhere") does it become entirely clear that the thought immediately antecedent to "Yes because" must have concerned Molly's suspicion of her husband's infidelity. But beyond this specific syntactic riddle, this beginning leaves unexplained whose voice speaks, where, when, and how.

The inception of "Penelope" points up the special limitations imposed on a fictional text if it is to create for the reader the illusion that it records a mind involved in self-address. Since it would be implausible for Molly to expound to herself facts she already knows, all exposition (in the usual sense of conveying information about past happenings and present situations) is barred from the text. The facts of Molly's life pass through her consciousness only implicitly, incidentally, by allusive indirection. And all that remains understood in her thoughts can be understood by the reader only by means of a cumulative process of orientation that gradually closes the cognitive gap.

Yet Joyce could not have exposed Molly's inner life without exposition if he had not placed her in a highly pregnant moment, a crisis situation that brings into mental play the key conditions of her life (and of life). Though Molly's may be an ordinary mind, Bloomsday is not—for Molly any more than for Bloom or Stephen—an entirely ordinary day. Its extraordinary events (the afternoon tryst, Bloom's tardy return) are necessary to awaken in her the thoughts that keep her awake, and thus to make what is implicit at least partially explicit. Though she does not tell herself the story of her day, nor the story of her life, both stories transpire through her agitated thoughts, or better, in spite of them.

Doubtless the most artful stratagem Joyce employed, however, is to set Molly's mind into its turbulent motion while setting her body into a state of nearly absolute tranquility. This obviates a major difficulty inherent in the autonomous monologue form: to present through self-address the physical activities the self performs within the time-span of the monologue. Molly, to be sure, does once rise from her bed, but her gestures during this brief interlude are so obvious and so elemental that they can be gathered without being directly recorded. As Dujardin's *Les Lauriers* and Schnitzler's *Fräulein Else* show, when monologists become much more enterprising they begin to sound much less convincing; forced to describe the actions they perform while they perform them, they tend to sound like gymnastics teachers vocally demonstrating an exercise.

But Joyce not only places the monologizing mind in a body at rest; he also places that body in calm surroundings. The sensations that impinge on Molly's consciousness are few and far between: the whistling trains, the chiming bells, a lamp, a creaking press, the sleeping Bloom. Only minimally deflected by perceptions of the external world, her monologue is "interior" not only in the technical sense of remaining unvoiced, but also in the more literal sense: it is directed to and by the world within. The perfect adherence to unity of place thus creates the condition for a monologue in which the mind is its own place: self-centered and therefore self-generative to a degree that can hardly be surpassed.

The classic unity (and unities) in the overall structure of "Penelope" are both matched and mirrored by its linguistic texture. Without intending a complete linguistic-stylistic description of the text, I will focus on three features of its language that spring directly from the autonomous monologue form, and at the same time contrast sharply with the language of retrospective narration: 1) the predominance of exclamatory syntax; 2) the avoidance of narrative and reportive tenses; and 3) the nonreferential implicitness of the pronoun system. . . .

The following excerpt from "Penelope" will serve as the starting point. I have divided it into thirty numbered segments, each of which corresponds to a "sentence" in the generally accepted sense of a syntactic unit of meaning, or (as one linguist defines it) "a word or set of words followed by a pause and revealing an intelligible purpose" (Alan Gardiner: *The Theory of Speech and Language*):

1. I bet the cat itself is better off than us
2. have we too much blood up in us or what
3. O patience above its pouring out of me like the sea
4. anyhow he didnt make me pregnant as big as he is
5. I dont want to ruin the clean sheets
6. the clean linen I wore brought it on too
7. damn it damn it
8. and they always want to see a stain on the bed to know youre a virgin for them
9. all thats troubling them
10. theyre such fools too
11. you could be a widow and divorced 40 times over
12. a daub of red ink would do or blackberry juice
13. no thats too purply
14. O Jamesy let me up out of this
15. pooh
16. sweets of sin
17. whoever suggested that business for women what between clothes and cooking and children
18. this damned old bed too jingling like the dickens
19. I suppose they could hear us away over the other side of the park till I suggested to put the quilt on the floor with the pillow under my bottom
20. I wonder is it nicer in the day
21. I think it is
22. easy
23. I think Ill cut all this hair off me there scalding me
24. I might look like a young girl
25. wouldnt he get the great suckin the next time he turned up my clothes on me
26. Id give anything to see his face
27. wheres the chamber gone
28. easy
29. Ive a holy horror of its breaking under me after that old commode
30. I wonder was I too heavy sitting on his knee

The most immediately apparent aspect of this language is its agitated, emotional tone. Leaving aside for the moment the several interrogatory sentences (2, 17, 20, 25, 27, 30), almost every sentence would, in normal punctuation, deserve—and some would require—a final exclamation mark: most obviously the seven sentences that are, or contain, interjections (3, 7, 14, 15, 16, 22, 28). But since the essence of exclamations is that "they emphasize to the listener some mood, attitude, or desire of the speaker," almost all the other sentences could be classed as exclamations as well. The passage abounds in emphatically expressive forms: wishes (5, 26), fears (29), disparaging generalizations (9, 10). A highly subjective tone pervades even those sentences that come closest to statements of fact. They are either marked by introductory verbs of conjecture: "I bet" (1), "I suppose" (19), "I think" (21, 23); or by patent overstatement: "divorced 40 times over" (11); or by omission of the copula (18); or by emphatic adverbs and conjunctions: "and" (8), "anyhow" (4), the thrice-uttered "too" (6, 10, 18). No sentence, in short, takes the form of a simple statement; all contain emotive, expressive signals, whether they concern past events or present happenings.

If we remember that interior monologue is, by definition, a discourse addressed to no one, a gratuitous verbal agitation without communicative aim, then this predominance of exclamatory syntax appears perfectly in keeping with the nature of monologue. As the form of discourse that requires no reply, to which there *is* no reply, exclamation is the self-sufficient, self-involved language gesture par excellence. Since interrogation, by contrast, is uttered in the expectation of a reply, and thus dialogic by nature, it at first seems surprising that this passage contains so many questions. But Molly's questions are of a kind fitting easily into a monologic milieu: they are themselves essentially exclamatory. This is most obvious where they are rhetorical, either implying their own answer ("wouldn't he get the great suckin the next time he turned up my clothes on me," 25) or uttered without the expectation of an answer ("whoever suggested that business for women," 17, "have we too much blood up in us or what," 2). The latter type is particularly characteristic for Molly: existential questions abound in her dialogue, questions pleading against the absurd order of the universe, especially its division into pleasure-seeking males and long-suffering females: "whats the idea making us like that with a big hole in the middle of us"; "clothes we have to wear whoever invented them"; "why cant you kiss a man without going and marrying him first"; "where would they all of them be if they hadn't all a mother to look after them"; and many more. But also when Molly asks herself genuinely interrogatory questions, she asks them in an exclamatory fashion, usually by introducing them with the phrase "I wonder": "I wonder is it nicer in the day" (20), "I wonder was I too heavy sitting on his knee" (30). A kind of pathetic anxiety or insecurity comes to the fore in this form of query, especially when the unknown is the impression she made on Boylan (cf. "I wonder was he satisfied with me"; "I wonder is he awake thinking of me or dreaming am I in it"). In this sense self-interrogation seems the natural complement to exclamation in the turbulent syntax of language-for-oneself, counterpointing attitudes toward the known with attitudes toward the unknown.

But even as exclamation and interrogation stamp Molly's discourse with subjectivity, these sentence forms also orient it away from a neutral report of the present moment, and away from the narration of past events. Since language-for-oneself is by definition the form of language in which speaker and listener coincide, the technique that imitates it in fiction can remain convincing only if it excludes all factual statements, all explicit report on present and past happenings. The various tenses in Molly's monologue further determine its antinarrative, antireportorial orientation.

I have intentionally chosen my sample passage from the section of Molly's monologue where she begins her most ambitious physical activity of the night—the excursion to the "chamber"—in order to show how Joyce manages to convey Molly's bodily gestures without a single direct statement of the I-am-doing-this-now type. If her activity becomes clear to an attentive reader, it is not because she explicitly reports what she does, but because what she does is implicitly reflected in her thoughts, roughly as follows: "O patience above its pouring out of me. . . . I dont want to ruin the clean sheets" (she decides to get a sanitary napkin); "O Jamesy let me up out of this" (she strains to raise her body); "this damned old bed too jingling" (she moves her body out of bed); "I think Ill cut all this hair off me" (she lifts her nightgown); "wheres the chamber gone" (she decides on the interim stop, and reaches for the needed object); "easy Ive a holy horror of its breaking under me" (she lowers herself onto it). Her subsequent performance—"O Lord how noisy," its conclusion—"Id better not make an all night sitting on this affair," the activity with "those napkins"—"I hope theyll have something better for us in the other world . . . thats all right for tonight," and finally the return to bed—"easy piano O I like my bed," are all rendered by exclamatory indirection as well. In sum, we search in vain through "Penelope" for a first-person pronoun coupled with an action verb in present tense—precisely the combination that creates that most jarring effect in less well-executed interior monologues (like *Les Lauriers sont coupés*), because it introduces a reportorial dimension of language into a nonreportorial language situation.

The first-person, present-tense combination in Molly's monologue occurs exclusively with verbs of internal rather than external activity. She supposes, thinks, wishes, hopes, and remembers many times over on every page, so that the punctual present of her inner discourse continuously refers to and feeds on the very activity she literally performs at every moment of her monologue. It is in this present moment of mental activity that all Molly's other verbal tenses and moods are anchored. And she uses them all: past, future, indicative, conditional, and quite prominently the present of generalization. This constant oscillation between memories and projects, the real and the potential, the specific and the general, is one of the most distinctive marks of freely associative monologic language. Our sample passage contains it in motley display, especially toward its end, when we get in rapid succession past (19), present (20–21), future (23), conditional (24–26), and again present (27–29) and past (30). Note how the punctual present of the mental verbs in turn subordinates the past ("I suppose they could hear us"), the generalizing present ("I wonder is it nicer in the day I think it is"), the future ("I think Ill cut all this hair") and the reversion to the past ("I wonder was I too heavy").

There are moments in Molly's monologue when she adheres more extensively to one or another of these tenses and moods. Since she is not much of a planner, her looks into the future verge on the imaginary, whether she uses the conditional or the indicative: thus "supposing he stayed with us" introduces the wish dream of the *ménage à trois* with Stephen, whereas her dreams of glory as a poet's muse and the alternate scenarios for seducing Bloom are cast in future tense. Her fantasies—"the cracked things come into my head sometimes"—cluster in the last third of "Penelope," whereas memories are denser in the first two-thirds.

In the earlier sections the recalls are so extensive that the past tense actually predominates over the present, with the past sentences at times in straight narrative form, unsubordinated by thinking verbs. Yet even where a consecutive sequence of events takes shape in her mind, the narrative idiom rarely prevails without being interrupted by opinionated comments. The following samples from the courtship scene alternate typically:

> he was shaking like a jelly all over *they want to do everything too quick take all the pleasure out of it* . . . then he wrote me that letter with all those words in it *how could he have the face to any woman*

> *after* . . . dont understand you I said and wasnt it natural *so it is of course* . . . then writing a letter every morning sometimes twice a day *I liked the way he made love then* . . . then I wrote the night he kissed my heart at Dolphins barn *I couldnt describe it simply it makes you feel like nothing on earth*   ·

I have italicized the sentences that regularly turn a reflective gaze back on each narrative sentence—generalizing, questioning, evaluating; and this discursive language retards, and eventually displaces, the narrative language, as the concern for the present moment again prevails. In this fashion even the moments of Molly's monologue when she comes closest to narrating her life to herself—see also the recall of the Mulvey affair and the love scene on Howth Head—never gain sufficient momentum to yield more than briefly suggestive vignettes.

Molly's memories occur to her in thoroughly random order, her mind gliding ceaselessly up and down the thread of time, with the same past tense now referring to the events of the previous afternoon, now reaching back to her nymphet days in Gibraltar, now again lingering on numberless intervening incidents. This achronological time montage—as Robert Humphrey (in *Stream of Consciousness in the Modern Novel*) calls this technique— provides the data for a fairly detailed Molly biography; but her monologue itself is autobiographical only in spite of itself.

A further, and perhaps the most telling, symptom for the non-narrative and non-communicative nature of Molly's language is the profusion and referential instability of its pronouns. This initially bewildering system puts the reader into a situation akin to that of a person eavesdropping on a conversation in progress between close friends, about people and events unknown to him but so familiar to them that they need not name the people or objects to which they refer. In this sense Molly's pronominal implicitness combines both traits of language-for-oneself discussed earlier in connection with Bloom's monologic idiom: grammatical abbreviation and lexical opaqueness—traits in other respects far less prominent in Molly's than in Bloom's language. But even as Joyce creates this impression of cryptic privacy he plants just enough signposts to guard against total incomprehensibility.

The only pronoun that has an invariant referent in "Penelope" is the first person singular. Since "I" is by definition "the person who is uttering the present instance of discourse containing *I*" (Emile Benvéniste: *Problems in General Linguistics*), and since an autonomous monologue is by definition the utterance of a single speaker, this fixity of the first person is endemic to the genre. So, of course, is its frequency. In the sample passage more than half the sentences contain a self-reference, and several contain more than one. This egocentricity is typical of Molly's entire monologue.

All her other pronouns confront the reader with more or less unknown quantities, mostly without immediate antecedent, identifiable only from the broader context. Third-person pronouns—particularly in the masculine gender—display the most obvious referential instability, and may contain significant equivocation as well. Molly presumably always knows the who-is-who of her pronouns, but the reader is sometimes left guessing as to which *he* is on her mind at any moment. The *he* who "didnt make me pregnant as big as he is" (4) is clearly Boylan (who must also be the owner of the knee in 30)—even though his name has not been mentioned for three pages. But the *he* whose face she wants to see "the next time he turned up my clothes" (25–26) could be either Bloom or Boylan. And watch the rapid shuttling of the he-reference (between Bloom and Stephen) in the following passage:

> he [Stephen] could do his writing and studies at the table in there
> for all the scribbling he [Bloom] does at it and if he [Stephen]
> wants to read in bed in the morning like me as hes [Bloom]
> making the breakfast for 1 he can make it for 2

On the larger scale of her monologue, a slower relay of he-men can be observed as the Bloom-Boylan alternation gives way to the Bloom-Stephen one, an evolution that coincides with the decreasing past and mounting future and conditional tenses. But the "he" of the exact mid-pages of "Penelope" is the explicitly introduced "Mulvey was the first," who will return only pronominally to fuse with Bloom at the very end: "and how he kissed me under the Moorish wall and I thought well as well him as another and then I asked him with my eyes to ask again yes and then he asked me would I yes." As Richard Ellmann has remarked, this is the point when "her reference to all the men she has known as 'he' has a sudden relevance" (*Ulysses on the Liffey*); for here the undifferentiated reference at the point of sleep underlines the contingency of the erotic partner. But this ultimate indifference is counterpointed by an overarching constancy, Bloom being the referent for the first "he" she uses in her monologue, as well as for the last.

In his play with the male pronoun, then, Joyce makes symbolic and amusing use of a realistic feature of speech-for-oneself. Other pronominal games attain their effect more by pointing to Molly's fixed ideas than to her fickle feelings. Their key lies in the discovery not of her past, but of her private logic and its system of notation. The neuter pronoun refers with comic constancy to her favorite unmentionable, most densely on the first pages:

> anyway love its not or hed be off his feed thinking of her so either it was one of those night women if it was down there he was really and the hotel story he made up a pack of lies to hide it planning it . . . or else if its not that its some little bitch or other . . . and then the usual kissing my bottom was to hide it not that I care two straws who he does it with.

The plural pronouns are equally specific in their generality: they express Molly's sexual polarization of the world. "We," whenever it does not signify the self and a specific partner (as in 19), signifies the genus women, as in "I bet the cat itself is better off than us have we too much blood up in us or what" (1–2). The pronominal enemy of this female kinship group is *they,* the genus men: "they always want to see a stain on the bed . . . all thats troubling them . . . theyre such fools too" (8–10). This meaning attends the third person plural in the clichés Molly coins: "they havent half the character a woman has," "1 woman is not enough for them," "arent they thick never understand what you say," "grey matter they have it all in their tail if you ask me," etc. But when Molly's kinship with other women turns to venom, *they* turns into a feminine pronoun: "lot of sparrowfarts . . . talking about politics they know as much about as my backside . . . my bust that they havent . . . make them burst with envy," etc. Our passage also shows Molly's feminine perspective on the second person pronoun in the impersonal sense of *one*: "to know youre a virgin for them" (8) or "you could be a widow" (11).

"You" as the pronoun of address, finally, is used very sparingly by Molly, and in this she differs from most other monologists. If we leave aside an occasional rhetorical phrase ("if you ask me"; "I tell you"), imagined interlocutors are almost entirely absent. I find only three exceptions: one is the "O Jamesy let me up out of this" (14) in our passage—with Molly perhaps calling on her creator-author in a spirit of Romantic irony; "give us room even to let a fart God" is her only address to another higher power; and "O move over your big carcass" her only address to a fellow human being. Molly also occasionally uses the second person for self-address, but only in brief admonishments: "better lower this lamp," "better go easy," "O Lord what a row youre making," "now wouldnt that afflict you." The extended inner debates that feature second- and even third-person self-references in some of her fellow monologists would be out of character with the single-minded monologist who spins her yarn here.

The Aesthetic of Delay

Hugh Kenner

In a foretime of uncomplicated pleasures, when pocketwatches were ubiquitous, before digital readouts and also before sweep second hands, the challenge ran, "Make a '6' like the one on your watch." This depended on the victim's not having noticed that his watch had no "6," its space being occupied by the little second dial. And yet he had looked at the watch a thousand times.

This information may help a modern reader with a much reprinted passage in *Stephen Hero,* where the terminology has attracted more attention than the example:

> He told Cranly that the clock of the Ballast Office was capable
> of an epiphany. Cranly questioned the inscrutable dial of the
> Ballast Office with his no less inscrutable countenance.
>
> —Yes, said Stephen. I will pass it time after time, allude to
> it, refer to it, catch a glimpse of it. It is only an item in the
> catalogue of Dublin's street furniture. Then all at once I see it
> and I know at once what it is: epiphany.
>
> —What?
>
> —Imagine my glimpses at that clock as the gropings of a
> spiritual eye which seeks to adjust its vision to an exact focus.
> The moment the focus is reached the object is epiphanised. It is
> just in this epiphany that I find the third, the supreme quality
> of beauty.
>
> —Yes? said Cranly absently.

From *Ulysses.* © 1980 by George Allen & Unwin (Publishers) Ltd.

The Ballast Office clock, an object of no special interest, was perhaps the most looked-at object in all Dublin. It was right at the gullet of the city, where O'Connell Bridge delivers flowing crowds to the south side of the Liffey for shops and offices to absorb. Seamen could set their chronometers by the drop of its timeball, and in a city of stopped and casual clocks, before homes had wireless or watches were cheap and reliable, the authority of its dial reassured countless glancing eyes daily, or else admonished hurrying feet to hurry harder. Does any of those many thousand pairs of eyes, Stephen is asking, ever *see* that clock? Could anyone, for instance, describe it, let alone contemplate its *quidditas*? One would need to look at it as frequently, as intently, as one looks at, say, a fine statue: in part to kill the habit of merely asking it the time, in part to grow used to it as more than a florid curiosity; for a while, as precisely "an item . . . of Dublin's street furniture"; then as itself.

Leopold Bloom does not see it, he who sees so much, when making his way southward through the city toward lunch he looks up at it for distraction from a painful thought.

> Mr Bloom moved forward raising his troubled eyes. Think no more about that. After one. Timeball on the ballast office is down. Dunsink time. Fascinating little book that is of Sir Robert Ball's. Parallax. I never exactly understood. There's a priest. Could ask him. Par it's Greek: parallel, parallax. Met him pike hoses she called it till I told her about the transmigration. O rocks!

This far into the book, we are meant to have acquired enough experience both of *Ulysses* and of Bloom to negotiate these sixty-four words without trouble. Bloom sees the dropped timeball but not the face of the clock because he is on the same side of the street as the clock is and has insufficient need of the exact time to crane his neck upward. (How do we know this? We know it because he started his southward walk on the same side—the west side—as Graham Lemon's and Butler's Monument House and will only cross to the east side a minute or so after his glimpse of the Ballast Office timeball.) He remembers that local time (twenty-five minutes later than Greenwich) comes to this timepiece by wire from Dunsink Observatory. "Observatory" aided by "time*ball*" reminds him of Sir Robert *Ball,* the Dublin-born Astronomer Royal of England. As for Ball's "fascinating little book," it is *The Story of the Heavens* (1885), as we shall learn when we eventually find it on Bloom's bookshelf. He remembers "parallax" from Ball's exposition, attributes the word's obduracy to its Greek origin, mistakenly etymologises *par-* instead of *para-,* supplies a related word, "parallel," the single *r* of which had detained his attention an hour earlier when thoughts of Martin Cunningham's conundrum set him spelling "unpar one ar elleled," and elides, via "Greek," to the Greek word he'd explained to Molly at breakfast-time: "metempsychosis." "O rocks!" was what she said when he told her it meant "transmigration"; "Tell us in plain words."

So here is the Ballast Office clock of Stephen's example, not manifesting "the third, the supreme quality of beauty"—it is not even seen—but still embedded in ambiguities of perception ("parallax"—seen from different spots, *Gestalts* alter); associated moreover with explanation, bringing light to another.

A dozen pages later, having walked the length of Westmoreland Street and passed Trinity, Bloom has another encounter with a timepiece, also unseen. Field glasses in the window of Yeates & Son, opticians and instrument makers, 2 Grafton Street, prompt him to look purposefully upward:

> Goerz lenses, six guineas. . . . There's a little watch up there on
> the roof of the bank to test those glasses by.
> His lids came down on the lower rims of his irides. Can't see
> it. If you imagine it's there you can almost see it. Can't see it.

This effort to perceive a watch that perhaps isn't there—Bloom groping to adjust not his spiritual but his corporeal eye to a correct focus—corresponds in Joyce's intricate bookkeeping to the earlier failure to so much as glance up at the dial of the blatant Ballast Office clock. And if that clock's exemplary status in a theory of perception is accessible to us only because some pages Joyce discarded from the Ur-*Portrait* chanced not to be lost we need no such happenstance, only an act of attention, to enjoy the fun when Bloom vainly squints his eye moments after an encounter with the incorporeal vision of theosophy. For just before his failure with the watch he had overheard "the eminent poet Mr Geo Russell" ("Æ") discoursing to a lady disciple of "the twoheaded octopus, one of whose heads is the head upon which the ends of the world have forgotten to come," and his only comment had been "Something occult. Symbolism." Such people he reflects, eat only vegetables, and "I wouldn't be surprised if it was that kind of food you see produces the like waves of the brain the poetical." So when he, by choice an eater of "the inner organs of beasts and fowls," bends his eye toward a sign of the time he can't see it. "If you imagine it's there you can almost see it. Can't see it."

Yet another twenty pages and this same Æ will be asserting in Stephen

Dedalus's hearing that art reveals "formless spiritual essences," and Stephen will inaudibly rebut him on behalf of what you can see.

> Streams of tendency and eons they worship. . . . Through spaces smaller than red globules of man's blood they creepycrawl after Blake's buttocks into eternity of which this vegetable world is but a shadow. Hold to the now, the here, through which all future plunges to the past.

The now, the here. Outside Yeates & Son Bloom's mind, responsive to optical instruments and invisible timepieces, is drawn back half a mile to the Ballast Office timeball.

> Now that I come to think of it, that ball falls at Greenwich time.
> It's the clock is worked by an electric wire from Dunsink.

He proceeds to query "parallax" again, and concludes: "Never know anything about it. Waste of time."

And yet he has just let slip through his mind unnoticed a homely example of parallax: two standpoints, two different alignments of phenomena. For not only have his thoughts in two different places assessed the dropped ball differently (metaphorical parallax); not only that, but the Ballast Office clock itself presents parallactic readings, two times simultaneously: Greenwich Time by the ball for mariners, Dunsink Time by the dial for pedestrians. And Greenwich Time and Dunsink Time differ by twenty-five minutes because astronomers in those two places observe the sun from stations separated by $6\frac{1}{4}°$ of longitude; this is, precisely and technically, parallax. (And the timeball fell at 12.35 by the dial, so when Bloom deduced "after one" from the fact that it had already fallen his correct conclusion, as so often, was drawn from false premises and correct by luck.)

Parallax makes possible stereoscopic vision: "In order to see that basket," Stephen instructs Lynch in the *Portrait,* "your mind first of all separates the basket from the rest of the visible universe which is not the basket," something the mind can do more easily since the eyes have presented it with separate versions of the basket's location. Two different versions at least, that is Joyce's normal way; and the uncanny sense of reality that grows in readers of *Ulysses* page after page is fostered by the neatness with which versions of the same event, versions different in wording and often in constituent facts—separated, moreover, by tens or hundreds of pages—reliably render one another substantial. Indeed, the book's first parallax is the double incident of the little cloud which occludes Stephen's sun in "Telemachus" and Bloom's sun in "Calypso," turning both men's thoughts deathward. Since the tower and Eccles Street are seven miles apart these occultations cannot be simultaneous; from the fact that the cloud seems to come later in "Calypso" we may judge that the winds over Ireland are blowing, as usual, westerly.

The poet Russell, pushing his bicycle along the kerbstone, passed Bloom from behind at the south-east corner of College Green and Nassau Street. That kerb, swerving left, will lead him straight as a tramline to the foot of Kildare Street, two minutes from the National Library. And, when the next episode opens an hour later, there is Russell ensconced in the Library, "oracling" out of its shadows. This does much to assure us that Bloom did really see Russell, a substantial Russell in motion through Dublin's Newtonian space. It does something, too, since Russell "existed," to help confirm the reality of Bloom. It is perhaps elementary narrative technique.

The technique of letting Bloom drop a phrase about Sir Robert Ball's "fascinating little book," to be complemented when Bloom's books are catalogued some 500 pages later, is harder to match in the work of antecedent writers, less scrupulous about trivia (but Joyce is all trivia). Both elements, book and title, are intelligible when we encounter them. The first creates no mystery to whet our alertness for the second; the second, so many pages later, quite likely stirs no memory whatever. Yet the two do something, minute, incremental, to help Bloomsday cohere in any mind that chances to unite them, if only by confirming that as the foxes have their holes and the birds their nests, so each speck in this book has somewhere its complementary speck, in a cosmos we can trust. Einstein thought that God did not play dice with the universe.

A device that can make dustmotes vivid has obvious power over scenes and incidents. Thanks to Bloom's busily associative memory, virtually every scene in Ulysses is narrated at least twice, and by varying what he tells and emphasises Joyce ensures that repetition shall not dilute but intensify. "Now, my miss," says the pork butcher Dlugacz to a customer, making "a red grimace." "Deep voice that fellow Dlugacz has," Bloom recalls nine pages later. "Now, my miss." Bloom's recall omits the red grimace, adds the deep voice; the incident has grown stereoscopic, stereophonic. But when he reappears in the phantasmagoria of "Circe" Dlugacz (dreams going by contraries) has become "a ferreteyed albino" who speaks "hoarsely," and the words he speaks are words he never spoke, merely words Bloom read on a handbill in his shop. This is normal operating procedure for Joyce. One effect is to thicken the book's human texture

without overpopulating it, another is to turn Moses Dlugacz from a su-
pernumerary into a Theme, and a third is to help us think "Circe" phan-
tasmal since what is transfigured there is elsewhere substantial, twice
testified.

Leopold Bloom is much pressed upon by his past. We must feel with
him how substantial is that past. The substantiality of past scenes, though
they exist for us only in his recollections, is achieved by comparable means,
each scene built up out of numerous partial recalls. There was an evening
at Mat Dillon's in Terenure "fifteen seventeen golden years ago" (Seventeen
is correct; it was May 1887), at which he and Molly first met; they played
musical chairs, and the game isolated the two of them (Molly got the last
chair). Later she sang; he turned her music. He was 21, she 16. This may
have been the same evening the solicitor John Henry Menton felt humiliated
because lucky Bloom bested him at bowls and ladies laughed; the same,
too, when a boy of five stood on a garden urn, supported by Molly and
by three of Mat Dillon's daughters, and declined to shake hands with the
21-year-old Mr Bloom. By outrageous coincidence . . . but we'll come to
that.

No single account governs our sense of all this. We cannot even know
whether one occasion or several is denoted by the four principal vignettes
which Dillon's name and the name of lilacs unify. Mat Dillon's and lilacs
come to stand for Eden, a fragrant girl-filled garden; nuance by nuance an
alluring past emerges. First the sight of Menton at Paddy Dignam's funeral
recalls the bowls and Menton's long-ago choler, and places theme-words
parallax will not alter:

> Solicitor, I think. I know his face. Menton, John Henry, so-
> licitor, commissioner for oaths and affidavits. Dignam used to
> be in his office. Mat Dillon's long ago. Jolly Mat convivial
> evenings. Cold fowl, cigars, the Tantalus glasses. Heart of gold
> really. Yes, Menton. Got his rag out that evening on the bowling
> green because I sailed inside him. Pure fluke of mine: the bias.
> Why he took such a rooted dislike to me. Hate at first sight.
> Molly and Floey Dillon linked under the lilactree, laughing.
> Fellow always like that, mortified if women are by.

Dillon and lilac trees are united, and Molly and Floey (special friends), and
Dillon's garden and good times gone. Some four hours later, while Bloom
sits in the Ormond in the knowledge that Molly is preparing to cuckold
him, words of a tenor song—"When first I saw"—bring back that time of
first sight.

First night when first I saw her at Mat Dillon's in Terenure. Yellow, black lace she wore. Musical chairs. We two the last. Fate. After her. Fate. . . .

—*Charmed my eye* . . .

Singing. *Waiting* she sang. I turned her music. Full voice of perfume of what perfume does your lilactrees. Bosom I saw, both full, throat warbling. First I saw. She thanked me. Why did she me? Fate. Spanishy eyes. Under a peartree alone patio this hour in old Madrid one side in shadow Dolores shedolores. At me. Luring. Ah, alluring.

Dillon's, lilac trees. Bloom, too, is plotting a (minor) infidelity; "what perfume does your" has strayed into his revery from his lady penpal's letter, one he's just on the point of answering under his postal-box pseudonym, Henry Flower. Still, the lost time shines in memory. It is clear why Bloom's dream cottage, focus of his habitual bedtime fantasies, will feature among its hundreds of amenities "a sundial shaded and sheltered by laburnum and lilactrees": lilacs to emblematise a magical evening, shading a sundial on which no minatory shadow will ever move; clear, too, why the mock Wedding of the Trees, in a context mocking Bloom, will cite two girls named "Lilac" as well as "Senhor Enrique Flor" (Henry Flower) who "presided at the organ with his wellknown ability"—here "organ" is a word that snickers—"and, in addition to the prescribed numbers of the nuptial mass, played a new and striking arrangement of *Woodman, spare that tree.*"

Another seven hours, and a chance word in a bitter harangue of Stephen Dedalus prompts one more evocation of the lilac-shaded scene. The word—unspecified—may have been "mother." Eden this time is distanced by elaborate cadences; a Victorian hand like Pater's is holding the pen, evoking "a shaven space of lawn one soft May evening, the wellremembered grove of lilacs at Roundtown, purple and white," and amid the lilacs "another as fragrant sisterhood, Floey, Atty, Tiny and their darker friend . . . Our Lady of the Cherries, a comely brace of them pendant from an ear." These are Dillon's daughters and Molly.

A lad of four or five in linsey-woolsey . . . is standing on the urn secured by that circle of girlish fond hands. He frowns a little just as this young man does now with a perhaps too conscious enjoyment of danger but must needs glance at whiles towards where his mother watches from the *piazzetta* giving upon the flowerclose with a faint shadow of remoteness or of reproach (*alles Vergängliche*) in her glad look.

"*Alles Vergängliche*" bids us see Stephen's mother not as the wraith who haunts his thoughts today but as the Mater Gloriosa who summons Goethe's errant Faust aloft. (An imitation of the *Faust Walpurgisnacht* will commence in just a few pages.)

Readers skilled in the clichés of Victorian fiction will expect the child in this tableau to have been Stephen; such a style cherishes that order of sentimental coincidence. Sure enough, when the two men are at last installed in Bloom's kitchen drinking cocoa, the catechist of Ithaca asks and is answered:

> How many previous encounters proved their preexisting acquaintance?
>
> Two. The first in the lilacgarden of Matthew Dillon's house, Medina Villa, Kimmage Road, Roundtown, in 1887, in the company of Stephen's mother, Stephen being then of the age of 5 and reluctant to give his hand in salutation.

They were all there together once in Eden, Bloom and a not yet unfaithful Molly, Stephen and a not yet spectral mother. Ministering to a cosy sense of the fitness of things, this sort of revelation would have served a Victorian novelist for the stuff of a climax. But making things fit together inheres in Joyce's method, and *Ulysses* abounds in coincidental alignments to such an extent that no one is especially crucial. This particular one, emerging slowly as we correlate several passages against the grain of styles that resist correlation, is likely to be missed altogether by the first-time reader. The last two episodes, "Ithaca" and "Penelope," supply missing facts for so many suspended patterns, momentous and trivial, that a reader who should work carefully through them sentence by sentence, equipped with perfect knowledge of the rest of the book, would experience bewilderment from the very profusion of small elements dropping into place.

And he would be deceived, this reader, if he supposed the whole book had declared itself to him. There are elements dropping into place among the late pages that effect clarifications only on early pages, and only when on a later reading those pages are revisited.

For consider the potato. Bloom's "potato I have"—as he checks his pockets on first leaving the house—is wholly unintelligible (what on earth does he want with a potato?). Still, the mystery is too slight to detain us; we have much else to attend to. Twice later we are assured that "potato I have" means something: that a potato is indeed in his pocket, from which a harlot's exploring hand can extract it. Later we find him firmly requesting its return: "It is nothing, but still a relic of poor mamma." Here, suddenly, is something new to correlate.

Points of correlation have already appeared: the phantasm of Bloom's mother with "a shrivelled potato" among her talismans—a phial, an Agnus Dei, a celluloid doll; Bloom's phrase, "poor mamma's panacea," as he feels his pocket (but does not then name the potato); finally, the disclosure of its principle in one of his hallucinatory speeches: "the potato . . . a killer of pestilence by absorption."

Sure enough, in the Litany of the Daughters of Erin we hear phantom voices chanting "Potato Preservative Against Plague and Pestilence, pray for us." Bloom carries a potato in his trousers pocket, has thought to transfer it to these black trousers from his everyday ones even though he has forgotten to transfer his latchkey, and *touches it as he crosses the threshold when a more orthodox Jew would touch the "mezuzah,"* all because his mother told him long ago that it would absorb disease from the air. And there is no one place where we are given this information.

Probably most students of *Ulysses* derive the doctrine of the potato from a commentary. Still, its elements are in the text, the most elucidative ones—"poor mamma's panacea"; "killer of pestilence by absorption"; "Potato Preservative Against Plague and Pestilence"—all in one episode and not many pages apart. Attention unassisted by commentary could unriddle the potato as it unriddles so much else. But the equivalence of the potato and the *mezuzah* (a small case containing Deuteronomy 6:4–9 and 11: 13–21, affixed to the right-hand doorpost for the devout to touch or kiss as they cross the threshold)—this, assuming even that we possess the lore and have the luck to make the connection—is not something we might hope to think of when we first read of how Bloom crossed his threshold and said "Potato I have," because at that time we have some hundreds of pages to traverse before the meaning of "potato" will have been disclosed. Nor, when we know the meaning, does it work retroactively, since by then we have surely forgotten the doorframe adjacent to the initial "Potato I have." The *mezuzah*-epiphany will occur at some future reading, perhaps even never. If it never occurs, still, others will occur.

Joyce's strange book has no stranger aspect than this, that no one comprehensive reading is thinkable. A book—certainly, a novel—normally presupposes that ideal attention will reap it at one traverse; if we need, as we frequently do, repeated readings, that is because our attention is plagued by lapses, or perhaps because the writing is faulty. But *Ulysses* is so designed that new readers, given, even, what cannot be postulated, ideal immunity to attention overload, cannot possibly grasp certain elements because of a warp in the order of presentation, and veteran readers will perceive after twenty years new lights going on as a consequence of a question they have only just thought to ask. Such a question would be: Why is Bloom made to advert to the potato just when he does, on a page where there seems no earthly reason for him to remember the potato or for us to be apprised of it? And when we think to ask something happens.

Clarifying early puzzles with late information, *Ulysses* resembles a detective story, paradigm of the nineteenth-century novel—*Great Expectations, The Moonstone*—in which all hinges on postponed revelations. Changing our earlier understanding with late facts, it resembles a plot like that of *Oedipus Rex,* where a terminal revelation alters all. But mutating each time it is reread, altering the very sense of early sentences as the import of later ones chances to come home, it resembles chiefly itself. Its universe is Einsteinian, nonsimultaneous, internally consistent but never to be grasped in one act of apprehension: not only because the details are so numerous but also because their pertinent interconnections are more numerous still. Why was young Poldy Bloom, of all people, invited to Mat Dillon's that evening? Why Molly was there we know—she was Floey Dillon's special friend; but Poldy? Was handsome Poldy perhaps invited as a partner for Molly? (Very likely, daughter of a girl named Lunita Laredo, she looked as exotic as he.)

Some possible interconnections, though mutually exclusive, are not interdicted. Is one of the numerous women whom we see by any chance Bloom's correspondent "Martha Clifford"? Very possibly. Possibly not. Is Cissey Caffrey, in Nighttown, really Gerty MacDowell's friend of the same name, "madcap Cis"? Possibly; it was only by unprompted inference that when we were detained with Gerty's friends we assigned them to the middle class. Did Molly Bloom really move all that heavy furniture, including a piano and a sideboard so high it cracked Bloom's temple? Thinkably; though there was also, that afternoon, a strong man on the premises named Boylan.

There are things we shall never know, and we think it meaningful to say we shall never know them, quite as though they were entities on the plane of the potentially knowable, forgetting that nothing exists between these covers after all but marks on paper, in a system very nearly consistent. (The great world offers experiences, too, that are very nearly consistent.) Joyce's aesthetic of delay, producing the simplest facts by parallax, one element now, one later, and leaving large orders of fact to be assembled late or another time or never, in solving the problem of novels that go flat after we know "how it comes out" also provides what fiction has never before really provided, an experience comparable to that of experiencing the haphazardly evidential quality of life; and, moreover, what art is supposed to offer that life can not, a permanence to be revisited at will but not exhausted.

There is sometimes a Heisenbergian trouble with the evidence itself. What did Molly say when she asked about "metempsychosis"? We are to believe that she found that word in a book called *Ruby, Pride of the Ring*. (Is that, by the way, believable?) The narrative runs:

> She swallowed a draught of tea from her cup held by nothandle and, having wiped her fingertips smartly on the blanket, began to search the text with the hairpin till she reached the word.
> —Met him what? he asked.
> —Here, she said. What does that mean?
> He leaned downwards and read near her polished thumbnail.
> —Metempsychosis, he said, frowning. It's Greek: from the Greek. That means the transmigration of souls.
> —O, rocks! she said. Tell us in plain words.

"Met him what? he asked." What does *that* respond to? A murmur the narrator has not transcribed? Or a no-murmur? (When a cup can be held by a nothandle, may an answer also be given to a no-question?) Or did he spot the word on the page, misread it, before her hairpin found it? No knowing. We do know, though, from that scene by the Ballast Office clock, that Bloom, remembering "Greek," says "Met him pikehoses she called it till I told her about the transmigration. O rocks!"

It is right that Ulysses should explain a Greek word to Penelope (one more thing to be lost on a first-time reader). Is it not also conceivable that Ulysses master of lies—you could not believe him, Homer avers repeatedly—should say to himself "Met him pikehoses she called it" if she called it nothing of the kind? (He has a stake in thinking Molly less astute than she is.) And the grotesque phrase comes up again and again and again, seven more times in all, till we're quite sure we heard her say it though we never did. Her own recall runs "that word met something with hoses in it and he came out with some jawbreakers about the incarnation." But that's seventeen hours after she'd heard him pronounce the word three times.

Parallax falsifies. But maybe she did say it, while Homer was nodding. It would be like Joyce, to insert an equivalent for that famous nod.

A Clown's Inquest into Paternity: Fathers, Dead or Alive, in *Ulysses*

Jean-Michel Rabaté

It is because the Unconscious needs the insistence of writing that critics err when they treat a written work in the same way as they treat the Unconscious. At every moment, any written work cannot but lend itself to interpretation in a psychoanalytic sense. But to subscribe to this, ever so slightly, implies that one supposes the work to be a forgery, since, inasmuch as it is written, it does not imitate the effects of the Unconscious. The work poses the equivalent of the Unconscious, an equivalent no less real than it, as the one forges the other in its curvature. . . . The literary work fails or succeeds, but this failure is not due to the imitating of the effects of the structure. The work only exists in that curvature which is that of the structure itself. We are left then with no mere analogy. The curvature mentioned here is no more a metaphor for the structure than the structure is a metaphor for the reality of the Unconscious. It is real, and, in this sense, the work imitates nothing. It is, as fiction, a truthful structure.

JACQUES LACAN

What is a father? Who is the father? What is common between my father, your father, me as a father, the man next door, the mailman, the commercial traveler or He whom we picture walking in the clouds? A father as Viconian giant, thundering, farting, belching, castrating sons and daughters alike, with his pockets full of sweets to lure little girls astray, or cakewalking as the cake that you can both eat and have in his last triumphal march, just to provide critics with one of their great white whales? Who can be sure to be the father, who can be so self-confident as to utter without faltering, "I am a fa . . ." and not crash down into the frozen lakes of doubt and

From *The Fictional Father: Lacanian Readings of the Text,* edited by Robert Con Davis. © 1981 by the University of Massachusetts Press.

incest that have nonetheless been safely crossed? Thus, *Finnegans Wake*: a list of names, all dubious, corrupted by tradition and oral distortion, voluntary manglings and unconscious censorship, all of which try to pin down the father to a definition or to a precise spot on earth. Among those, one appellation seems to offer a clue, which might serve as a point of departure: "apersonal problem, a locative enigma." This can lead to three sets of preliminary remarks. A father is not simply an "individual," but mainly a function; paternity is that place from which someone lays down a law, be it the law of sexual difference, the law of the prohibition of incest, or the laws of language. A father is not a person but the focal point where castration can be brought to bear on the structure of desire; as such he is the knot binding the anarchic compound of drives and the realm of cultural codification. Next, a father is not a "problem," but a nexus of unresolved enigmas, all founded on the mysterious efficacy of a Name, which in itself remains a riddling cipher. And lastly, Joyce's formulation helps us to replace the question of designation by an exploration in positioning; if, as we shall see, a father is defined by his absence, paternity and patriarch are set adrift in a world of substitutes, in which everybody is endlessly elsewhere.

I am not setting out to give a psychoanalytic reading of "the father in *Ulysses*; indeed Lacan's epigraph should rather come as a warning not to apply Freudian hermeneutics to a text which already uses and makes fun of so many Freudian, Jungian, and Rankian tags. Lacan's statement could also suggest that a psychoanalytic interpretation, although now wary of unlocking the "author's psyche" behind his text, has its limits, to be found not in a textual uniqueness or irreducibility, but in the deliberate manipulation of uncertainties through which Joyce sought to infinitize the possibilities of language. If the unconscious works like a text, as a text, what Joyce may imitate of its effects in his "epical forged cheque" of "many piously forged palimpsests" only bursts through at times as symptoms. And the symptoms do not so much betray Joyce himself as a state of language in its overdetermined and complex articulation with politics, sexuality, and history. In these language-symptoms, released and not simply created by Joyce, the role of paternity is perhaps not so ominous as one could be tempted to believe, yet surely more problematical, more elusive, and more perverse. . . .

Ulysses begins in the atmosphere of the pervading presence of the mother and ends with a hymn to femininity; the reader can even conjure up the unwritten text that would join Molly Bloom's final "yes" to Stephen's melancholy musings on his dead mother, if the circularity of *Finnegans Wake* could apply to *Ulysses*. It is fitting to remember that the concept of "atonement" is dropped like a brick upon Stephen's theory of paternity in *Hamlet* precisely by Haines, the usurping Englishman coming to rescue Mulligan the Irish usurper: "I read a theological interpretation of it somewhere, he said bemused. The Father and Son idea. The Son striving to atone with the Father." Despite the vagueness of the reference, an imprecision which Stephen would never allow since he almost always quotes by name, this remark only then prompts Stephen's thoughts on the "consubstantiality of the Son with the Father." Now, the very origin of this "interpretation" ought to invite suspicion and prevent us from too glibly glossing over the text in the same way. Moreover, at the close of the book, the question of atonement is met with an offhand dismissal in the abortive conclusion to Bloom's proposal that Stephen (as Telemachus who has found Ulysses at last) should spend the end of the night in his house. Bloom ponders on the difficulty he will have to keep in touch with the young poet as he meditates on the "irreparability of the past" and remembers an incident which had taken place in a circus: "once . . . an intuitive particoloured clown in quest of paternity . . . had publicly declared to an exhilarated audience that he (Bloom) was his (the clown's) papa." The answer is the curtest of the sarcastic comebacks contained in the catechistic chapter of "Ithaca": "Was the clown Bloom's son? / No." This little scene quite deftly sketches the whole structure of the book, placing Stephen as clown, jester, or fool, not too far from the laughing audience; it shows, by a kind of *reductio ad absurdum* of the basics of the theme of paternity, that the "fusion of Bloom and Stephen" which Joyce had contemplated, as the Linati scheme reveals, was at best temporary and bound to fail. Therefore, the claim to paternity on which the greater part of *Ulysses* seems founded is now challenged by the widening gap which sets "father" and "son," like Bloom and his notched coin, drifting further apart. "Had Bloom's coin returned? / Never."

The "possible, circuitous or direct, return" Bloom had hoped for never really occurs in *Ulysses*. . . . I shall try to trace out the path opened by the concept of "atonement" in *Ulysses* to show how the shift from a living "impossible" father to a dead father, one reduced to his pure function, governs the basic unit of the family and generates a radically new orientation in the language of fiction. If the father is a "legal fiction" in *Ulysses*, in *Finnegans Wake* he opens the door to the laws of fiction as "truthful structure."

THE FIGURES OF INCESTITUDE

Investigations into paternity are forbidden.
Code Napoleon, 1804, article 340

One of the basic elements of *Ulysses* is the duplication of the father figure, and the relationship between the real father (Simon Dedalus) and the symbolic father (Bloom as Ulysses) is a first key to the function of paternity in the book. The dissociation is established progressively between the two, and at the start there seems to be a close link between Stephen and his father; at least there is evidence for this link in the words of others as recalled by Stephen. Two physical motifs, the voice and the eyes, recur to stress this resemblance, so that a certain degree of "consubstantiality" seems to unite father and son in the flesh. The editor of the newspaper exclaims that Stephen is a "Chip off the old block!" when Stephen suggests a pause in a pub; likewise, Kevin Egan had told him in Paris: "You're your father's son. I know the voice." In the same way, when Bloom thinks about Rudy, his only son who did not live, he mentions the two features: "If little Rudy had lived. See him grow up. Hear his voice in the house. . . . My son. Me in his eyes." Late until the *Walpurgisnacht* of the "Circe" chapter, Stephen, who tries to kill the "priest and king" in his mind, has not killed his father yet, for he still imitates his prodigal father by being consistently prodigal: "Play with your eyes shut. Imitate pa. Filling my belly with husks of swine. Too much of this. I will arise and go to my. . . . No voice. I am a most finished artist." Stephen imitates the mannerisms of his father when he sings, but in his drunken state, the blindness and the voicelessness alone reveal that Stephen is closest to his real father: he is about to return, although he represses the mention of his father. No voice, no eyes, a closed, opaque body—already caught up in the cycle of repetition in which failed artist and failed gentleman merge their shortcomings. In fact for Joyce the voice and the eyes seem to have embodied the true clues to affiliation, since when he proudly announces Giorgio's birth to his family back in Dublin, he writes, "The child appears to have inherited his grandfather's and father's voices. He has dark blue eyes," and this is enough of a description.

These distinctive features loom out again when Stephen imagines the love-making of his parents. But, though his vampiric and necrophiliac fantasies revolve around his mother's corpse, they are blended with theological speculations on paternity, for Stephen identifies himself with a divine form, revealed in the likeness of physical characteristics (eyes, voice), a form which lends to his contingent existence the ineluctable necessity of a law. "Wombed in sin darkness I was too, made, not begotten. By them, the man with my voice and my eyes, and a ghostwoman with ashes on her breath." Stephen implies that he has not merely been generated in the flesh by his parents, but has been *made,* or willed eternally by a divine Creator.

The transmission of a pure form thus seems instrumental in canceling all reference to the sexual role of the mother, and the *lex eterna* of the father's law prepares the way for the assertion of a "divine substance wherein Father and Son are consubstantial.

But Stephen is betrayed by the ambiguity of his images, as he feels locked in a postmortem embrace with a mother who haunts him, and he only refutes the Arian heresy to fall into the trap of an unnamed heresy which would interpret the "substance" as the womb of imagination. If Stephen's first temptation is to rule out the Oedipal triangle so that he may enhance a dual relationship to his Maker, it then appears that he has never killed his mother and cannot take his father's place. For him, to kill the mother would mean to deny this substance without an origin which fascinates him, and whose truth he ultimately discovers in the materiality of the act of writing: "Belly without blemish, bulging big, a buckler of taut vellum, no, whiteheaped corn, orient and immortal, standing from everlasting to everlasting. Womb of sin!" The white vellum or parchment is Eve's sin as well as the future blank page kept waiting for Stephen's traces and signs, "signs on a white field."

By a very telling shift in Stephen's reflections, which shows the ambivalent nature of the *lex eterna,* the imagined voice of Simon Dedalus proceeds with an attack, although oblique, on the incestuous potentialities of the family pattern. Just after these thoughts, Stephen wonders whether he will visit his aunt: "Here. Am I going to Aunt Sara's or not? My consubstantial father's voice." Stephen is deterred from such a visit by the sneers he has often heard: "Did you see anything of your artist brother Stephen lately? No? Sure he's not down in Strasburg terrace with his Aunt Sally. . . . And and and and tell us Stephen, how is uncle Si? . . . And skeweyed Walter sirring his father, no less. Sir. Yes, sir. No, sir." Through Simon's voice, we hear uncle Richie's stammer and Walter's obsequious sirring. This voice conjures up a series of vivid pictures in a spirited ventriloquism which fuses with the rhythm of Stephen's musings. The "old artificer" even parodies the Daedalan myth in a sordid fall: "Couldn't he fly a bit higher than that, eh?" Such a flexible idiom lends itself perfectly to mimicry and abuse while it achieves its aim: the scene is so effectively reconstructed that Stephen, walking along the strand, passes the house and forgets to call on them. The father's voice has been powerful enough as to shunt Stephen's thoughts to another track, and yet reveals even more of the incestuous nature of his link to his "in-laws," and by way of another detour, to Bloom's possible fosterage.

All this becomes clearer and more pointed when the same sequence recurs in a different context, during the funeral procession, as Bloom, Simon Dedalus, and friends are driving to the churchyard. Bloom tells Mr Dedalus that he has just spotted Stephen, "your son and heir," walking on the beach, thus giving the cue for what seems to be one of Simon's clichés: "Down with his aunt Sally, I suppose, Mr Dedalus said, the Goulding faction, the drunken little costdrawer and Crissie, papa's little lump of dung, the wise child that knows her own father." Simon Dedalus no longer responds to Walter's servility but Crissie's love, and his insinuations modify the previous remark made by Stephen about Crissie ("Papa's little bedpal. Lump of love"); now the scatological abuse makes clear the incestuous relationship between Richie Goulding and his daughter. For Simon, this is what characterizes the mother's side of the family: it is a faction involved in a continuous intrigue, always plotting against the supremacy of the real head of the house. As such, it threatens the orthodoxy of the father's law; it questions the original atomic or adamic structure. The mother's family is a constant reminder of degradation ("O weeping God, the things I married into"). When Stephen is tempted for a while by this possible shelter, he may well be looking for a temporary substitute home, by anticipation finding in his "fraction" of an old decaying unity the maternal and heretical shelter only Bloom can offer. The displacement of the incestuous nexus toward Bloom's paternal attitude is then made more obvious before reaching a climax in Molly's dreams of seducing a "sonhusband" (as *Finnegans Wake* neatly puts it).

The specific meaning of incest entails a pun on blindness and insight contained in the verb *to know*. The phrase "wise child that knows her own father" echoes proverbially and also recalls *The Merchant of Venice*. Launcelot tells his blind father who does not recognize him, "Nay indeed, if you had your eyes you might fail the knowing of me: it is a wise father that knows his own child" (2.2). But then he adds confidently, "Murder cannot be hid long: a man's son may; but, in the end, truth will out"; Bloom, who must be confusedly remembering those lines, distorts their impact as "The body to be exhumed. Murder will out." Bloom also has his skeleton in a cupboard, and through the associations with the Childs murder he is led to his own fifteen-year-old daughter Milly: "She mightn't like me to come that way without letting her know. Must be careful about women. Catch them once with their pants down. Never forgive you after. Fifteen." The equating of love-making with murder—soul-murder, as Schreber would say—is a typical feature of the Oedipal fantasies linked with the hallucinated primal scene.

Bloom and Richie Goulding thus have been connected, for the reader at least, heaped together as they are by this "lump of love." This connection is emphasized by the parallelism of their situation in "Sirens," when both are silently listening, enthralled by Simon's superb tenor voice; "married in silence" they talk a little.

> A beautiful air, said Bloom lost Leopold. I know it well.
> Never in all his life had Richie Goulding.
> He knows it well too. Or he feels. Still harping on his daughter.
> Wise child that knows her father, Dedalus said. Me?

On the one side, there is a "Master's voice," the voice of a man "full of his son" and endowed with a rich voice all others admire; on the other side are two fathers who are hampered by their half-conscious incestuous wishes and who can only literally "harp" on that theme. Bloom is quite right to describe the "relations" of the two "brothers-in-law" with the musical simile: a rift in the lute. Thus, will it finally "make the music mute / And ever widening slowly silence all" (song quoted in Gifford and Seidman: *Notes for Joyce: An Annotation of James Joyce's* Ulysses.)

The gap between the right lineage and the maternal line of descent already introduces the contrast between the symbolic order as defined by the law of the father and the prohibition of incest, and an imaginary realm where the fantasies of incest merely cover the wish to return to the womb. This contract explains why a qualification needs to be made about Bloom's role as a symbolic father. To be a father, symbolically, does not imply merely a real paternity; on the contrary, it takes death, absence, and radical otherness into account. Bloom can be said to become Stephen's father only after they have parted; it is when they are closest that this relation is impossible. Contact is the reverse side of the coin of mystical fatherhood. Because of Bloom's offer and Stephen's subsequent refusal of hospitality, Stephen has to choose for himself in order to father himself: he accordingly begins the new cycle of dawn while Bloom is getting buried in his deep night (according to the Linati scheme). A symbolic father is not simply the father of a son, as such can be left to the real father's function; a symbolic father is as it were the father of a father—a grandfather, in a way—who fades away to become increasingly identified with a pure name. But Stephen's new home can be only a text which he still has to sign as he incorporates Bloom's name to it.

The way to such a symbolic father can only be discovered if the refusal of any acknowledgment it implies is based on the ignorance of the real father. Stephen and Simon, in spite of their objective complicity, have to ignore their respective presence in the blind link which prevents them from knowing each other. Simon Dedalus fails to recognize his son several times, as for instance when Lenehan praises him with, "Greetings from the famous son of a famous father." Simon's "Who may he be?" expresses his lack of concern, and after he has admitted his oversight ("I didn't recognize him for the moment") he rapidly shifts the conversation to another subject. Stephen similarly does not aspire to have "a wise father who knows his own child": such would be the imaginary father as Bloom dreams of himself ("Now he is himself paternal and these about him might be his sons. Who can say? The wise father knows his child"). Stephen has had the opportunity to reflect earlier in life upon certain ambiguous expressions of his father's; for instance, the scene in the pub during the visit to his father's hometown in the *Portrait* showed the rivalry to be more apparent. Stephen would probably have failed by his father's standards and those of his friends: "Then he is not his father's son, said the little old man.—I don't know, I'm sure, said Mr Dedalus, smiling complacently." What a wry remark on the dictum, *Pater semper incertus!*

But this uncertainty cannot be pushed to its end in a denial of filial or paternal ties. And Stephen makes an interesting parallel between John Eglington (Magee) and himself when in *Ulysses* he accuses Magee of "denying his kindred." Magee deals the most decisive blow to Stephen's theological and para-psychoanalytical theory of creation in Shakespeare when he says, "What do we care for his wife and father? I should say that only family poets have family lives." Stephen's paradox lies precisely in the fact that he needs to present Shakespeare in the midst of family rivalries, usurpations, and treacheries in order to free paternity as creation from the power of the mother. Magee is in fact a sort of alter ego for Stephen, but is as yet unaware that he has had to deny his heritage in order to live on romantic and outdated principles. Stephen thinks: "He *knows* your old fellow. The widower. / Hurrying to her squalid deathlair from gay Paris on the quayside I touched his hand. The *voice,* new warmth, speaking. Dr Bob Kenny is attending her. The *eyes* that wish me well. But do not *know* me" (italics added). The widower refers to Stephen's father, and the phrase "He knows your old fellow" was said by Mulligan about Bloom, whom Mulligan jokingly suspects of pederasty ("He knows you. He knows your old fellow. O, I fear me he is Greeker than the Greeks"). Bloom is already the "jewgreek" combining incest with homosexuality.

It is only then that Stephen finds the courage to develop his theory with the famous statement, "A father is a necessary evil." While Magee places Shakespeare as a creator alone in a mythic space, surrounded by the figures of Falstaff and others, Stephen sees him as the representative of paternity as artistic creation: this "mystical estate" can only be transmitted to a son; it cannot be made conscious. Thus, "Fatherhood, in the sense of conscious begetting, is unknown to man." The "mystery" of fatherhood is this unconscious begetting through which an artist feels the unconscious to exist. The consciousness is reserved to the mother: every man "knows" his mother and "does not know" his father, because his father himself is unaware of the nature of their link. Only a mother's love can mean truth, since the evidence of the senses proves the filiation and also since the son shares with the father the unmentionable privilege of having crossed in person, once at least, the threshold of her womb. "What links them in nature? An instant of *blind* rut" (italics added). *Amor matris*, a true "genitive" subjective and objective, but *Caecitas patribus*, an "ablative" plural: desire and castration, places and replacements. This blindness anticipates the full treatment of the incest theme and of the post-Oedipal symbolic castration. Stephen has already defined incest, following St. Thomas, as "an avarice of emotion," which he relates to the Jews, "the most given to intermarriage." Stephen still attempts to reach a definition of the "mystical father," and he gets lost in his self-contradictory developments; he finally locates the elusive relationship in a complete refusal of incest. For Stephen, there can be no reconciliation without first a "sundering," and the father and son are "sundered by a bodily shame so steadfast that the criminal annals of the world, stained with all other incests and bestialities, hardly record its breach." Incest marks the negative limit of paternity, incest literally taken as the love between father and son. In the vast array of perversions one taboo still holds, stronger than the forbidden yet tempting intercourse of the son with the mother. The "bodily" shame is confirmed by the common "transgression" of the mother's sex. Therefore, if the rapport between the mother and son is one of prohibition and transgression, the relation between father and son is what constitutes the essence of the law; it lies at the very core of the Oedipal pattern which introduces the subject to the symbolic realm of language. Without the mother, the son could not *not know* his father. But the mother by herself is unable to tell her son the way to his origins, or his name even.

The famous remark of Telémakhos to Athena in the first book of *The Odyssey* underlines all this discussion: "My mother tells me that I am his son [of Odysseus], but I know not, for no one knows his own father." Through language, a play of absence, difference, and incertitude are brought to bear upon one's own kinship. The mother's voice is not forceful enough to prove the truth of her motherhood: her love has to be true since it can do without proof. Now, as soon as the subject attempts to define himself, he needs the symbolic order of language as conditioned by the absent father, so that he may wander through meaning in quest of a father. For Lacan, the acquisition of language is contemporary with the Oedipal stages. When first I speak, I accept a symbolic castration in that I have to renounce my intense desire for fusion with the mother: as I learn the rules of language, I accept the externality of a symbolic code which existed prior to my unique connection with the other and even predetermined it. The Church is for Stephen such a symbolic world of discourse and culture, which ought likewise to renounce the lure of a madonna "flung to the mob of Europe" in order to found its world "upon the void," "upon incertitude, upon unlikelihood." If the mother's self-sufficiency is denied, the father is not, for all that, a presence embodying the legitimate succession. Language is a system of differences, a power of death and absence in which he too is caught up. This paternal complicity explains the guilt lying within language's very foundation, the guilt of having to displace the mother and to kill the father as presence. Hence, the shame which makes up the voice of the artist, "Shame's voice" as the voice of Shem the artist in *Finnegans Wake.*

Castration and incest thus are played off one another to define the symbolic order of the written text. Paternity is reduced to being a name, which can be separated from the bearer and transmitted to an heir, as Shakespeare did when he transferred his power to Hamlet. Hamlet, "disarmed of fatherhood, having devised that mystical estate upon his son." The divine procession of the Logos needs no virgin to encourage believers, but a name is necessary. It is then striking to notice that the first time Joyce wrote the phrase "legal fiction" to define fatherhood, he used it in connection with his own son's name: "The child has got no name yet, though he will be two months old on Thursday next. . . . I don't know who he's like. . . . I think a child should be allowed to take his father's or mother's name at will on coming of age. Paternity is a legal fiction." The same expression sounds quite different in *Ulysses,* since Stephen has to ascertain at once the fiction of paternity and the ineluctable power of a name; this difference explains the shift to a modal phrase ("Paternity may be a legal fiction"): any "definition" of paternity has to be hypothetical. And the suspension of the imposition of the name cannot last very long, since a name implies this "mystical" function—a mystique without love or belief—binding heredity to the law. The name becomes a signifier, as Lacan expresses clearly: "the attribution of procreation to the father can only be the effect of a pure signifier, of a recognition, not of a real father, but of what religion has taught us to refer to as the Name-of-the-Father."

Stephen does not really claim his name. It is imposed on him from the outside; even his listeners refer his subtle digressions back to his name:

"Your own name is strange enough. I suppose it explains your fantastical humour." Although a name explains nothing in such a direct way, indeed its function is to raise the physical resemblances (eyes, voice) to the power of a symbolic signifier. Only a signifier can be related to a voice, in a pattern which opposes name and bearer, inherited signifier and speaking subject. Stephen has then to choose a delicate balance between usurpation and right lineage. He says: "I am tired of my voice, the voice of Esau." Thus, although he is really the first-born and hardly seems to care about his brother Maurice, he is both Esau and Jacob in his double role of actor and acted upon: as actor, he displaces both brothers and father; as acted upon, he obeys the mother's wishes ("Act. Be acted upon."). The course of his self-generation is a journey through writings, from the Bible to Shakespeare, in which he sets out to assume his father's name in full ("Dedalus"), after having passed the labyrinths of his own logics: "Lapwing. Icarus. *Pater, ait.* Seabedabbled, fallen, weltering. Lapwing you are."

So the voice is less of a clue revealing one's descendance than a symptom of a division within the subject; it is less "his master's voice" as Paddy Dignam exclaims than a cracked reproduction which splits asunder in the effort to maintain warring opposites in the same position of discourse. Just before Dignam's exclamation, Father Coffey's voice was heard: "Namine, Jacobs Vobiscuits. Amen," in a sacrilegious variation on Jacob's biscuits. The name-of-the-father as received must be written down to be efficacious as signifier, but in this very movement, the play of differences opens up and fastens the subject in a knot tying Jacob to Esau. Stephen had wondered: "What's in a name? That is what we ask ourselves in childhood when we *write* the name that we are *told* is ours." This statement is a new departure from what Telémakhos said when he mentioned that no one knows his father by himself. No one knows for himself, but everyone, even a poor schoolboy has a signature, a name that becomes a coat of arms, a personal emblem or simply the illegible cipher of the most common signature: "a crooked signature with blind loops and a blot. Cyril Sargent: his name and seal." A name entails a writing, a hand reappropriating what another's voice says of it. This hand and voice are here locked together in the blind gaze of a signifier which has to reconcile the name-of-the-father with the mother's desire. Now, the voice of Esau is twice absent: a first time because it has been usurped by Jacob's voice, a second time because it has been replaced by his handwriting. When this problematic knot is linked to the creation of a text, the antagonistic elements are integrated into the machinery of sense which adequately uses the brothers' conflict to bring about the father's fall. Such a scenario adumbrates the nuclear organization of *Finnegans Wake*.

In *Finnegans Wake*, the story of Jacob and Esau, exploited to satiety, offers the model of a potent performative function of language, a paradigm even more interesting than the divine *fiat lux,* since it works with a deceived paternal namer. Isaac, whose name is already a pun ("laugh!"—"When is a pun not a pun?" asks the textbook, with the answer "Isaac" in the margin, suggesting that the answer is "when it is a name"), cannot alter his benediction after he has realized Jacob's ruse. Now Esau stems from his father's side; he is the natural heir of patrilineal descent, while Jacob the second-born is his mother's favorite. The mother needs the paternal benediction to place Jacob at the head of the family: she needs the ritual power of a name. Jacob obeys his mother's *voice*; Rebekah tells him, "Only obey my voice" (Genesis 27.13). When later the blind father feels his son's body hidden beneath a goatskin, he seems to renew a sensual contact with his wife. His lyrical benediction takes the form of a fresh alliance with a feminine earth: "*See,* the smell of my son is as the smell of a field which the Lord hath blessed." In his blind vision, through the almost homosexual contact of a trembling hand with a son's fake skin, the old father turns back to the mother and her heir to bless the erotic gift of food and a body fetishistically identified by hair. All this is bartered against this name. In his voice, something is inexorably written, a signature which becomes a fate: *fari fatum.* Speech is a production which entails irreversible action as soon as it is undersigned by a name: "Speech, speech. But act. Act speech. They mock to try you. Act. Be acted on."

The same division between name and bearer reappears in Bloom's complex relationship with his father's name. This theme is introduced when Bloom remembers the words his father was fond of quoting: "Nathan's voice! His son's voice! I hear the voice of Nathan who left his father to die of grief and misery in my arms, who left the house of his father and left the God of his father. Every word is so deep, Leopold." These lines from the play *Leah* are said by Abraham, a blind Jew who recognizes the voice of the villain, Nathan, a recanted Jew who changes his name and abjures his faith. He persecutes Leah (who bears the name of one of Jacob's wives in the Bible), a jewess, as he attempts to erase his origins. The scene, vividly evoked by Bloom's father, recurs in Bloom's mind to mark his guilt when he thinks of his father's suicide. The coming anniversary of his death sends Bloom's thoughts spinning around his inheritance of a changed name, a name which is never exactly fitting nor properly placed. "Bloom" is a translation from the Hungarian name "Virag," which means flower. Hence Bloom's pen-name of Henry Flower. In this exile from an origin, the name has suffered a certain degradation. This instability is enhanced by the absence of any male heir in Bloom's family. Throughout the book Bloom mourns both his father and his son, poised between a transcribed origin and a nameless issue. As such, he can only imagine a substitute heir, like Stephen, and must also use pseudonyms. This prudence makes him unable to sign his own real name; that is confirmed by the gossip in a pub: "O Bloom has his good points. But there's one thing he'll never do. / His hand scrawled a dry pen signature beside his grog."

Whereas Stephen balances between a father's and a son's name, Bloom's own signifier is unstable, a prey to transformations: "Bloom" will never acquire the status of symbolic signifier. One relevant instance of that general distrust for his name—which, like the name of Odysseus, *Outis*, allows for all sorts of puns—lies in the obvious legal action which changed Virag to Bloom. Martin Cunningham explains the procedure to his drinking companions: "His name was Virag. The father's name that poisoned himself. He changed it by deedpoll, the father did." The pub idiom ("father's name that") opens a significant ambiguity here, since the sentence could even imply that the name was poisoned by itself(!), or simply that the father's suicide could be due to a certain flaw in his name. The same type of idiotism occurs to question Bloom's ability to stand as a real father. A certain J. J. continues with: " . . . every male that's born they think it may be their Messiah. And every jew is in a tall state of excitement, I believe, till he knows if he's a father or a mother." Here, of course, father and mother refer to "father of a son" and "father of a daughter" but if we are to take this literally, Bloom is then only a mother, an insinuation which will be acted out in one of the most paroxysmal hallucinations of "Circe," when he gives birth to eight children.

The transformation of the name and the suicide can then arise from similar causes; a suicide like that of Rudolph Bloom is a desperate act, committed in isolation, while the *deedpoll* which ratified his new name is a deed executed "by one party only" ("I Rudolph Virag . . . hereby give notice . . . at all times to be known by the name of Rudolph Bloom"). To poll means to cut off or to cut even, as with a sheet of paper for instance; this practice of polling the edge of the paper is opposed to the practice of indenting it, which supposes two parties at least and is meant to reconstitute the original sheet, "each section being later fitted if necessary to the sections having an exactly tallying edge as proof that the sections are parts of an original authentic document" (*Webster's Dictionary*). *Finnegans Wake* mentions for instance a certain Mr Cockshott, "present holder by deedpoll and indenture of the swearing belt" in a passage introducing the father's bisexuality. Since the change of names has been, in a way, unilateral, its symbolic function as name-of-the-father is more than problematical. The real *symbolon,* an object cut into two halves that can be reconstituted as a token of identity, implies that dented edge which is lacking in the case of a deedpoll. "Cockshott" is here a signifier of the phallus; one of the most enigmatic recurrent names of *Finnegans Wake,* he unites the broken line of the symbol (indenture) and the clean edge of castration (deedpoll). It is no surprise then to see Bloom's grandfather, Leopold Virag, in one of the visions of "Circe," holding a parchmentroll, which among other things is the text of his son's deedpoll (he provides us with a hint when he exclaims "Pretty Poll!"). The old Virag, more than Rudolph Bloom, appears as Bloom's real father in this scene, since he at least is an authority on sexual matters: "(He taps his parchmentroll energetically.) This book tells you how to act with all descriptive particulars." He is also a master over his son's fate and toys with the anxieties of his grandson: "Consult index for agitated fear of aconite. . . . Virag is going to talk about amputation." Sex and death are reconciled in Virag's hysterical ramblings, and the sequence of the first names: Leopold-Rudolph-Leopold-Rudy offers a pattern which goes beyond the change of surname. Virag in fact initiates the series of metamorphoses which affects the Blooms; Virag calls up the apparition of Henry Flower in persona and is described aptly as "sloughing his skins, his multitudinous plumage moulting." As "Basilicogrammate," he is "Lord of letters"; like Thoth, the god of letters Stephen invokes, he welcomes all the travesties, transsexualisms, and metempsychoses of the book.

It is not because Stephen and Bloom are not really father and son that they fail to "atone," for Stephen sees even less of his father during Blooms-day; it is because Stephen is the son-type in the process of fathering himself, approaching the creative stage, at least one hopes, and Bloom is the imperfect father in the process of husbanding all his forces to find himself. Bloom's absence from home, his Homeric pilgrimage, has started in 1893, at the time when he had his last complete sexual intercourse (i.e., coitus non interruptus) with Molly; his physical and intellectual absence has increased ten years later, in 1903 since his daughter Milly's puberty. The wider frame of Absence covers the minor "temporary absences" in which Bloom feels his freedom inhibited by the female alliance of Molly and Milly. The nine months and one day that have come between the "consummation" of her puberty and the date of June 16, 1904 indicate that Molly's adultery with Boylan is nothing but the natural outcome of the symbolic incest which both links and separates Bloom and his daughter. So the different triangles overlap and displace each other successively. We shift from Molly—Bloom—Rudy, the early Oedipal triangle ended by the death of Rudy, to Molly—Bloom—Milly, the familial triangle, and to Molly—

Bloom—Boylan, the triangle of adultery. The next triangle would of course be Molly—Bloom—Stephen, a triangle that would be both incestuous and adulterous, since "the way to daughter led through mother, the way to mother through daughter." Molly, who entertains thoughts of seducing Stephen, could still be a foster mother for him; by the possible offer of her daughter, she would become Stephen's mother-in-law, thus finding a new point of return to her husband, freed at last from his Oedipal infatuation with his daughter. Hence the impossible superimposition of the two basic triangles, Molly—Boylan—Bloom and Molly—Bloom—Stephen, ideally would give rise to the one stable lozenge, Molly—Milly—Bloom—Stephen. But this superimposition does not happen.

Such a combination would bring about the ideal fusion of the contradictory "French triangles" Stephen had discovered in Shakespeare's life and creation. "You are a delusion, said roundly John Eglington to Stephen. You have brought us all this way to show us a French triangle." Their fusion would build one of the *French lozenges* which are passed around in Bella's brothel: "No objection to French lozenges?" This pattern will in turn be included in the expanding sex of the mother who *Finnegans Wake* presents with "the no niggard spot of her safety vulve, first of all usquiluteral threeingles": she is drawn as A.L.P / παλ, and her figure sums up the different possible positions in the family: "it will be lozenge to me all my lauffe" (with a note referring to the sigla of the family).

In the *Portrait,* the young Stephen who still has to "encounter" experience denies family ties as well as all triangular relationships. He seems to be a victim of the delusions of grandeur that, according to Freud, accompany those family romances most children evolve around their origins. Stephen stands aloof and in proud isolation, cut off from his relatives despite his father's awkward attempts at intimacy with him. "I treat you as your grandfather treated me when I was a young chap. We were more like brothers than father and son." Typically, Stephen sees himself as the foster child of Irish lore: "he felt he was hardly of the one blood with them but stood to them rather in the mystical kinship of fosterage, fosterchild and fosterbrother." His vocation of artist, which is yet a pure promise, implies a severing of the most immediate ties, and this process goes on well into *Ulysses.* But in the *Portrait,* this romantic attitude is left without any complementary positive father figure, and his temporary hope to "save" his family from chaos, thus becoming too slackly his parents' father, is undermined by parodic economic metaphors, much in the same way as the image of a "cash-register" comes to debunk the masturbatory enthusiasm of his first creative act, the composition of his villanelle.

Stephen then tries to use his family as a secure bolt-holt from which he could define himself, in spite of its evident frailty. The values embodied by the family could have served as a "bulwark" or a "mole" against the mounting "tides" of desire which threatened to overcome him, but the only effective check to his impulses can come from religion. Stephen generously places the money he got from his school prizes at the disposal of his family, hoping to give a new vitality to their life, "by rules of conduct and active interests and new filial relations." But, as soon as the money is spent, "the commonwealth fell, the loan bank closed its coffers and its books on a sensible loss"; Stephen is no longer able to resist the call of Nighttown. The latent ironical tone of some sentences which stress his wish to promote quasi-usurious practices, all in a noble cause of course, shows Stephen "press[ing] loans on willing borrowers so that he might have the pleasure of making out receipts and reckoning the interests on the sums lent." This situation is paralleled in *Ulysses* as the hesitation between squandering and lending at interest takes on heightened significance when Stephen explains in the library that for St. Thomas incest is a kind of usury of emotions. The "breakwater of order and elegance" which Stephen wants to erect was a desperate attempt at limiting the circulation of desire to the little microcosm of the family, and when it crumbles for want of money, he measures his failure in terms of a renewed sundering of ties: "He had not gone one step nearer the lives he had sought to approach nor bridged the *restless shame* and rancour that had divided him from mother and brother and sister." The single difference is that here the "shame" does not apply to his relationship with the father. In *Ulysses,* a physical shame dividing father and son gives them both the impetus to travel to the ends of the world in order to avoid meeting the other with the same voice and eyes.

A father is "what went forth to the ends of the world to traverse not itself": the prohibition of the shameful proximity of parenthood brings about a circuit, a bend and swerve through language, thanks to which the subject indeed traverses himself precisely because of this movement of self-avoidance. The subject travels through the panorama of styles, literatures, and speeches, and generates the complementary image of self as other. This very movement finally rests upon the assertion of a capitalized Other, a place where the unconscious molds from the outside the serial discourses through which one passes, dying and being born again. In Stephen's musical theory, the father and the son are compared to the "fundamental" and the "dominant" on a scale, as Stephen plays a series of "empty fifths" on the piano: they are "separated by the greatest possible interval which is the greatest possible ellipse consistent with the ultimate return."

The greatest possible interval is both castration as embodied in the father's law and the tabooed, almost perverse, love of castration for itself. In Lacanian terms, Stephen is the phallus for Bloom even more than for Molly, the phallus as a signifier of absence; this representation triggers the movement of ellipse back to the mother. In *Ulysses,* ellipsis is constantly a precondition to the ellipse or transmigration through language: the ellipsis or omission of the prohibited love for the father. This condition also explains why Stephen refuses religion not as a structure of thought, but as a theology of divine and human love. The ellipsis of sexual intercourse conditions the heavenly and terrestrial ellipse centered around Gea-Tellus, Molly as *ewig weibliche*. And Molly, who is perhaps the only "present" character in a text woven by the apparitions and fade-outs of various absent males, can rightly pun on Bloom's omissions and her own emission. At one point, she remembers the doctor who was to cure her venereal disease that was contracted during her too frequent masturbations due to Bloom's inspired erotic letters: "that doctor one guinea please and asking me had I frequent omissions." She still thinks he had guessed the cause of her ailment, which she of course "omits" ("and I said I hadnt are you sure O yes I said I am quite sure"). When she later considers diverse ways of seducing Bloom, she imagines his discharge on her drawers: "then Ill wipe him off me just like a business his omission then Ill go out." Bloom, the "commercial traveller" who follows his son in his wanderings, has perhaps chosen the longest loop round sexual commerce; but if this "wiping out" is by no means an "atonement," no more than a promise of a fulfilled and generative sexuality, it can tentatively point to an issue. After all, to cancel an omission may asymptotically approach the shortest route to a direct statement. The father's loss is his gain, in a perpetual displacement; the lack of intercourse finally spins the courses and recourses of the Viconian history on which *Finnegans Wake* elaborates.

Righting *Ulysses*

Fritz Senn

Early readers of *Ulysses* had a hard time just finding their way around the book, distinguishing between tale and talk, or separating either from thought. Joyce, in this respect behaving like a divine judge of sins, did not appear to differentiate much between "thought, word and deed," as the Catechism and *A Portrait* put it. To us latecomers such distinctions have become much less problematic, and we have also learned that some distinctions are futile. A passage may well be a third-person report and yet suggest the articulations of some character who may not be articulating anything aloud. Joyce changes from one track to another without notice and on occasion moves happily along two or more at the same time.

Whoever makes an effort nowadays will usually step cautiously through the first three chapters, perhaps with a few tutorial nudges, then progress fairly well through the early Bloom parts and, in the course of this apprenticeship, pick up some basic knowhow which will help to cope with most of the looming extravagancies. At every turning there are stumbling blocks, irritations, erudite clusters, unannounced references, dislocations, and our attention is generally directed towards them. Much later, however, our interest may well return to other, less remarkable, parts which we overlooked in our first tentative navigation. We are now—to judge from a recent burst of studies in narrative technique—more and more fascinated also by the "easy" passages. Many of the following samples are therefore taken from the Bloom chapters in the first half of the book, that is, before

From *James Joyce: New Perspectives,* edited by Colin MacCabe. © 1982 by the Harvester Press Ltd.

the novel changes its character so radically (as we have been told). Many of the novel's strident departures from habit (our habits as readers, perhaps, more than anything else) have been quietly foreshadowed in those muted openings. A schoolmaster of 1922 might well have objected or an editor interfered where now we would hardly care to stop.

At the beginning of the "Hades" chapter, for example, Bloom enters into the funeral carriage and sits "in the vacant place":

> He pulled the door to after him and slammed it tight till it shut
> tight.

This will hardly confuse us on a first reading, though we might well focus on the strangely echoing "tight." Perhaps we can accept it as the awkwardness, and most likely the silence and constraint of social occasions like a funeral procession, being carried into the sentence itself. We can share Bloom's sense of decorum and his self-consciousness; treated almost as a non-person when he enters, he feels ill at ease. Which may also explain why he concentrates so intently on a less than perfect door mechanism.

Leopold Bloom is not an indiscriminate slammer of doors. Not long ago, at his own house and with competent ease, "He pulled the halldoor to after him very quietly, more, till the footleaf dropped gently over the threshold"—a similar statement for a similar action, with obvious differences (already, we notice, the book gently varies its own phrases). Leaving home, Bloom is methodical about creating an appearance ("Looked shut"), but does not, for good reason, actually shut the door. In the carriage the required shutting comes about only by a renewed effort. Both actions are repetitive, threefold, they take time, and in each case a "till" points the way towards achievement.

But only the "Hades" sentence is awkward, as though the act were made even more difficult by the others (we can assume) watching Bloom. The first "tight" in the sentence is the odd one, and we can imagine an early editor insisting on its excision. For if it were justified in its place, then the following clause would be redundant. It is only today's modern reader, schooled in writers like Joyce, who has learned to appreciate stylistic inadvertance as an expression of clumsiness or a sign of inner turbulence.

What does emerge from this minuscule linguistic fluster is Bloom's perseverance. On the smallest possible scale he is what Joyce said of Odysseus, "a jusqu'auboutist." As we can see from an earlier version, now called the Rosenbach Manuscript, Joyce had originally written: "and slammed it twice till it shut tight," a wholly unobjectionable phrasing. The substitution has changed a lot and introduced some nervousness. We might say, pedantically, that the first "tight" will at the end come to mean "*not* tight," so that further efforts are needed. Or we might say the first adverb refers to appearance, the second to reality. The first one will be recognised, in hindsight, as a fumble, the last one as a hit. The second one makes us doubt the validity of its identical predecessor. Or, to try again, "he slammed it tight" expresses an endeavour, "till it shut tight" the fulfillment. That a trivial insistent act calls for such a lot of descriptive expenditure is not very surprising, for we are already dealing with eminently Ulyssean concerns and techniques. It is also not surprising that the rebarbative duplication does not translate itself very well. The French version of it is a simple sequence, "Il tira la portière après lui, la claqua et reclaqua jusqu'à ce qu'elle tînt bon," like the Italian one: "e lo sbatte finché non fu ben chiuso"; in German too the sentence is smoother, "schlug sie fest zu, bis sie fest schloss," and renders a somewhat different action.

Even in that "initial style" of *Ulysses* a harmless word like "tight" may stand for a disquieting semblance or for the reality of its meaning, and we have an early instance of the weaving and unweaving of a texture, a word retroactively changing its being. Furthermore the whole sentence, with its reiteration before a door gets finally shut, could be reinterpreted entirely if we were, as well we might, to comb the "Hades" chapter for metaphors of death.

Much of *Ulysses* has to do with the deceptive identity of appearance. Close to the beginning of book 2 there are two sentences of almost parallel construction. "Gelid light and air were in the kitchen" resembles, on its surface, the preceding: "Kidneys were in his mind." But clearly, kidneys are not in one's mind in quite the same sense that air is in one's kitchen. No reader has trouble adjusting to the minor discrepancy within the range of the idiom, in fact few readers will notice it at all. But if we turn to our control group, the translations, we will hardly find one rendering which retains the spurious parallelism. The target languages cannot, it seems, simply put kidneys into a mind. A Portuguese version is here representative for most of the others: "Rins tinha em mente . . . Luz e ar gélidos havia na conzinna."

It is perhaps in little low-key miracles like "kidneys were in his mind" that *Ulysses* departs from the smooth level of conventional novels. This occurs when Joyce shifts from Bloom's mind to his surroundings and allows us, for the first time, to locate him in space:

> Kidneys were in his mind as he moved about the kitchen softly, righting her breakfast things on the humpy tray.

Early readers probably balked at the abrupt possessive "her" and its lack of an antecedent and, therefore, its pointed dependence on, precisely, "his mind." But we might still wonder for a moment what exactly Bloom is doing, "righting" her things; the verb is not often used in such a non-figurative sense. Translators tend to settle for some kind of arrangement, a disposition of objects, unless they leave it at some vague "preparation"; "disposant," "sistemando," "dispondo," "preparandole," "richete," "zu-rechtmachte," etc. In none of these samples do we get the impression of Bloom striving for some kind of satisfactory array which can then be called "right," as the sequel bears out: "Another slice of bread and butter: three, four: right. She didn't like her plate full. Right." But while one can deter-mine whether a door is shut tight or not, this "right" of approval is far less objective (we may remember that Stephen Dedalus, in the first chapter of *A Portrait,* had a tough time learning its tricky applications). Standards differ. And in fact we never know if Bloom's judicious structuring of cup and plate, toast and cream actually satisfies "her," for when the humpy tray—not the only defective gear in the house, as we will also have learned by that time—is served upstairs, both Molly Bloom and her husband have other arrangements to think of.

"Righting" is a particularly human activity, and a common one. Be-cause it is the first endeavour of a new character, prototypical of him and of *Ulysses,* it may pay off to study the hand-righting. The sketch is char-acteristic, Bloom moves about a good deal righting things, literally and figuratively. He is concerned with a different spatial arrangement the next morning: "So saying he skipped around nimbly, considering frankly, at the same time apologetic, to get on his companion's right, a habit of his, by the by, the right side being, in classical idiom, his tender Achilles." His ameliorative pains often go unappreciated: "of course he prefers plottering about the house," says Molly, not applauding. Bloom sees a dinge in John Henry Menton's hat and—this as the last thing Bloom does at the end of the introductory triad of chapters—instigates a remedy, with success, "It's all right now, Martin Cunningham said," but little thanks. Bloom is always full of projects for civic improvements.

The "Aeolus" chapter presents Bloom busy to right the conditions for an advertisement. The newspaper offices assemble a group of professionals whose functions are to prepare and edit news (including a letter for vet-erinary remedies), to set or proofread type. Within that chapter Bloom will self-edit a belated retort to Menton and fail at it. The concealed activities of "Aeolus" include one of the novel's main chains of mismanaged recti-fication, the naming of M'Intosh in the obituary report. This communi-cative misadventure was caused by Bloom supplying the right word which, written down, became the wrong name. One of the chapter's captions is "ORTHOGRAPHICAL" (the right way of writing words). (This caption is missing from the Penguin edition of *Ulysses*. It should occur above the lines beginning "Want to be sure of his spelling").

Bloom is not the only character who permutes objects towards a more satisfactory end. His own efforts are often wasted, but on his late return he comes up against an unexpected rearrangement of the furniture, "alterations effected . . . to a more advantageous . . . position." This change, more difficult to ignore, leaves a lasting impression on his forehead.

As it happens, "Ithaca" also arranges data and themes previously encountered, while at the same time supplementing new features and angles for the reader to take into account. The chapter in particular offers new recapitulations (scientific, statistical, categorical, budgetary, ritualistic, etc.) — "recapitulate" means finding new unifying perspectives, appropriate headings (from *caput,* "head," which, Bloom might agree, is perhaps the *mot juste*). In a purely figurative and wholly painless sense, the reader in turn is also "knocking his sconce against" restructured realities.

Bloom is adept at mental rectification, which does not mean that he usually gets things right. Experience is forever conducted through, or reflected (is it perhaps refracted?) in, a mind which remains cautious and ready to adjust. A few minutes after his breakfast preparations we watch him rehearsing an address to Larry O'Rourke, pub keeper, trying out an alternative (inwardly), but opting for a simple salute. Even before that he wonders how he compares in size to his cat—from her point of view (already a corrective change of viewpoint): "Height of a tower?" He instantly checks himself: "No, she can jump me." This *No* sets him off from his monocular fellow citizens. He can sense his wrongness, recognise his own limitations or the illusions he sometimes gives in to. After conjuring up a scene of the East, full of memories of the stage, of *Arabian Nights,* popular poetry and stereotypes, he deflates his own day dream: "Probably not a bit like it really. Kind of stuff you read." Such a corrective can even be taken up by the narrative itself, as in "Eumaeus," when an earlier statement is abruptly cancelled with the same negation that Bloom often uses: "No, it was the daughter of the mother in the washkitchen," the narrative consciousness, as it were (and it has clear affinities with Bloom), having second thoughts and even going on to challenge all variant versions: "if the whole thing wasn't a complete fabrication from start to finish." By the time we have progressed this far in the book we know, or should know, that such caution applies fairly generally.

It is fitting that one of the apotheoses of the "Circe" chapter has Bloom enthroned as a versatile Reformer and Righter of errors, mistakes and injustices. On occasion his inclinations bore or irritate the others: "he'd try to downface you that dying was living." In quick succession Bloom appreciates (in fact, like any good reader, interprets) Molly's erroneous but witty remark on Dollard's "base barreltone" voice, and then fumbles at a literary conceit of his own, a satirical sketch of a Laestrygonian eater: "Born with a silver knife in his mouth." Then, typically unsatisfied, he corrects himself: "Or no." This time no improvement is at hand: "Silver means born rich. Born with a knife. But then the allusion is lost." Molly's accomplished witticism and Bloom's abortive one look like examples of what composing *Ulysses* must have been: hits and misses and hazards in the shaping of resistant material.

Explaining an eccentric word to his wife, "metempsychosis," a word he first has to extract correctly from her garbled, tell-tale assimilation "Met him pike hoses," Bloom shows Odyssean resilience. A first attempt, "the transmigration of souls," is adequate but ill-adapted to the audience and leads to a rebuff. Undaunted, after some stalling he comes up with an alternative, embedded in simple instruction: "Some people believe . . . that we go on living . . . They call it reincarnation." His shrewd didactic sense prompts him to look for an illustration, and he picks the nymph over the bed for visual aid. But because of Molly's diminished attention and her sudden sensual response to the downstairs smells, most of Bloom's exertions are in vain. Instead he is precipitated down to the kitchen. He retrieves the kidney (a real one, not just in his mind), and he is brought, along with the reader, to the chapter's starting point, the kitchen. At this point the narrative—after allowing Bloom an excursion into the world of classical reverberations (which, in the overall assignment of duties, is more Stephen's domain)—has adjusted itself and called him back to the appropriate mundane level.

Already it has proved impossible neatly to separate one character's corrective urge from the way in which the novel handles its many concerns. Like Bloom, it tends to counteract whatever it has been doing, contradict whatever it has been saying. We may now observe that the sentence which was here singled out as being somehow representative occurs within an opening where the author is softly moving about from one narrative stance to the next. He introduces, according to well-known convention, a character by means of some dominant trait, with the unconventional difference that it is a preference of taste:

> Mr. Leopold Bloom ate with relish the inner organs of beasts and fowls.

This continues in the same vein thematically, but with a tonal drop from a formal "ate with relish" to the homely translation "liked"; from the stylised (even biblical) general to the itemised particular of a menu:

> He liked thick giblet soup, nutty gizzards, a stuffed roast heart,
> liver slices fried with crustcrumbs, fried hencod's roes.

The details amount to one of the earliest catalogues in the novel, to which the third sentence adds one superlative item which will become, as it turns out, the final selection. But a new note of reflection and causality is also noticeable:

> Most of all he liked grilled mutton kidneys which gave to his
> palate a fine tang of faintly scented urine.

The shifting of gears may be slight, but the narrative progression is not uniform, though it is not at all easy to pin down the faintly scented variations. With the second paragraph (already looked at), however, a strikingly new perspective comes into play:

> Kidneys were in his mind as he moved about the kitchen.

From this we can orient ourselves in two ways: we have, at last, a setting in the external world, and it becomes clear that all along we have been obliquely sharing what goes on in Bloom's mind as it was considering tasty alternatives for a breakfast meal. The next sentence, "Gelid light and air were in the kitchen," takes us completely outside, with a widening angle of vision, but by now we are assured of also being given impressions of Bloom: no doubt *he* now becomes aware of what is around him. But then a really unmistakable change of direction occurs with a first grammatical lapse, the elliptic:

> Made him feel a bit peckish.

This is the closest so far to how Bloom may actually phrase to himself something that he is unlikely to verbalise at the moment. But we have now been initiated to Bloom's rhythm and his cadences, even though we cannot as yet be sure that these are in fact his characteristic thought patterns. At this point the narrative veers again, back to a descriptive statement:

> The coals were reddening.

Formally this looks like a regression to the earlier type of sentence, the so-called objective, but (we have somehow learned by now) obviously not *just* objective. We sense what we cannot prove—that Bloom is now also looking at those coals. And once more we adjust the focus in the opening paragraph: the tending of the fire, presumably, caused Bloom to think (but, on our first run through, we couldn't realise that he *was* thinking this) about delicacies whose preparation depend on heat. And we might now try out too, moving from our minds to our tongues and palates, that second sentence again, that little festival of food fried or roasted, and to articulate it with our own vocal instruments. We will feel that, because of its obstacular consonant clusters, it is not a sentence that we can formulate without considerable lingual effort:

> He liked thick giblet soup, nutty gizzards, a stuffed roast heart,
> liver slices fried with crustcrumbs, fried hencod's roes.

Our lips get busy and our tongues have to do an awful lot of moving about the palate: we come in fact as close to imitating what happens when we taste and swallow—or when we imagine it very vividly. As deglutitory a sentence as ever there was. When the "Sirens" chapter first appeared, readers were taken aback by its acoustic assimilations, the bold innovation of making language (as it seemed) conform to music. Few may have noticed that the technique is anticipated in a sentence which brings language as near to gustative articulation as seems possible—taste-speech. It is continued in that next saporific lump, "grilled mutton kidneys," of the following sentence and, later on, extensively in "Laestrygonians."

After some initiatory jockeying of narrative slants, then, the style at last settles down, more or less, to the typical movements of the Bloom chapters, a blend of direct "interior monologue." "Another slice of bread and butter, three, four: right," narrated monologue, "She didn't like her plate full," and third person report, "He turned from the tray." A complex arsenal of terminology has recently been marshalled to label the various modes with some show of precision and, as current discussions indicate, no narrative terms are likely to prove convincing enough to be above further righting and modification.

Irrespective of how we name them, a whole series of narrative relations has been conjugated already in about half a page. On a modest scale, most of the prominent stylistic excesses of the latter part of the novel have been subtly prepared for.

As though to corroborate the constant need for modulation, Bloom's cat exemplifies change on a prelinguistic level, proceeding on a similar principle of rhetorical variation for a strategic end. In three stages,

> Mkgnao! . . . Mrkgnao! . . . Mrkrgnao!

there is continuity (a basic "gnao" remains stable and, incidentally, looks like a Greek verb, though it isn't) as well as modification. The initial consonant structure—like the whole of *Ulysses*—gets more elaborate. Feline critics may interpret the increase of *r's* as a gradual transition from plaintive plea to anticipatory purr, culminating in "Gurrhr!" Cat and author, in any case, adapt their style to new contexts.

Explicitly or not, as readers we have been composing the novel just as the author has done. "Art," as a youthful Stephen Dedalus lectured long ago to an audience of one, "is the human disposition of sensible or intelligible matter for an esthetic end." Writing, in particular, is a matter of arranging, adjusting, getting words right, revising. Joyce, one of the most obsessed righters of them all, chose words with care, scrupulously, from the outset; and in *Finnegans Wake,* as he told us, the words of the English Language were no longer the "right" ones any more. He had already put them in some optimal order. The shaping of *Ulysses* was a laborious development from short story to multidimensional epic. In 1915 an outline in Joyce's mind assigned four, fifteen and three chapters, respectively, to the book's three parts; these were then trimmed to a symmetrical arrangement in a triptych which balanced swelling disproportions. A detailed "Schema" helped to shape the writing, but was also determined *by* the writing; but the Schema was righted into a final one, so that now we have at least two systems of authorial designs, and thereby a constant invitation to the critical reader to devise further metaschematic refinements.

We can now assess Joyce's indefatigable revisions by the many studies of the process, such as Michael Groden's *Ulysses in Progress,* and also by leafing through a score of facsimile volumes, with notes, drafts, fair copies, typescripts, corrections and proofs. But externally too, in writing after Easter 1916, Joyce was restoring central Dublin to its pristine state before the destruction: The General Post Office, O'Connell Street and much of the city furniture had to be fictionally re-erected.

No special virtue inheres in the clue "righting" as picked up from an early passage; it calls up merely one more way of rereading, which would supplement all the other approaches. Righting, as developed here, is convenient shorthand for at least four interconnected processes: (1) characters in the book, mainly Bloom, amending their practices or conjectures in what they momentarily believe to be improvements; (2) Joyce revising and retouching his own handiwork; (3) the reader/critic adjusting to the text; and (4) the book itself tending towards ameliorative diversity. We can almost personify the novel, in a metaphorical shift, as though it had its own self-critical consciousness, were "selfrighting the balance" of its own being. This later quote is brought back from *Finnegans Wake,* the self-righting literary work *par excellence*: it never lets you forget its inevitable wrongness, which it signals, and aims to correct, by its glaring heterography and its lexicological and syntactic fusions. It may also be called, with equal justice, the first self-wronging book: "Wringlings upon wronglings."

The *Wake* of course no longer keeps writing apart from righting, nor right from rite, nor either from wright(ing). Evidence abounds: "the rite words by the rote order," "righting his name," "the wright side," "you could wright anny pippap passage" and so on. But *Finnegans Wake* is far removed in time and concept from a straightforward sentence introducing Bloom which was wrought no later than 1918. And yet the sound-connected activities have something in common and take over ritual overtones in the luxuriating novel which begins with an elaborate rite on top of a Martello tower, which is then counterpointed in Bloom's lowly kitchen. The rite, we learn, is the poet's rest; and the book rests precariously for a moment with a later rectified account of the day's deeds given in terms of Jewish observations and rites.

But no claim is made here that Joyce intended to implement all such potential readings; these are in fact already the subjective rightings of one particular reader. In Joycean critical practice, readers tend to rewright the text; this is called interpretation. Readers returning from *Ulysses* and *Finnegans Wake* can be irreversibly conditioned, prone to retouch the earliest works in ingenious ways the young author may never have thought of, to realign the short stories or *A Portrait* in accordance with themes later encountered or discovered through cognitive skills later acquired. After *Ulysses*, the "faints and worms" of "The Sisters" become very intriguing, multilayered things, not at all constricted by whatever the original intentions may have been.

The homophone "wright," enlisted here in this retroactive way, is cognate with "work" and such Greek words as "energy," "organ," or even "demiurgos": the reader's function becomes that of a *demiurgos* (from *demos*, people, and *ergos*, workman). In the *Odyssey* (17.383) the term is applied to seers, healers, joiners, and even singers; Greek philosophers applied it to a creator, either divine or, later, a subordinate craftsman (it surfaces in *Ulysses* in this capacity: the ground "sounds solid: made by the mallet of *Los Demiurgos*"). Readers are mediators who shape, or forge, the matter at hand.

Moving about and righting entails a lot of inceptive groping, trial and error, possibly false steps. Success is never guaranteed. Bloom may never get his advertisement from Keyes. His very profession deals with improvement. Remedies are promised but not invariably effected. The home, even with Catesby's cork lino or Plumtree's Potted Meat, may become neither "bright and cheery" nor "an abode of bliss."

We have no reason to believe that our interpretations work much better than Plumtree's potted meat. What we regard and present as essential, remains dubious and, at best, incomplete. We tend to rephrase *Ulysses* in our own favourite terms (witness this performance). Awareness of this tendency might militate against the rigidity with which we single out, at times, arbitrary aspects or glorify one particular scene, image, symbol, act or analogy as though it moved, like Mr Deasy's history, to one great, nameable goal.

The righting urge is always present in the reader—to give or find direction, to align elements, to complete; the urge has been felt even by the dreary criticism of the middle period which streamlined *Ulysses* to some kind of dismal diagnosis (as often as not tied to "paralysis") and managed to disregard the myriadmindedness of the work in favour of some privileged cure for Bloom or Stephen.

That *Ulysses* variegates forms of righting would not put it into a special class, but merely into a long tradition, often called humanist. What makes *Ulysses* different in kind is that the processes are not just described but integrated, acted out, and that the book seems to want to redress, emend, adjust, itself continually, and that it involves the reader in these processes.

Even righting *Ulysses* in the elementary sense of rescuing the text from the errors and falsifications which its complicated gestation made inevitable is a tricky task demanding expert skills. It is being undertaken right now, with the help of computers, so that in a few more years we may finally have a text which resembles best what the author wanted us to read. In the meantime it is small comfort to know that the *Odyssey*, too, differs essentially and irretrievably from whatever it was that a Greek poet made up around the eighth century B.C. Every Homeric critic presents a variant account of the author, or authors, compilers, and the genesis of the epic, including Athenian and Alexandrinian editors and commentators. A scholar like Victor Bérard moreover considered the whole epic a cross-cultural assimilation of Phoenician nautic lore to Greek notions, a Hellenising of some earlier material. And every translation of the poem that we use adds its own priorities and adjustments. The *Odyssey* belongs to a group of tales which take as their theme the restoration, through vengeance, of some lost order, a particularly violent form of righting which Joyce toned down considerably. The same is true of *Hamlet* (here, too, as with all of Shakespeare's plays, the text can never be authoritative) and of Don Giovanni; in each case the new order brought about differs from the old one.

Some corrective touches in the novel are structural or have thematic impact. The Bloom chapters revise much of the Telemachiad, and with the advent of Bloom we get new points of view for confirmation, or for questioning, at any rate for our comparison. Parallax will stalk into the book a bit later as an instance of Bloom's curiosity and as a concept, but it has been applied from the beginning, in the narrative shifts or in the setting off of Stephen's musing against Mulligan's posing. The first chapter elevates common things like teeth, navels, or the sea into classical Greek. In the fourth chapter Bloom tries to render a Greek word into ordinary English (which Molly has done already, through ignorance). For him a navel is something in which dirt gets rolled up, not some Homeric-Delphic *omphalos*.

The best known example of parallax is the cloud which turns, first, Stephen's mood and then affects Bloom, fifty pages and a few minutes of actual time later. Parallax, an apparent displacement, allows scientists to measure with Euclidian precision distances that could never be traversed; it here allows readers to objectify the cloud itself and measure character differences. It is thus all the more instructive to ponder the novel's prime instance of a scientific method of verification, a matutinal cloud, which is also duly noted in the "Ithaca," the book's most scientific report. Clouds are something that can never be fixed with accuracy; they change both shape and their position, are one of nature's least stable items, so that they have become proverbial notations for dreamy lack of determination. No accumulation of parallactic information can pinpoint that cloud, or any other. They fit the "Proteus" chapter because of their mutability; and one famous cloud, especially, is lifted from a play where it exemplifies change, gullibility and the mind's projective capabilities, "Ay, very like a whale." Such an early nebulous cluster shows *Ulysses* already counteracting itself, scientific procedure and imaginative flexibility holding each other in check.

Each Ulyssean chapter reprocesses its material according to a different programme and new priorities. Our attempts even to describe what each chapter "is" never quite succeed. We still have not yet assimilated a performance like "Oxen of the Sun," a jerky array of fake-historical rerightings modelled on the styles of particular authors or periods, but with anachronistic checks working against facile systematisation. The chapter induces us to recreate, paraphrase, extract a text to our own liking. There is a strong temptation to talk about its action in the manner of what we have become used to, say, of the "Hades" chapter, to expound what the characters do, what exactly they may be saying or thinking. The final pages of "Oxen" are perhaps the most sustained challenge to our adjustive skills. No reader absorbs them as they are. We accommodate each phrase within some plausible context. What in fact we usually do is to translate it into a kind of script—precisely what it is not. A phrase like "The least tholice" remains irksome until it is seen as a variant of "The Leith police dismisseth us" immediately preceding; and we feel more at ease when we are given the "right" information that this latter sentence is, not some provincial aside, but a standard enunciation test for one's sobriety (Bloom's "liver slices fried with crustcrumbs," incidentally, might serve the same purpose). So we may deduce that someone present (and we are provoked into finding out who) has playfully worked in this line and that someone else is offering a variant, perhaps drunkenly incapable or merely pretending. In some such way we change the debased quotation into its "correct" form and setting, which of course still does not account for the specific whatness of "least tholice," which needs further adjustment. What we have done could conveniently be presented by the typographical layout which characterises the "Circe" chapter:

1. NAME OF SPEAKER (in capital letters)
2. (*parenthetical stage direction, in italics, indicating speaker's gestures or mannerisms*)
3. The least tholice.

But "Circe" would most likely conjure up a transient scene in a police station, perhaps even in County Leith. And in "Circe" as well as in "Oxen" we would have to speculate on whether the words given are actually spoken or not. We would have to argue, in fact, about every single item in the above transcription, but we would agree that *some* such rearrangement is implied when we try to come to terms with the elusive lines.

By having subsequent chapters (often parts within them) righting what went before, *Ulysses* demonstrates our own practice as readers. When we talk about the "Sirens" chapter we usually take the music out and report *on* it, or report on the characters' problems, or talk *about* its music. In effect and for practical purposes, we all punctuate "Penelope" by parcelling out its components or themes for critical retailing. But let us descend again, from interpretative restructuring to the ordinary business of simply reading the novel correctly on the factual level. At one time no one could do it, and even today it remains so hard that most readers, and conscientious scholars, ask for assistance. Within 60 years we have, collectively, learned a great deal, and still not enough. Where else in literary criticism would one find a whole volume which sets out to do nothing but rectify wrong readings, that is, not tenuous interpretations, but demonstrable falsifications of the text at some elementary level. A Dutch scholar, Paul P. J. Van Caspel, has undertaken the task in *Bloomers on the Liffey,* and the task, unfortunately, is necessary. Van Caspel's list could even be expanded (most of us probably have a list of our own); weeding out the hardcore errors in *Notes for Joyce* alone would be a sizeable venture. In his useful though somewhat disproportionate strictures, however, Van Caspel just stops short of asking why *Ulysses,* of all novels, has caused such numerous sloppy and faulty readings. This seems to be one of its characteristics, in fact *Ulysses* is almost defined by the way it provokes misreadings at each of its levels; it does indeed deceive, puzzle, mystify, trick, mislead its readers. (Its own characters, after all, misread in the same way.)

Many errors are forgivable enough, although perhaps not their perpetuation. It was easy to suppose, on first experience, that "Married to Bloom, to greaseaseabloom" and similar hints at the beginning of "Sirens" means that the two barmaids in the Ormond hotel are making fun of Bloom passing by outside: they aren't and he isn't. But it takes a lot of exegetical and topographical rummaging to show this. A reader unfamiliar with Dublin also cannot tell whether some paragraphs in "Wandering Rocks" are interpolated from elsewhere or not. Passing "Farrell's statue" and then "Gray's statue," how can we possibly know that the first statue is *by* and the second *of* the person named? For a long time it seemed understood that the two women whom Stephen sees coming down to Sandymount strand are midwives, named Florence MacCabe and Anne Kearns. Or when documents came to sight which showed that Oliver Gogarty had rented and paid for the Martello tower in Sandycove it seemed necessary to point out that Joyce altered a fact for the fiction: in the book Stephen, and not Gogarty-Mulligan, pays the rent. And perhaps he does. But who is to say that Stephen's "It is mine. I paid the rent" recalls his own deed and status, and not something Mulligan has said or might say? We always have to sort out voices in a regress of quotations, to distinguish external saying from internal thought, all amidst pitfalls we never thought of. (Regarding sandy towers on the coast of Dublin, how many tourists have been directed to the Martello tower in Sandy*mount* by helpful locals, it being much closer to the city than Sandy*cove*? Quite a few, but even more have been offered the wrong tower in a documentary book.)

In the sex life of the Blooms, we read, "something changed. Could never like it again after Rudy." *Who* never like it? The French translators (who could have approached the author if they liked) say: "Elle ne s'y plaisait plus"; the Italian version opts for Bloom: "Non ci ho mai preso gusto." We may settle this question, perhaps, by recourse to further parallactic evidence, but even parallax may cloud the issue.

Translators have to put their cards on the table. What would one do with "loom of the moon"? Is "loom" something Penelopean to weave on (as most translators have decided), connected with a following "toil" (from *texere,* weave): or else something dimly visible and looming—perhaps taken up by "shining" in the next line? You pays your money . . . A simple question like "Who is the long fellow running for the mayoralty?," though not ambiguous when spoken, is tricky in print. The Italian translation, "Chi è quel lungo manigoldo che è candidato sindaco?," is wrong: the long fellow (Long John Fanning, not named), is not running for office, but backing candidates. But all wrong readings at least tell us something about *Ulysses,* and the examples given in particular about the hazards of identification. It is from the "Cyclops" chapter where traps of naming or grammatical agreement become thematic concerns.

Stephen's dictum about Shakespeare's errors as portals of discovery seems to apply to the most humble readers. To define any reading as absolutely wrong may be futile, especially when semantic, homophonic and etymological coincidences are freely enlisted. "Ties," which Stephen borrows from Mulligan are something to wear for decoration; but every loan is also a bond. Bloom watches, from the funeral carriage, a woman's nose "whiteflattened against the pane," later he eats his lunch while "stuck on the pane two flies buzzed." Both of these are window panes and nothing else, and yet the themes in residence, love and death, also cause pain. In "Hades" Bloom remembers the man in charge of the protestant cemetery: "His garden Major Gamble calls Mount Jerome." The name was not invented but merely exploited by Joyce, who fitted it into his arrangement of mortality and thereby gave the reader a chance—never an obligation— to see in it yet one more circuitous reminder of death. "Desolation," a weighty word forming a whole paragraph, has nothing to do with Latin *sol,* sun, but with *solus,* alone. Yet this is the moment when that remarkable cloud begins to "cover the sun slowly wholly" and Bloom's morning becomes in fact de-sunned for a while. *Finnegans Wake* will later purposefully take such accidental concurrencies of etymology in its semantic stride. One didactic value of *Ulysses* lies in its capacity to alert our senses, to train our skills, to confront us with decisions which no authority can make for us. Readings like the above are frank falsifications of the text, but they can be recircuited into patterns which are not entirely extraneous.

Since all the processes so far described, including the process of "meaning," *are* processes they would be best expressed by active verbs. The pivotal sentence of Bloom's breakfast arrangements depends, not on "things," "breakfast," "tray" or "kitchen," but on the actions of moving and righting. As critical readers, we might take up the hint and do what we can to counteract the Western mind's tendency towards objects, things, nouns, categories.

Processes elude us while things can be handled, ordered, administered, categorised, classified, filed away, as nouns. Perhaps all we can do, given the nominal bias of our language habits, is to signal, from time to time, that we are dealing essentially, not with rigid substances, but with dynamic doings, relatings, meaning or rightings. Our own categories are necessary, but they remain *our own* categories. And perhaps we can guard against talking of structures, schemas, themes, narratives, etc., as though these were solid fixtures and not somehow encapsulated doings. Remember only those once-fashionable interpretations which consisted in a run through the text, as with a Geiger counter, marking out passages which were termed epiphanies or symbols, as though these were things. That method of interpretation has outlived its usefulness, but the continued reification of terms like allusion, pun, or parody (all essentially actions) has a similarly deadening effect.

Much sterile arguing concerns what *Ulysses* "is"; whether Bloom for instance "is" or else "is not" a Jew. To claim that *Ulysses* is a novel is as correct and inconclusive as to claim that Joyce is a Dubliner, an exile, a symbolist, a humorist, a perhapsed catholic, or a case of particular neurosis. If such formulas as "*Ulysses* is X; M'Intosh is Y; this is a symbol of Z . . ." could give way to phrasing like "*Ulysses* behaves in part like X," we would at least avoid the semblance of laying down a law. Verbs like "This passage/phrase/chapter . . . performs, provokes, incites, questions . . ." frankly admit to their purely metaphorical function as convenient illustrations and could less misleadingly pose as the momentous truths which nominal fixations have a way of projecting.

Verbs have the added advantage of being formally less fixed, of changing with different persons, numbers, voices, moods. Their tenses reveal that they change with time, which in itself qualifies them for *Ulysses*; they don't even suggest the stability vitiating some otherwise valuable criticism. In its most naive, pedestrian sense, time infuses *Ulysses*. It is not just that the action naturally evolves in time; nor that we are made aware of clocks and watches, of a funeral looming at eleven, and a visit at four; nor that simultaneity is emphasised; nor that several times and cultures (the present, the characters' pasts, Irish history, Homeric, Semitic, Christian, Shakespearean ages, etc.) are conflated; nor even that the novel goes out of its diurnal way to compress centuries of linguistic growth into one chapter. *Ulysses* literally (in its letters) changes with the time the reading takes, and these temporal changes affect the reader. Bloom catches short his images of the East, the "Kind of stuff you read: in the track of the sun." At this stage we can do little more than connect the phrases with Bloom's ideas of travelling around the earth in front of the sun. Hundreds of pages later we find out that Bloom actually has read something of the sort; his library contains the book *In the Track of the Sun*. The earlier passage can then no longer remain what it has been (but it is questionable whether a first reader should already be short-circuited to Bloom's bookshelf by a well-meaning, interfering commentator).

That "bowl of lather" in the book's first line is *not* a chalice, as *Notes for Joyce* misinforms its public (Don Gifford with Robert J. Seidman). But the bowl—in a manner of speaking—*will be* transformed into the chalice of the Mass just a few moments and three lines later, as soon as Buck Mulligan distinctly switches on his priestly role—just as the bowl will be reduced back to mere matter when it again becomes a "nickel shaving bowl." This may amount to the tiniest qualitative difference in phrasing, but it is a vital one within the text's protean lifestyle.

The effect of delayed recognition is a Wakean feature. When we first come upon "Pinck poncks that bail for seeks alicence," we may play around with pick, pock, ping-pong, bail, licences, Alice, perhaps Belle Alliance, and many other things (and try to right them on our humpy tray). But we will not hear "the bell for Sechseläuten," not until we come to the end of the first book, in Anna Livia's "Pingpong! There's the Belle for Sexaloitez!" and even then the meaning will only emerge if we have been told that "Sechseläuten" (as its name is) is an annual spring rite, when winter is driven out and the bells start ringing ("läuten") at six o'clock again in Zürich (where Joyce often attended the festival). Without such information a reader is still left with sexy bells loitering and a number of guesses. Once primed with that knowledge, the reader on a recircling tour will tackle the earlier sentence by changing it into an echo of something which it precedes.

Such temporal rightings occur in *Ulysses* too. (In a way, this whole essay is one.) "O, lust," initially, is simply lust; but the sequel, "our refuge and our strength," transforms the beginning into a prayer and the whole into a blasphemous parallel reading. *Ulysses* changes, on rereading, its letters and words and generates more configurations than could ever be recognised a first time, and it changes even more so if, between readings, one has visited Dublin, studied Aristotle or music hall songs, or taken a course in semiotics. It also changes because our previous moving about makes us aware of more contexts and alignments. Furthermore the book also seems to provide a narcissistic comment on its own idiosyncrasies (or should we say, with a verb "its own behaving"?). In the "Aeolus" chapter, Professor

MacHugh steadies his glasses "to a new focus." This further instance of righting is applicable to the chapter itself with its new technique and different perspectives which require the reader to adjust his own focus. "Righting" has been treated here as such a narcissistic touch.

Temporal expediency should not be disregarded in the classroom or in guidebooks or notes. Not all information is equally helpful at all times, for certain insights would only confuse the novice and are better detained for opportune passages. Some relations simply do not "make sense" at first, such as presenting the first chapter right away as some analogy to Homer and Telemachus. A student has many good reasons for remaining unconvinced and finding the correspondences forced. But later it might be a rewarding exercise to treat the whole chapter, for the sake of an argument, as though it were nothing but some adaptation from the Greek, or a continuation of *A Portrait,* or a reenactment of the Mass, or a choreography of roles. It may be didactically useful to extract some kind of narrative "norm" from the early chapters against which later extravagancies can be measured. But by the same token, a subsequent corrective reading can also help unmask such an empirical norm as yet another convention, no more and no less artificial and arbitrary than any that follow. Interpretations, too, have to be timed or, to return to the grammatical analogy, conjugated through the tenses and moods.

The model of some sort of conjugation helps to highlight a few facets of *Ulysses,* such as its gradual departure from the indicative mood (closer to reality) early on to more subjunctive, conditional, conjunctive, or optative ones, expressing wishes, hypotheses, contingencies, mere conjectures. The chapters of the second half seem based on various suppositions, *what if . . .* , and Molly's monologue would in part be a return to the indicative mood.

But *Ulysses* never conforms very smoothly. At least one chapter, "Ithaca," yields more inert data than verbs. In its diabolical advocation of substances and its accumulation of solid, factual information, measurements, statistics and inventories like department store catalogues, it reminds us more of things than of processes. Never are finite verbs less frequent than in this orgy of nominal fixation. We are aware of much abstract verbiage and of little syntax. Even visually the chapter is a series of separate blocks. It glorifies the Western mind's trust in systematisation and its proclivity to freeze, take apart, order and pigeonhole experience. One could redistribute most of the contents of the chapter in some different order (according to subject matter or even alphabetically) without violating its administrative spirit as much as one would similarly falsify the mood of "Sirens" or "Circe."

And yet the "Ithaca" chapter, almost more than any other, invites us to process the material it presents in such arid abundance. Even Joyce implied this when he confessed to Frank Budgen that the chapter, his favourite, was "the ugly duckling of the book." Ugly ducklings are notorious for changing into something one would not expect. Our trial run here is a sequence in which Bloom and Stephen urinate side by side in the back garden. Information is accumulated on issues we would never think of investigating, such as the position or visibility of "their organs of micturition." After learning that their gazes are elevated to what must be a lighted window, we may find the next question difficult to account for: "Similarly?" It is far from clear which action may be similar to what other action, and we would never predict the kind of answer that is offered, in the terms of classical sciences like ballistics and physiology:

> Similarly?
>
> The trajectories of their, first sequent, then simultaneous, urinations were dissimilar: Bloom's longer, less irruent, in the incomplete form of the bifurcated penultimate alphabetical letter who in his ultimate year at High School (1880) had been capable of attaining the point of greatest altitude against the whole concurrent strength of the institution, 210 scholars: Stephen's higher, more sibilant, who in the ultimate hours of the previous day had augmented by diuretic consumption an insistent vesical pressure.

In sorting out the data, we gain little insight by concentrating on the verbs: "were . . . had been capable of attaining . . . had augmented," they perform mere ancillary or copulative functions. What the almost forty substantives and adjectives do, is, primarily, to spawn more questions. It takes time—not much perhaps, but nevertheless time—just to figure out what it all means. And we may wonder how the whole tangential sketch fits into the narrative framework. Perhaps this is something like a scientific transcript of what goes on in the mind of, presumably, Bloom. We may sense the silence of the occasion and even that strange constraint of male timidity which often goes with it. In such a moment Bloom might compare the jets in front of him, and his memory might lead to a juvenile achievement and Bloom's only Olympic feat we hear of in the whole book, a veritable victory over strong competition. This allows for a Homeric sideglance too: Odysseus beating all competing suitors at wielding the bow. Bloom's interest in causality is prominent in general, so that here too he might relate Stephen's previous drinking with his present performance. But this is not what the text says, only what we can possibly extrapolate from it. There must be other ways to account for the why and the wherefore of the sequence; again the point is simply that reading means giving some kind of account, we bring back (or perhaps tra-ject) the passage back to some of the norms it questions.

This we can do by releasing the verbs from their nominal wraps, obvious enough with "urination" or "consumption." A trajectory has to do with something thrown (*Ulysses* takes great interest in everything "thrown away," and in making water). We can extract motion from "irruent" or "insistent," and noise from "sibilant," which may in fact lead us to reconsider even "dissimilar" and its circumambient esses for acoustic effect. Above all we can savour the reticent beauty of a participle, Bloom having triumphed over "the whole *concurrent* strength" of his High School, in a word which runs many meanings together.

The two curves, the main topic of the paragraph, are laid out, so to speak, for inspection and comparison and for us to wonder what else these graphs may tell us about the protagonists, the symbolic relationships or the novel itself. The two oddly misplaced relative clauses link the present urination to Bloom's remote past (by association) and Stephen's recent past (by causality). But a future is codetermined too: altitude is an attainment of youth. Bloom, 24 years from his apogee, may be conscious of his waning powers, and we may find ourselves transferring a word like "strength" to a different context (just as we do when Molly Bloom thinks of "the strength those engines have in them like big giants").

Scientific terminology purports to be accurate as well as non-distractive. The passage strives for this but does not quite succeed; against its overt intentions it suggests spurious patterns. Stephen's higher trajectory connects with "altitude," but only coincidentally with "High School." Is there any meaningful relation between the conspicuous clutter of "ultimate year . . . ultimate hours of the previous day" and the intrusive "penultimate letter"? A ghostly configuration of ultimacy arises, to be relegated, most likely, to some more remote level of significance, but vaguely disturbing in the foreground. Many such polysyllabic signposts in the "Ithaca" chapter seem more useful as markers for the various subsections than for instant communication.

And how to accommodate that gratuitous "bifurcated penultimate alphabetical letter," worked in, it seems, to illustrate a shape (but incompletely at that)? It waits for further coordination among the primary concerns of the passage. It is up to us to speculate, at some further remove, that Stephen's and Bloom's ways will soon bifurcate. Incomplete form characterises much in the lives of the characters, it is a strategy of the text and demands the readers' supplementation (there is thus also a return to a remote beginning, "The Sisters," with incomplete sentences and deficient information—the first injunction to readers is to complete the forms). And we happen to be in the book's penultimate chapter. Homer's works were divided, by later editors, into twenty-four books designated by the twenty-four letters of the Greek alphabet. The penultimate book of the *Odyssey* concerns itself with the recognition of Odysseus and Penelope: the corresponding scene in *Ulysses* is close at hand. But in the Greek the second last letter was *Psi* and not *Y*. By grace of English homophony, however, the sound of the penultimate letter is identical with a potent interrogative: this "why" is behind Bloom's curiosity, and it introduces many of the questions in the chapter, including many a reader will ask on top of it. The urge to look into cause, motive, reason, purpose, etc. was perfected by the Greeks, among them thinkers like Pythagoras, a man who held forth about numbers, triangles and heavenly bodies, as well as about metempsychosis. He might well be the patron saint of "Ithaca" (one could not, in those times, go through High School without hearing about him). He never, as far as we know, lectured on micturition, but because he used the letter *Y* to illustrate the divergent paths of virtue and vice, it came to be known as the "letter of Pythagoras." All of which may have very little to do with the passage except that the text by its odd concatenations seems to provoke a search for centrifugal justification.

But—to return to the matter at hand—what exactly did happen at that unique exploit which Bloom recalls, his attaining "the point of greatest altitude against the whole concurrent strength of the institution, 210 scholars"? Raleigh states succinctly that "Bloom wins a contest by urinating higher than any of his 210 classmates" (John Henry Raleigh: *The Chronicle of Leopold and Molly Bloom: Ulysses as Narrative*). How did they organise those contests, back in 1880, in the limited area of a Dublin school? Surely not by lining up 210 athletes, vesically ready at the word "go"—that is, not simultaneously. Then perhaps "sequently," with markings on a wall (and with no spoilsport cleaning staff to intervene)? Such was in fact the practice at British schools, but if we accept that version, then the contest was not, strictly speaking, "concurrent." We cannot trust the vocabulary which makes such a show of being objective. And once distrust has set in—and it is general all over "Ithaca"—confidence is basically undermined: we are thrown back to guesswork, precisely what the elaborate wording strains to eliminate. What *really* (the chapter fills us in on reality) took place? The school presumably *had* 210 (or perhaps 211, counting Bloom extra) students at one time; which looks like a verifiable fact, but the stylisation of them as "scholars" itself throws some odd light on it. It is just conceivable that a smaller group of boys discovered at one time Bloom's prowess (habitual or accidental), and that someone offered a remark that Bloom must be the champion of the whole bleeding school, and that some such memory, in the pedantic deadpan nature of "Ithaca" (which has not been programmed to register irony, levity or hyperbole) would become objectified. This would be similar to Bloom's having been "baptised," as another paragraph has it, "under a pump in the village of Swords." One thing all the Nostos chapters do is to question the relationship between a report and the event itself.

The passage poses as an answer, but it offers solutions to questions we would never have asked in the first place. Whatever our interest focuses on, we will have to interpret and sort out, supply the verbs of action. As it happens, High School pupils often encounter the symbol Y (a bit less often than its companion X, which is scattered all over *Ulysses*): inevitably and kinetically it stands for something to be figured out. The teacher insists that it be righted, translated into some satisfactory arrangement of letters and numbers which is then called the solution.

The preceding chapter, "Eumaeus," has prepared us for the chanciness of equations: "as to who he in reality was let XX equal my right name and address, as Mr Algebra remarks *passim*." Mr Algebra and his colleagues have taken over the later chapters and spare no efforts, but theirs have to be supplemented by ours. Innumerable new sets of approaches, different systems of reprocessing, alternative points of view (some entirely irrational), but none of the new equations are solutions, the meaning, if any, seems to consist in the equating processes.

The retarded sting of "Ithaca" lies in the defamiliarised terminology, which diversifies itself into the language of emotion, values, decisions and doings, of verbs simple and complex. One such verb is laboriously introduced, but not named, in grammatical paraphrases: "the natural grammatical transition by inversion involving no alteration of sense of an aorist preterite proposition (parsed as masculine subject, monosyllabic onomatopoeic transitive verb with direct feminine object) from the active voice into its correlative aorist preterite proposition (parsed as feminine subject, auxiliary verb and quasimonosyllabic onomatopoeic past participle with complementary masculine agent)." Molly will translate that one later on, in plain words. Joyce elaborately and deviously works in the conjugation of a verb around which some of the offstage action of *Ulysses* turns. From hints such as these many critics have concentrated, perhaps rightly, on conjugal relations and, perhaps less rightly, on conjugal imperatives.

Here the emphasis is on conjugation itself, one of many names for a dynamic process. *Ulysses* refuses to stay put. Once we know what it *is* we are sure to be wrong. The nominal inertia of the "Ithaca" chapter, the book's most solid fixation on the surface of it, vexes us into reconjugating, yoking and joining, its elements and treating anew whatever went before. In the beginning was the verb, and it energises everything from breakfast preparation and morning shave through all the fumbles and trials of Blooms-day and night down to Molly's final turnings, and even more the lettered choreography of the next work, the "reconjungation of nodebinding ayes" of *Finnegans Wake,* a book with one humpy character and much moving about, many "curios of signs" in wrong writing, blatantly in need to be righted by its own re-formations and the rightings of every mutable reader.

Bloom's Metaphors
and the Language of Flowers

Ramón Saldívar

*Je dis: une fleur! et hors de l'oubli . . . musicalement se lève, idée même et
suave, l'absente de tous bouquets.*

MALLARMÉ, Crise de vers

Language is among the several of Leopold's preoccupations as he emerges
into the sunlight on Bloomsday. It is a preoccupation which in the course
of the day will take various forms. Now, as he steps into the sunlight, he
begins to muse: "Somewhere in the east: early morning: set off at dawn,
travel round in front of the sun, steal a day's march on him. Keep it up for
ever never grow a day older technically . . . .Kind of stuff you read: in the
track of the sun. Sunburst on the title page." Dublin, bathed in radiance,
will become for Bloom a scene of writing and interpretation, as if the sun
"Wants to stamp his trademark on everything," as Joyce explores the possibilities of metaphorical language and of its role in the dialectical relationship between life and art.

In the "Lotus Eaters" episode, the text shifts from solar to floral metaphors as Leopold blossoms into "Henry Flower." Reacting against the
frustrations of his nonexistent sexual life, he has begun an affair with Martha
Clifford, an affair, however, that exists only on paper. The improper "anonymous letter" which becomes the sign of his guilt and humiliation later in
the nightmares of the "Circe" episode ("He implored me to soil his letter
in an unspeakable manner, to chastise him as he richly deserves") here create
a Bloom where there is none. This proxy flower represents a nonexistent

From *James Joyce Quarterly* 20, no. 4 (Summer 1983). © 1983 by the University of
Tulsa.

figure, for Bloom, even in his own *persona,* is always someone other than himself: cuckolded husband of Molly, usurped protector of Milly, dupe of Dublin's Irish citizenry, son-seeking father of Rudy.

Walking along, he opens a letter newly arrived from Martha to find a flower enclosed. He tears the flower from its pinhold and smells its "almost no smell" and thinks: "Language of flowers. They like it because no-one can hear." He reads the letter again: "Angry tulips with you darling man-flower punish your cactus if you don't please poor forgetmenot how I long violets to dear roses when we soon anemone meet all naughty nightstalk wife Martha's perfume." A few pages later, at the end of the chapter, Bloom thinks of taking a bath and foresees his own body becoming a flower: "He saw his trunk and limbs riprippled over and sustained, buoyed lightly upward, lemonyellow: his navel, bud of flesh: and saw the dark tangled curls of his bush floating, floating hair of the stream around the limp father of thousands, a languid floating flower."

Both Bloom's severe parody of Martha's letter and his more luxurious vision of his own body transforming into a flower are manifestations in the "language of flowers" of a thought which remains to be deciphered from the text. As a puissant rhetorician, Joyce would know that "flowers of speech" is a traditional designation for the metaphors and figurative language that characterize literary discourse and distinguish it from refer-ential or more scientific kinds of writing. Joyce now links figurative lan-guage, or flowers of speech, with the "language of flowers," or the principle of euphemistic or courtly diction. He depicts what are in the eyes of Dublin bourgeois society Bloom's perverse and unspeakable desires by a flowery style. When unspeakable thoughts do emerge into the light of language, metaphor too of necessity arises, for it is precisely the work of metaphor to disguise the impropriety of the literal signified behind the transforming mask of the figural signifier. So Bloom's expressions of sexual desire, of love for a departed son, of nostalgia for a past time of sensual wholeness can only be spoken through an indirection which names something else as a preoccupation of the mind. For Bloom, this indirection is both the origin of metaphor and the condition of sense. Metaphor has become the only vehicle for expressing his "unspeakable" desires. As a consequence, expres-sion which resists the "Flower to console me . . . language of flow" must remain foreign and unvoiced on Bloomsday.

In "Nausicaa," Bloom's language of flowers becomes literally a flowery rhetoric, but even there metaphoric flowers arise to name indirectly the notions of sensuality and desire. After her self-exposure (a "wondrous revealment half offered") Gertie McDowell meets Bloom's glance with her own full "sweet flowerlike face." As she turns to leave, she wafts her handkerchief in the breeze. Slowly, across seven pages of text, the scent of her perfume floats toward Bloom, a synaesthesia of the silent sexual language that had passed between them: "Wait. Hm. Hm. Yes. That's her perfume. Why she waved her hand" and Bloom proceeds to read its import. "I leave you this to think of me when I'm far away on the pillow. What is it? Heliotrope? No, Hyacinth? Hm. Roses, I think . . . .Molly likes opoponax . . . with a little jessamine mixed. Her high notes and her low notes." Here again, the language of flowers, itself a figural displacement of sexual deprivation, fills the space between Gertie and Bloom, as if promising to close the all too real distance between them. And then that displacement into the flowery speech is itself immediately displaced by metaphors which lead to Molly as an emblem of plenitude and self-sufficiency. Gertie remains a mere *simulacrum* of Molly, as her perfume is a poor imitation of Molly's scent, which is also her voice.

The interesting flower in this garden is the Heliotrope. Formerly, heliotrope was the name applied to the sunflower, marigold, or any plant the flowers of which turn toward the sun. Now it names a plant with small clustered, purple flowers commonly cultivated for fragrance. Bloom has both meanings of the word in mind, for as he sits on the beach, the sun begins to set and his mind begins weaving together the solar and floral images into a single pattern. He recalls first that the "Best time to spray plants [is] in the shade after the sun," and then returns to the idea of the heliotrope: women are described as "Open[ing] like flowers, know their hours, sunflowers." This confluence of thought figured by the sunward-turning flowers is the metaphor of the single overriding obsession on Bloom's mind today—the possibility of stamping his mark (as the sun "Wants to stamp his trademark on everything") on the fluid phenomena of everchanging differences by the conception of a son to be in the place of the one he has lost. But the possibility that such a script will come to pass seems now impossibly remote.

In succession, then, the various solar and floral metaphors which name the intersection of the concepts of sexuality, paternity, and even language, increasingly create a weave of metaphoric inter-reference. And while Bloom becomes more and more associated with the sun-tending heliotrope, Stephen comes increasingly to stand for the lost son (sun) until, in the "Oxen of the Sun" episode, the association is made virtually explicit.

In the maternity hospital, "Leopold that had of his body no manchild for an heir looked upon him [Stephen] his friend's son and was shut up in sorrow for his forepassed happiness and as sad . . . that him failed a son of such gentle courage." Further on, Bloom again in reverie ("a mirror within a mirror") becomes amid the boisterous students "paternal" and imagines that "these about him might be his sons." "Who can say?" the narrator asks, for "The wise father knows his own child." But memory and daydream soon recede and Bloom is left with neither son nor woman to "bear the sunnygolden babe of day: No, Leopold! Name and memory solace thee not . . . .No son of thy loins is by thee. There is none now to be for Leopold, what Leopold was for Rudolph." Through their power to substitute and displace the *literal* and *figural* levels of words by manifesting the shared *proper* elements among them, metaphors will be for Bloom a means of conceiving one "to be for Leopold, what Leopold was for Rudolph." Failing to be content with mere metaphor, Bloom continues to seek a form of discourse which will lead to peace in all its fullness. Rather than finding peace, however, Bloom continues to find only other metaphors which in an impossible combination attempt to describe the fact of paternity.

Since Molly is unavailable to bear the son, Bloom creates replacements, metempsychotic Mollies, and metaphors to take the place of the real source of life. As he does so, a totalizing vision seems to arise before Bloom:

> And, lo, wonder of metempsychosis, it is she, the everlasting bride, harbinger of the daystar, the bride, ever virgin. It is she, Martha, thou lost one, Millicent, the young, the dear, the radiant. How serene does she now arise, a queen among the Pleiades, in the penultimate antelucan hour, shod in sandals of bright gold, coifed with a veil of what do you call it gossamer! It floats, it flows about her starborn flesh and loose it streams emerald, sapphire, mauve and heliotrope, sustained on currents of cold interstellar wind, winding, coiling, simply swirling, writhing in the skies a mysterious writing till after a myriad metamorphoses of symbol, it blazes, Alpha, a ruby and triangled sign upon the forehead of Taurus.

Martha, insubstantial lover, and Millicent, the departed daughter, merge into one figure who traces an interstellar script which seems to refer to the source of all meaning, Alpha. The feminine form is simultaneously lover and daughter, sun-seeking heliotrope and author of revealing signs. As a paranomasia, the ruby sign of Alpha represents both the deceased son Rudy and his metaphoric substitute, Stephen (whose own signature in the heavens is "delta in Cassiopeia"). But the veiled stellar script of "sapphire, mauve and heliotrope," which seems to provide Bloom with a sign of salvation from the meaningless language of flowers, is itself metaphoric and continues to bear the kinds of ambiguities which have coursed through Stephen's own unsuccessful attempts to authenticate the meaning of words. After the heavenly writing fades there remain only further repetitions and elaborations of other versions of each of these metaphors. But whether in isolation, in new configurations, or in new permutations, they continue expressing the same distressing lack of certainty.

In their exchange of desires, Stephen (the father-seeker soaring sunward) and Leopold (a son-compelled flower) align along an axis of paradigmatic compatibility. Yet even Stephen, who "likes dialectic, the universal language," is free enough from illusion in "Ithaca" to see that the ideal synthesis of antitheses, which all good dialectics and effective metaphors hope to achieve, is still but a remote possibility. Reduced to their simple reciprocal forms, and substituted by chiasmic exchange, "Stephen for Bloom Stoom" and "Bloom for Stephen Blephen," each represents only a composite, asymmetrical image which cannot endure as a meaningful personality. The omniscient narrative voice of "Ithaca" foresees that the reduction of Bloom by such cross substitution could render him "a negligible negative irrational unreal quantity."

As soon as either Dedalus or Bloom begins to think that reconciliation, coherence, and stability in their various forms might be accessible, each discovers that the terms of the analogizing statements which facilitate the expression of those reconciliations are individually set in metaphorical relations. Bloom the "suncompelled" figure "obey[ing] the summons of recall" and Dedalus, the hawk-like man "soaring sunward," thus find their metaphoric Sun to be not a source of truth but rather a *simulacrum* of it. That central ruling Sun remains invisible, veiled by darkness and eclipsed by linguistic illusions. Its traces, "Holy Writ," as the narrator informs us, are always found to be but "genuine forgeries."

If Bloom's story is not a tragic one, and certainly it seems more comic than tragic, it is because he manages in his innocence to create a manner of self-integration by his equanimity before the meaninglessness of his cuckolded, sonless existence. The narrator of "Ithaca" poses the possibility that Bloom might smile as he crawls back into the "bed of conception and of birth, of consummation of marriage and of breach of marriage, of sleep and of death":

If he had smiled why would he have smiled?
To reflect that each one who enters [the bed of marriage] imagines himself to be the first to enter whereas he is always the last term of a preceding series even if the first term of a

succeeding one, each imagining himself to be first, last, only
and alone, whereas he is neither first nor last nor only nor alone
in a series originating in and repeated to infinity.

From a narrative point of view, the narrator's questions and answers
in "Ithaca" shift the pattern of referential authority from a mimetic mode
(which has been prevalent throughout Stephen's philosophizing) to a die-
getic mode: "If he had smiled . . . [he might have smiled] To reflect that."
Bloom is thus held capable of positing a vision of integration which is
significantly different from any that Stephen has articulated. Whereas Stephen's aesthetic theory and Shakespearean myth depend on the existence
of an ideal, original point as a source and guarantee of meaning, Bloom is
now said to be capable of conceiving a system of reference, structured as
a chain of spatial juxtapositions, underwritten by no definable origin. The
indeterminacy of this chain's origin, rather than being a source of frustration
and despair, as it is for Stephen, is for Bloom a situation with which one
can live. Bloom sees himself as merely another cipher within that long,
hidden sentence which leads neither back to the one proper Word of creation
nor forward to the teleologic end of history.

A variant of this umbilical chain had already appeared in Stephen's
thoughts about the human chain of history leading back by *anastomosis* to
the primal Eve: "The cords of all link back, strand-entwining cable of all
flesh," to "our mighty mother" to whom "we are linked up with by
successive anastomosis of navelcords." Stephen's anastomotic views of history (and narratives of history) imply that words proceed from and are
supported by a transcendentally self-present Word: God to Christ, Shakespeare to Hamlet, Dedalus to Icarus, in a kind of umbilical relation. From
this perspective, the artist's task is simply to recover the linguistic signs
most appropriate for the "expression" of that link between a self-present
immanent core of meaning and its radiated significations. Artists conduce
meanings from the world into language, while readers deduce those meanings from the proffered words. In contrast, Leopold's anastomotic chain
challenges this unidirectional flow by conceiving it as a channel without
detectable origin, and oriented toward no predictable end. Stephen's figure
of "anastomosis," as reiterated by Bloom, is thus a felicitous one, for it
simultaneously designates a physiological interconnection between bodies
of any kind, and also the rhetorical process of intercommunication. As a
concept of displacement and transport, anastomosis is precisely a consti-
tutive property of metaphor.

In accordance with the semantic pattern established throughout Joyce's texts, however, it is nonetheless uncertain whether or not the word "anastomosis" communicates a determinate meaning. Possessing as it does two distinct senses, one connoting a literal transmission or propagation, the other denoting a figural dissemination of a semantic content, it is not justifiable to define *anastomosis* as the communication of any one particular meaning.

For Stephen, however, this communicating chain does form a fixed, directional, telic axis, which carries within itself the hope of transmitting some sort of life-sustaining force from an original (procreating) to a secondary (procreated) body. Bloom, in contrast, entertains no such delusion: his metaphoric chain "originates in and repeats to infinity," and in accepting the "apathy of the stars," posits "nolast term," no determinate end or accomplished communication. Bloom's anastomotic chain acknowledges no definitive beginning or end to the story of human destiny in either its individual or abstract form.

Ineluctably multiplying the tender relations that its linked couples implacably displace, Bloom's "infinite chain" represents the necessity of the mirage that an original source of meaning can be conceived. The act of copulation, which for Bloom forms the emblem of the anastomotic human chain, is the living sign of asymmetrical difference in human affairs. It is, as the narrator grandiosely puts it, the "natural act of a nature expressed or understood executed in natured nature by natural creatures in accordance with his, her and their natured natures, of dissimilar similarity." This copulative play of dissimilar beings, which allows the momentary illusion of spiritual unity, designates for Bloom the possibility that existential meaning is a function not of an immanent core of truth within each of the copulating elements, which can be genetically transmitted through a kind of racial system of telecommunication, but is instead a function of the network of oppositions that simultaneously *distinguishes* the dissimilar pair and *relates* them to one another and to every other combination of copulating pairs.

Bloom can thus be said to imagine with convincing equanimity that "From outrage (matrimony) to outrage (adultery) there arose nought but outrage (copulation)," and that in the exchange of terms within that chain of copulating pairs, "the natural grammatical transition by inversion involv[es] no alteration of sense." His model of humanity (linked to one another by the anastomotic phallus but tied to no primal, original source) creates by contingency a provisional semantic field free of the illusion of pre-existing "ideas" and can be read as an emblem of the processes of the Joycean narrative itself in *Ulysses*. In Joyce's narratives, every metaphorical system which arises to define an independent, pre-existing, and authoritative truth always reveals itself to be necessarily inscribed in a relational chain or system within which it refers to other concepts, concepts which are themselves produced by the systematic by-play of the differences between them, and not by any privileged source of intrinsic value.

The effects of this anastomotic structure upon the notion of a "classical" narrative are striking indeed. Since language in *Ulysses* has not been carried down to humanity whole, significant, and free of differences by a Thoth-like heavenly messenger, it is clear that whatever meaning does exist has been produced by the interactions among Joyce's fictional characters. Stephen's words, therefore, certainly are the effects of a cause, as he imagines. But they have as their cause neither a Transcendental Subject, nor a Radiant Essence that is somewhere present (even if hidden), and which itself escapes the play of linguistic difference. The traces which Stephen, and sometimes Bloom, appear to find of such a Primary Cause are themselves the results of the system which gives metaphor a privileged place in the dialectical movement which is to produce that fabled "universal language" of Stephen's dreams.

Stephen's and Bloom's metaphoric attempt to encounter the totalizing word of such a universal language forms an allegory of the indeterminacy of meaning. But though driven by a desire for transcendence, allegories always remain schematic. Allegories are emblems, not archetypes of the universal Logos within which man, woman, and God might exist in perfect unity. If at any point the narrative of *Ulysses* were to have succeeded in creating such a heliotropic archetype of unity, the text might have been able to cease discarding alternative narrative voices and styles. But in fact the closing period to that multi-perspectival structure remains unattained, even beyond the final word of the "Penelope" section. Molly's "yes" answers no questions, resolves no contradictions, hypostatizes no distinct links in the copulative figural chain which is *Ulysses*. Molly's voice returns, as the other narrative voices return, from its digressionary movement to the central pattern of metaphor. It is a pattern, however, that cannot reduce polarities or resolve contradictions. To interpret those figures of speech as signs of consubstantial union between man and wife, Father and Son, word and idea, or signifier and signified, is to fall into the intoxicating delusion of Joyce's synthetic metaphors.

Stephen's "actions" in the text are the result of a nostalgia for a mythic universal language which is described in *A Portrait of the Artist* through the indirection which names the aesthetic theory as a model for the proper reading of the world. According to that theory, meaning and materiality can be reconciled in a transfigurative flash; for one fragile, heroic instant, a surge of spirit illuminates and redeems the material world from within. In *Ulysses,* that nostalgia for harmonious totalization is named in the form of the allegory of the self-begotten Son. Bloom's actions are the reciprocal movement of Stephen's word-play. The narrative of their quests for organic unity and coherence is repeatedly displaced by other narratives which parody that quest by expressing it in ever-proliferating styles and narrative modes. And perhaps we may go one step further to suggest that Stephen's and Bloom's constantly deferred goal of recreating a self-constituting, self-referential, and unmediated Word which will order the system of discourse is the analogue of the author's own attempt to encounter the proper narrative mode for the expression of their story. Had a universal language for the reconciliation of differences emerged from the text, Father and Son might have been reconciled and a genealogical chain linking them back to a proper origin might have been forged. But at every point in the narrative the linguistic sign marks out a systematic anarchy which does allow the creation of a provisional semantic field, but which also traces the law of arbitrariness and ambiguity which governs the creation of meaning.

Metaphor, "in the track of the sun," is not itself a presence but a simulacrum attempting to fill that semantic void. The heliotropic flowers of the Joycean narrative, always tending through metaphor toward a darkening sun, as if to form its substitute ("the condensation of spiral nebulae into suns"), point to no stable source. Rather, they remain unstable and ready to efface themselves from the text. And yet those metaphors are also the sources of the novel's soothing pathos, for *Ulysses* testifies on every page to the fact that there can be no essential expression, nor any understanding, of essence without metaphor. Nietzsche describes this need for metaphor in human affairs:

> Only by forgetting that primitive world of metaphors, only by the congelation and coagulation of an original mass of similes and percepts pouring forth as a fiery liquid out of the primal faculty of human fancy, only the invincible faith, that *this* sun, . . . is a truth in itself: in short only by the fact that man forgets himself as subject, and what is more as an *artistically creating* subject: only by all this does he live with some repose, safety and consequence.
>
> ("On Truth and Falsehood in Their Extra-Moral Sense")

Even in the face of such Dionysian truths, Apollonian illusions of Radiance will also persist. This is the source of Joyce's, and Bloom's, comic, not to say joyous, wisdom: that outside the myth of a universal language, the paternal language belonging to the lost fatherland of plenitude and truth, only the "interstellar void" exists. It is a void that can be read, as Leopold Bloom reads it, without nostalgia, but humanely, and perhaps even with equanimity, realizing that language "in the track of the sun" cannot be easily deflowered. Beneath the void, provisionally filling its space, lies only what Joyce will name later in *Finnegans Wake,* "the panaroma of all flores of speech."

Nature and Culture in the "Sirens" Episode of Joyce's *Ulysses*

Cheryl Herr

When Walter Pater insisted that all art "aspires towards the condition of music," he advanced a concept of music that became widely accepted by the end of the nineteenth century. A literary generation later, this same tradition of music as the highest and purest of the arts shaped in various ways much of James Joyce's linguistic experimentation with musical form. As critics have often commented, from the technically refined lyrics of *Chamber Music* to the polyphonic prose of *Finnegans Wake,* Joyce's work seems at times to differ by imitation to the aesthetic effects that music commands. Our knowledge of Joyce's personal reverence for music supports this interpretation of his work. For example, in 1934 Frank Budgen reported, "When Joyce talks 'tenor' one has the idea that he sees in the tenor organ not only an instrument of musical expression but also an adornment and a justification of humanity" (*James Joyce and the Making of "Ulysses"*). A similar sentiment informs a letter Joyce wrote in November 1930 to ask his friend Paul Ruggiero for Greek and French texts of a song Ruggiero had composed. Joyce had purchased a French recording of the piece, and he commented, "By the way, the words are different in the French text. There is nothing about the sea in it, no laughter and no blonde, but great sadness. My wife cried when she was listening to it. What the deuce is there in music, and above all in singing, that moves us so deeply?" Significantly, this emotional response to Ruggiero's music directly echoes that of some characters in the "Sirens" chapter, for after Ben Dollard con-

From *Essays in Literature* 11, no. 1 (Spring 1984). © 1984 by Western Illinois University.

cludes his performance of "The Croppy Boy," Simon Dedalus and his cohorts are described as "deepmoved." Joyce's letter, like the eleventh episode of *Ulysses,* accepts on some level the idea that music has mysterious powers. However, in "Sirens" Joyce's weaving together of several such received ideas tends to discredit this myth of the powers of music, especially the idea that music can intensify a listener's apprehension of self.

The word *move,* which Joyce used both in his letter and in "Sirens," holds one explanation for this apparent tension in Joycean attitudes about musical effect. As any reader armed with an *American Heritage Dictionary* can testify, modern English derivatives of the Indo-European root of *move* include *momentum, motif, motive, movingly, emotion,* and *remote.* The mixture in such cognates of spatial and psychological meanings mirrors the range in typical connotations of *move:* to progress in sequence or follow a specific course (on the model of the constellations), to change hands, to evacuate or void (of the body), to dislodge, to actuate, and to agitate, arouse, upset, excite, or affect deeply. Idiomatically, we may even "move heaven and earth." Thus, when we speak of the movement of emotions, we employ a redundancy that carries with it suggestions of both the movement of physical organs and the movement of the stars.

This connection of body and cosmos is, of course, implicit in the theories of early Greek cosmologists, for whom the momentum of the spheres created an ethereal music that could not be heard by mundane mortals and that took its harmonic order from the intricate holism of the First and Unmoved Mover. Just as Aristotle assumed the reality of the First Mover and the ordered cosmos which It moved, so our culture has long accepted the idea that those things that move, including music, may link us to the primal or natural self as well as to an intuited site of divinity.

The use of the word *move* to describe, however vaguely, the effect of music on a listener thus implies an ideological affirmation of art as a mode of knowledge. Along this line, Bloom's cryptic comment in "Circe"— "University of life. Bad art"—is significant, for Bloom implies that culture in Dublin is somehow spoiled, unable to generate the kind of art that educates and uplifts the human spirit. Bloom's confusion here about what is natural and what is cultural is not necessarily a measure of ignorance. He speaks for a tradition which has always sought in art a connection to a reality outside the artifact, whether Platonic essence or Aristotelian substance. But close attention to the figurative and descriptive language in "Sirens" reveals that the text blocks any achievement, through either music or literature, or such philosophic certitude. When one listens to music, the "Sirens" episode suggests, the self stirs to play only a highly conventional score. Given that from such conventions there is no possibility of removal, Bloom has no choice but to participate in the cultural constellations that shape both his consciousness and the text of "Sirens."

I

The power of the conventional in "Sirens" can be demonstrated on a number of fronts, especially in Bloom's thoughts about the sensory, the sexual, and the musical. Bloom, of course, uneasy at being emotionally touched against his will or control by the singing in the Ormond bar, attacks head-on the question of why music moves the listener. He sees the individual (as performer and audience) and his culture as interdependent in musical creation and perception. Further, Bloom probes the connection, which he perceives only peripherally, between the effect of music and the nature of sexual attraction. In addition, the narrative effort to name characters and to describe the sources and effects of musical power points to the highly conventional nature of language itself. And the songs that are sung or played in the episode suggest how far from natural inevitabilities are the popular sentiments of a culture. Both Bloom and the narrator register the peculiar effects of music, and both demonstrate the difficulty of transcending or seeing through received ideas.

Bloom's attempts to come to grips with musical effect are neither systematic nor consistent. As Father Cowley plays "Love and War," Bloom thinks, "Piano again. Cowley it is. Way he sits in to it, like one together, mutual understanding." Bloom then disparages "Tiresome shapers scraping fiddles," and, later, girls learning their scales and singers who spoil their voices by drinking. That is, from a simply mechanical standpoint, Bloom admires careful and sensitive execution of musical pieces. But his sense of a "mutual understanding" between Cowley and the piano picks up the common notion that real musical talent or genius is something as ill-defined as the performer's feeling of the music; to Bloom, the music plays Cowley as much as he plays the music.

Yet this sense of that somewhat mysterious power of music gives way to Bloom's skepticism over Richie Goulding's enthusiasm about performances he has witnessed: "Coming out with a whopper now. Rhapsodies about damn all." Nevertheless, when Richie whistles an air, Bloom ponders punningly about Goulding's ability to split-whistle: "Rich sound. Two notes in one there. Blackbird I heard in the hawthorn valley. Taking my motives he twined and turned them. All most too new call is lost in all. Echo. How sweet the answer. How is that done? All lost now. Mournful he whistled. Fall, surrender, lost." The description of sounds as "rich," "sweet," and "mournful" underscores the reason for Bloom's puzzlement over the twining of his motives by music. The whistle is, for Bloom, "rich" because of the doubling of notes and because of his recollection of a blackbird's song, and these two phenomena blend in Bloom's thoughts with his feeling of loss and his everpresent agony over Molly's infidelity. This narrative organization of ideas suggests that a listener's response to music depends on the sum of his experiences, each one a packet of cultural data. In *Ulysses* the power of music is attributed to a mechanism of tapping, rapidly, and blending in varying patterns a series of personal associations.

Of course, such personal memories are also highly conventional. In particular, the experience of being cuckolded was given literary shape and social weight long before 1904. Bloom's eventual labor is to separate a culturally predictable response (confront Boylan, make love to Molly, secure a divorce) from a truly individual one, but the "Ithaca" narrative, in its increasingly comprehensive perspective, enables us to see Bloom's attempt as doomed to failure; each of Bloom's choices of action is already part of or contingent on a social framework. Similarly, music takes the "motives" of the individual and works with them as cultural motifs to be variously interwoven and repackaged.

The nature of musical effect is not always clearly seen by Bloom, but the description of Simon Dedalus' rendition of "M'appari" confirms this analysis. As Si begins to sing in what Richie and Bloom agree is a magnificent—if not mint condition—tenor voice, we read: "Braintipped, cheek touched with flame, they listened feeling that flow endearing flow over skin limbs human heart soul spine." It would be difficult to find here ironic or satiric pointers that would demand our reading the passage as critical of this familiar goose-bump response to song. In this moment not just Bloom but the reader too can accept only what the text renders—a sentimental but also presumably accurate description of the effects that Si's voice creates in his audience: a flush in the cheeks, a shiver in the spine, and a sensation of being "moved." The description places these sensations firmly within a tradition that gives credence to the human "heart" and soul, and that values human emotions.

Obviously, the male and female behavior that Bloom notices in the Ormond bar depends on the same patterning culture as the perception of music does; for Bloom, the two phenomena participate in a received concept of love that both art and experience feed. As the words touch both "still ears" and "still hearts of their each his remembered lives," Bloom thinks, "Love that is singing: love's old sweet song." Si's listeners plug into the love mystique: love is joyful; love demands full consummation; lovers become one and grieve endlessly if they are separated. Western tradition plays Bloom as the piano plays Cowley.

While Dedalus sings, stereotyped ideas and behavior surface both in Bloom's thoughts and in narrative commentary. For instance, Bloom thinks, "Tenors get women by the score. Increase their flow." When, for Bloom, the song becomes one of predictable "joygush" and "tupthrop," his thoughts of a "Flood of warm jimjam lickitup secretness" are comically set off in the text against Lydia Douce's "so ladylike" response to George Lidwell's tentative courtship. Almost all actions center on the social contexts of the sexual in this chapter, from the bargirls' ridicule of the unmarrigeably greasy "old fogey in Boyd's" and Bloom's thoughts of the "Bluerobed" but "white under" plaster virgins that lure "those rakes of fellows" into Catholicism to the attempts of Miss Douce to discourage Lenehan but to attract, always in a genteel way, the attentions of Blazes Boylan. From Simon's racy comments in the bar ("Mrs Marion Bloom has left off clothes of all descriptions," "Sure, you'd burst the tympanum of her ear, man . . . with an organ like yours") to Bloom's recollections of his early, joyful days with Molly, the narrative is woven from references to the social customs and jokes that define the sexual in Joyce's Dublin. To find in *Ulysses,* as Marilyn French does, an implied argument for a realistic acceptance of sexuality as natural is to miss the implication that there is no way to de-conventionalize either sex or music (*The Book as World: James Joyce's* Ulysses); the culture of *Ulysses* binds its characters to infinite stylizations of the erotic and the aesthetic.

This ponderous idea finds repeated comic expression in the episode. For example, Bloom is aware that in Dublin farting is antisocial ("Now if I did that at a banquet") but goes on to think, "Just a question of custom shah of Persia." Further, Bloom's later reference to the shah reminds the reader of a focus on the themes of music, women, and custom that occurs as Bloom listens to Ben Dollard singing "The Croppy Boy":

> Bronze, listening by the beerpull, gazed far away. Soulfully. Doesn't half know I'm. Molly great dab at seeing anyone looking.
> Bronze gazed far sideways. Mirror there. Is that best side of her face? They always know. Knock at the door. Last tip to titivate . . . .
> What do they think when they hear music? Way to catch rattlesnakes. Night Michael Gunn gave us the box. Tuning up.

Shah of Persia liked that best. Remind him of home sweet home. Wiped his nose in curtain too. Custom his country perhaps. That's music too. Not as bad as it sounds . . . .

She looked fine. Her crocus dress she wore, lowcut, belongings on show. Clove her breath was always in theatre when she bent to ask a question. Told her what Spinoza says in that book of poor papa's. Hypnotized, listening. Eyes like that. She bent. Chap in dresscircle, staring down into her with his operaglass for all he was worth. Beauty of music you must hear twice. Nature woman half a look. God made the country man the tune. Met him pike hoses. Philosophy. O rocks!

Miss Douce's soulful look and seductive pose make Bloom wonder what women think of "when they hear music." Like the shah of Persia, women are, to Bloom, alien beings; always observant, he notes their behavior, but he cannot understand it *beyond* seeing that the women he knows share certain traits, that is, beyond the point where the behavior is culturally determined. Hence he turns, in wondering about Molly's choice of him as a mate, to the hazy idea of "Fate" as an explanation, really no explanation at all. Bloom backs off from concluding that perception of beauty, in woman and in song, is culturally shaped; instead he retreats to platitude: "God made the country man the tune." But the female viewpoint, or at least Molly's version of it, here explodes behind Bloom's refusal to recognize the standardization of his responses. Molly's deforming of the word "metempsychosis" to the Freudian "Met him pike hoses" punctures the "Philosophy" which pretends to explain life by labeling and relabeling it (compare Bloom's pedagogic technique) in quest of a final elucidation. There being no way out of this semiotic whirlpool, Molly's "O rocks" constitutes a reasonable response.

Because in this chapter the narrative stresses the customs by which sounds and words become musical and by which men and women become mutually attractive, it is intriguing to examine closely those moments when musical conventions, indicated in the narrative by various kinds of repetition, are purported to "move" characters in the narrative. Such a potential epiphany occurs in the consummation of Simon Dedalus's song when Si, Bloom, and Lionel are denoted as "Siopold."

—*Come!*
It soared, a bird, it held its flight, a swift pure cry, soar silver orb it leaped serene, speeding, sustained, to come, don't spin it out too long long breath he breath long life, soaring high, high

resplendent, aflame, crowned, high in the effulgence symbolistic, high, of the ethereal bosom, high, of the high vast irra-
diation everywhere all soaring all around about the all, the
endlessnessnessness . . .
   —*To me!*
Siopold!
Consumed.

Along one line of interpretation, it would be possible to take "Siopold"
as a sign of the perfect epistemological fusion of audience, performer, and
expressive object. As knower, Bloom would abstract from his sensory
experience the formal *quidditas* of the performance and would become cog-
nitively changed by this incorporation of knowledge; this fusion of knower
and known would involve both Dedalus's knowledge of the part he sings
and Bloom's complete apprehension of Si's rendition. The epiphany signified in the word "Siopold" might then involve a recognition of spiritual
consubstantiality achieved through aesthetic experience. This interpretation
finds apparent support in the fact that after the song's conclusion, the
narrative stresses a gradual movement by the audience away from a state
of unity: "All clapped. She ought to. Come. To me, to him, to her, you
too, me, us . . . .Encore, enclap, said, cried, clapped all, Ben Dollard, Lydia
Douce, George Lidwell, Pat, Mina, two gentlemen with two tankards,
Cowley, first gent with tank and bronze Miss Douce and gold Miss Mina."

However, to look in naming for evidence of ontological status is a
risky business in "Sirens." For example, as the barmaids laugh about the
"old fogey," their "goldbronze voices" merge, and they become "bronze
gigglegold," "Kennygiggles," "bronzegold goldbronze," almost indistin-
guishable in the description of their laughter. In turn, their fused ridicule
of the "greasy nose" is transferred in the narrative to Bloom, who is called
"greaseaseabloom." As we segment this word, we note that it does not
identify the Bloom we think we know. Why might Bloom be made linguistically consubstantial with an apothecary? Is Bloom greasy? in the sea?
at his ease? a seabloom (Henry Flower underwater)? Seemingly pretending
to name, the text thwarts identification. Possibly indicating consubstantiality, the narrative threatens to dissolve Bloom to the state of semiotic
mush. The narrative, in fact, frequently toys with Bloom's identity:

   —Bloowho went by by Moulang's pipes.
Bloowhose dark eye read Aaron Figatner's name.
Winsomely she on Bloohimwhom smiled.

Bloom's name notably does not become one with the name he reads (as in

Bloomgatner or Figbloom). Rather, he wonders, "Why do I always think Figather? Gathering figs I think. And Prosper Loré's huguenot name." Loré is not a huguenot, nor does Figatner gather figs; names, the reader is not surprised to find Bloom discovering, do not identify either denotatively or connotatively. Whatever consubstantiality is implied in a word like "Siopold" (that is, whatever unity inheres in the linguistic state that everything in the novel shares), and whatever epistemological or aesthetic condition the narrative evokes—all must be qualified radically by recognizing the narrative's persistent, playful questioning of naming, of identity, and of cognition, often under the guise of the customary repetitions of musical form.

Evidence of this playfulness abounds in "Sirens," but a few more quotations easily demonstrate the point. For instance, Simon's examination of the newly tuned piano is rendered with interpolations by a questioning, exclaiming narrative voice: "Upholding the lid he (who?) gazed in the coffin (coffin?) at the oblique triple (piano!) wires. He pressed (the same who pressed indulgently her hand), soft pedalling a triple of keys to see the thicknesses of felt advancing, to hear the muffled hammerfall in action." When Lydia sees Boylan, the narrator waxes metonymic: "Sparkling bronze azure eyed Blazure's skyblue bow and eyes." And the discussion of Molly by the men in the bar comically plays at pinning down her full identity and current estate:

> Mrs Marion met him pike hoses. Smell of burn of Paul de Kock. Nice name he.
> —What's this her name was? A buxom lassy. Marion . . .
> —Tweedy.
> —Yes. Is she alive?
> —And kicking.
> —She was a daughter of . . .
> —Daughter of the regiment.
> —Yes, begad. I remember the old drummajor.
> Mr Dedalus struck, whizzed, lit, puffed savoury puff after.
> —Irish? I don't know, faith. Is she, Simon?
> Puff after stiff, a puff, strong, savoury, crackling.
> —Buccinator muscle is . . . What? . . . Bit rusty . . . O, she is . . . My Irish Molly, O.

Earlier in the day Molly has tried to make Paul de Kock's name into a statement about his nature, and she is subjected to the same kind of jesting definition by the men in the bar, a naming in which the men use song-

tags. "Daughter of the regiment," the translated title of an opera by Donizetti, gives way to the even more indiscriminate "My Irish Molly," a
phrase so general that Zack Bowen sees it as an allusion to several popular
Irish songs (*Musical Allusions in the Works of James Joyce: Early Poetry through
"Ulysses"*).

Similarly difficult to nail ontologically is Ben Dollard, who is variously
referred to as "Ben bulky Dollard," "Bensoulbenjamin," and "Big Benaden
Dollard. Big Benben. Big Benben." When asked by two customers who
Dollard is, Miss Kennedy identifies the singer only to have the narrative
muddle this identification: "Tank one believed: Miss Kenn when she: that
doll he was: she doll: the tank./ He murmured that he knew the name. The
name was familiar to him, that is to say. That was to say he had heard the
name of Dollard, was it? Dollard, yes." And Ben is finally made part of a
"fifth" in the post-song clinking of glasses: "First Lid, De, Cow, Ker, Doll,
a fifth."

The playful naming in "Sirens" clearly testifies to the conventional
nature of language, and it also points to the philosophic ambiguities that
result from the customs of cultural expression, either literary or musical.
Bloom, for all of our problems with his identity in "Sirens," speaks effectively to this problem of philosophic certitude. He recognizes that, given
the right "mood," "you think you're listening to the ethereal" if music is
well executed and has appealing words: "*Blumenlied* I bought for her. The
name." Given the "proper disposition" of cultural associations, the name
alone—malleable and arbitrary as it is—is enough to create for Bloom a
liking, even, one suspects, a sense of being in touch with some stable and
permanent part of himself and the cosmos.

It would be unwise simply to write off a sense of movement to some
higher or deeper recognition, a sense that Joyce himself gave voice to, as
a "sweet cheat" (see Joyce's schemata to *Ulysses*) or simple illusion, but it
is undeniable that in *Ulysses* moments of characters' being "deepmoved"
are followed by moments of emotional or intellectual letdown. Such a
rhythm could, of course, be read as validating an intermittent human capacity to achieve knowledge of the self and of the cosmos, a knowledge
intuitive but non-sustainable. But this most positive of the metaphysical
ideas possibly implicit in the *Ulysses* theme of consubstantiality finds no
absolute confirmation in the text.

Even the moment when Si's song is most effective falls far short of
any specific communication of knowledge, validation of intuition, or affirmation of consubstantiality. Rather, the description stresses its metaphoric nature. The cry, both "orb" and "bird," soars and leaps into an

"effulgence symbolistic," and "ethereal bosom," an irradiated endlessness, and the upward movement that we expect of transcendent experiences blends with the ambiguous image of the soaring bird. Earlier, while listening to Richie Goulding whistle, Bloom describes the sound as "A thrush. A throstle," and Goulding's breath is called "birdsweet." As noted before, his song reminds Bloom: "Blackbird I heard in the hawthorn valley." From the "hawthorn valley," the site of the marvellous birdsong, to the Boylan-signifying "haw horn" is little distance graphically, but the removed "t" changes music to lust, romance to adultery, birdsong to disenchanted "tup-throp." Bloom is not aware of this textual counterpoint, but he does reflect further on the two whistlings and on the moving of motives they engineer, and he wonders of this movement and of the doubling sounding of an echo, "How is that done?" Bloom has as much trouble describing these sounds as the narrative does Si's high B flat. Further, the blackbird in the valley and the bird-notes of Richie and Si are images made comic in the puzzle that Bloom recalls Ben Dollard's trying to solve: "Thinks he'll win in *Answers* poets' picture puzzle. We hand you crisp five pound note. Bird sitting hatching in a nest. Lay of the last minstrel he thought it was." Thus, the image of a bird can take on many metaphoric implications, as can the sound of a song—all inscribed in the individual by the experiences that create him. From birdsong to birdflight is an easy linguistic move, and so Si's "high" note may be located figuratively in the heavens (witness Bloom's "Thanks, that was heavenly"), but in this context the ethereal has only a metaphoric import.

If the sounds of music do not define for the reader anything permanent within the shifting waters of "Sirens," the words of the five principal songs recorded or alluded to in the episode similarly strand the reader on the rocks of convention, far from the home ports of meaning and nature. Both in the love songs ("Goodbye, Sweetheart, Goodbye," "All Is Lost Now," "M'appari") and in the patriotic songs ("Love and War," "The Croppy Boy"), the speakers and situations are strictly stylized, the roles typical, the songs pastiches of convention.

"All Is Lost Now" and "M'appari" provide excellent examples of this stylization. In both cases the operatic situation makes a lover appear to be false or departed when in fact the lover is true or present. Both songs are uncompromising; when the loved one is near, all hope, joy, and delight belong to the lover; when the woman seems to be false, everything turns to clay. That the lovers misinterpret their situations, however, makes comically suspect the attitudes of the characters in "Sirens." Bloom's sense that all songs are about loss and that he has lost all is, of course, inaccurate.

Though lost, Molly is everpresent in his thoughts. Though the songs in "Sirens" are about losses, the losses are provisional. In one sense, the songs undo the losses; in another sense, the personae have always been bereft. The music that Bloom finally sees as a sweet cheat is just that; far from providing evidence for Bloom's fatalistic conviction that Molly's adultery was inevitable, the popular songs he hears are collections of cultural motifs most noteworthy for their arbitrary stylizing of behavior and idea.

Insofar as "Sirens" builds for a reader an illusion of musicality and of an experiential dimension above the ordinary, "Sirens" seems to argue that music is a mode of knowledge which provides access to information about the nature of the self and of a larger reality. But the chapter itself becomes, more aggressively than some other episodes of *Ulysses,* a gathering of cultural topoi. The reader finds that in "Sirens" conventions fabricate both art and life. Perhaps this emphasis on the endless repetitions of culture accounts for Joyce's agonized and well-known statement to Harriet Weaver (July 20, 1919) that "each successive episode, dealing with some province of artistic culture (rhetoric or music or dialectic), leaves behind it a burnt up field. Since I wrote the *Sirens* I find it impossible to listen to music of any kind." Joyce seems to have leveled all the arts to the misleading condition that music achieves in *Ulysses,* but when he discussed music, he did not always speak out of the post-creative depression of 1919. The time would come when he could listen to a popular song and wonder still, "What the deuce is there in music . . . that moves us so deeply?"

Chronology

1882   James Augustine Aloysius Joyce born in Dublin on February 2 to John Stanislaus Joyce, tax-collector, and Mary Jane (May) Murray Joyce. He is the eldest of ten children who survive infancy, of whom the closest to him is his next brother Stanislaus (born 1884).

1888–91   Attends Clongowes Wood College, a Jesuit boarding school. He eventually is forced to leave because of his father's financial troubles. During Joyce's childhood and early adulthood, the family moves many times, from respectable suburbs of Dublin to poorer districts, as its size grows and its finances dwindle. Charles Stewart Parnell dies on October 6, the young Joyce writes an elegy, "Et tu, Healy." His father, a staunch Parnellite, has the poem printed, but no copies survive.

1892–98   Briefly attends the less intellectually prestigious Christian Brothers School, then attends Belvedere College, another Jesuit school.

1898–1902   Attends University College (another Jesuit institution); turns away from Catholicism and Irish nationalist politics. Writes a play, *A Brilliant Career,* (which he later destroys) and essays, several of which are published. Graduates in 1902 with a degree in modern languages, having learned French, Italian, German, Norwegian and Latin. Leaves Dublin to go to Paris and study medicine.

1903   Joyce works primarily on writing poems (which will be published in 1907 as *Chamber Music*) and reading Jonson at the Bibliothèque Ste. Geneviève. Receives a telegram from his father ("Mother dying come home Father"). Returns to Dublin, where May Joyce dies of cancer on August 13, four months after her son's return.

1904   An essay-narrative, "A Portrait of the Artist," is rejected for publication; several poems are published in various magazines, and a few stories, which eventually appear in *Dubliners,* are published. Stays for a time in the Martello Tower with Oliver St. John Gogarty (Malachi Mulligan in *Ulysses*). Joyce takes his first walk with Nora Barnacle on June 16 ("Bloomsday" in *Ulysses*). The daughter of a Galway baker, she is working in a Dublin boarding house. In October, Joyce and Nora leave for the continent, where they will live the remainder of their lives. Joyce finds work at a Berlitz school in Pola (now in Yugoslavia).

1905   The Joyces (as they are known, although they do not marry until 1931, for "testamentary" reasons) move to Trieste, where Joyce teaches at the Berlitz school. Birth of son Giorgio on July 27. Joyce submits manuscript of *Chamber Music* and *Dubliners* to Dublin publisher Grant Richards. Joyce's brother Stanislaus joins them in Trieste.

1907   After a year in Rome, where Joyce worked in a bank, the Joyces return to Trieste, where Joyce does private tutoring in English. *Chamber Music* published in London (not by Grant Richards). Birth of a daughter, Lucia Anna, on July 26. Writes "The Dead," the last of the stories that will become *Dubliners*. Works on revision of *Stephen Hero,* an adaptation of the essay "A Portrait of the Artist," later to be *A Portrait of the Artist as a Young Man.* Begins writing articles for an Italian newspaper.

1908   Abandons work on *Portrait* after completing three of five projected chapters.

1909   Joyce pays two visits to Dublin: in August, to sign a contract for the publication of *Dubliners* (not with Grant Richards), and in September as representative for a group who wish to set up the first cinema in Dublin. Returns to Trieste with sister Eva, who will now live with the Joyces.

1910   Cinema venture fails; publication of *Dubliners* delayed.

1911   Publication of *Dubliners* is held up, mainly because of what are feared to be offensive references to Edward VII in "Ivy Day in the Committee Room." Joyce writes to George V to ask if he finds the story objectionable; a secretary replies that His Majesty does not express opinions on such matters.

1912   Final visit to Dublin with his family. Printer destroys the manuscript of *Dubliners,* deciding the book's aims are anti-Irish. Joyce takes the proofs of which he has gotten a copy from his equally unsympathetic publisher, to London but cannot find a publisher for them there, either.

1913   Joyce's original publisher, Grant Richards, asks to see the manuscript of *Dubliners* again. Ezra Pound, at the urging of William Butler Yeats, writes Joyce asking to see some of his work, since Pound has connections with various magazines, and might be able to help get Joyce published.

1914   Grant Richards publishes *Dubliners.* At Pound's urging, *A Portrait of the Artist as a Young Man* is published serially by the London magazine *The Egoist.* Joyce begins work on *Ulysses.* World War I begins on August 4.

1915   Joyce completes his play, *Exiles.* After Joyce pledges neutrality to the Austrian authorities in Trieste who threatened to intern him, the family moves to Zürich, with the exception of Stanislaus, who is interned. Joyce awarded a British Royal Literary Fund grant, the first of several grants he will receive.

1916   Publishes *A Portrait of the Artist as a Young Man* in book form in New York.

1917   Undergoes the first of numerous eye operations.

1918   Grant Richards publishes *Exiles* in London; it is also published in the United States. The American magazine *The Little Review* begins serializing *Ulysses,* which is not yet complete. Armistice Day, November 11.

1919   Joyce refuses to be analyzed by Carl Jung. *The Egoist* also begins serializing *Ulysses.* The U.S. Post Office confiscates issues of *The Little Review* containing the "Lystrygonians" and the "Scylla and Charybdis" chapters.

1920–21   More issues of *The Little Review* confiscated. In September, John S. Sumner, the secretary of the New York Society for the Prevention of Vice, lodges a protest against the "Nausicaa" issue. The case comes to trial, and the *Review* loses, in February 1921. Publication ceases in the United States. Joyce and family move to Paris. Joyce finishes *Ulysses.* Sylvia Beach agrees to publish it in Paris.

1922   Shakespeare and Company, Sylvia Beach's press, publishes *Ulysses* in Paris on February 2, Joyce's birthday. Nora takes children to Galway for a visit, over Joyce's protests, and their train is fired upon by Irish Civil War combatants.

1923   Joyce begins *Finnegans Wake*, known until its publication as *Work in Progress*.

1924   Part of the *Work* appears in the Paris magazine, *transatlantic review*.

1926   Pirated edition of *Ulysses* (incomplete) serialized in New York by *Two Worlds Monthly*.

1927   Shakespeare and Company publish *Pomes Penyeach*. Parts of *Work* published in Eugene Jolas's *transition*, in Paris.

1928   Joyce publishes parts of *Work* in New York to protect the copyright.

1929   Joyce assists at a French translation of *Ulysses*, which appears in February. Lucia Joyce operated on unsuccessfully to remove a squint. She gives up her sporadic career as a dancer; her mental stability seems precarious. To his father's delight, Giorgio Joyce makes his debut as a singer, with some success.

1930   At Joyce's instigation, Herbert Gorman begins a biography of Joyce. Joyce supervises a French translation of *Anna Livia Plurabelle*, part of the *Work*, by Samuel Beckett and friends, which appears in the *Nouvelle Revue Française* in 1931. Marriage of son Giorgio to Helen Kastor Fleischman.

1931   Joyce marries Nora Barnacle at a registry office in London. Death of Joyce's father.

1932   Helen Joyce gives birth to a son, Stephen James, on February 15; Giorgio and Helen have the baby secretly baptized so as not to upset Joyce. Joyce writes "Ecce Puer," a poem celebrating the birth of his grandson. Daughter Lucia suffers first mental breakdown; she is diagnosed as hebephrenic (a form of schizophrenia). Bennett Cerf of Random House contracts for the American publication of *Ulysses*.

1933   On December 6, Judge John M. Woolsey admits *Ulysses* into the United States, declaring that "whilst in many places the effect . . . on the reader undoubtedly is somewhat emetic, nowhere does it tend to be an aphrodisiac." Lucia Joyce hospitalized, as she will often be until her permanent hospitalization.

1934   Random House publishes *Ulysses*.

1934   Publishes *Collected Poems* in New York, and *A Chaucer A.B.C.* with illuminations by Lucia.

1939   *Finnegans Wake* published in London and New York. War declared. The Joyces move to Vichy, France, to be near Lucia's mental hospital.

1940   Herbert Gorman's authorized biography of Joyce appears. After the fall of France, the Joyces manage once more to get to Zürich.

1941   Joyce dies following surgery on a perforated ulcer on January 13. He is buried in Fluntern Cemetery, in Zürich, with no religious ceremony, at Nora's request.

1951   Nora Barnacle Joyce dies in Zürich on April 10. She is buried in Fluntern as well, but not next to Joyce, since that space has been taken. In 1966, the two bodies are reburied together.

Contributors

HAROLD BLOOM, Sterling Professor of the Humanities at Yale University, is the author of *The Anxiety of Influence, Poetry and Repression,* and many other volumes of literary criticism. His forthcoming study, *Freud: Transference and Authority,* attempts a full-scale reading of all Freud's major writings. A MacArthur Prize Fellow, he is general editor of five series of literary criticism published by Chelsea House.

RICHARD ELLMANN, formerly Goldsmiths Professor of English at New College, Oxford, is now Research Professor at Emory University. Perhaps the leading modern literary biographer, he is best known for his books on Joyce and Yeats. His long-awaited biography of Oscar Wilde promises to be the definitive study.

WOLFGANG ISER teaches English and Comparative Literature at the Universitat Konstanz in Germany and the University of California, Irvine. A pioneer of "reception aesthetics" criticism and a founder of the "Poetics and Hermeneutics" research group, he has written books on Fielding, Pater, Spenser, and Beckett as well as *The Act of Reading, The Implied Reader,* and *Der Appelstruktur der Texte.*

A. WALTON Litz is Professor of English at Princeton University. He is the author of *The Art of James Joyce* and of *James Joyce.*

DORRIT COHN is Professor of German at Harvard University. She is the author of *The Sleepwalkers: Elucidations of Hermann Broch's Trilogy* and of *Transparent Minds: Narrative Modes for Presenting Consciousness in Fiction.*

HUGH KENNER, Professor Emeritus of English at The Johns Hopkins University, is the leading critic of the High Modernists (Pound, Eliot, Joyce) and of Beckett. His books include *The Pound Era, The Stoic Comedians, Dublin's Joyce,* and *Ulysses.*

Jean-Michel Rabaté teaches English and American literature at the University of Dijon. He is the author of *James Joyce: Portrait de l'auteur en autre lecteur* and *Language, Sexuality and Ideology in Ezra Pound*. He has edited *Beckett avant Beckett,* and published essays on Joyce, Pound and Hermann Broch.

Fritz Senn, a Swiss scholar, has worked on Joyce for many years and published articles on Joyce in many languages. He is affiliated with *A Wake Newsletter* and the *James Joyce Quarterly*. A collection of his essays has been edited under the title *Joyce's Dislocations: Essays on Reading as Translation*.

Ramón Saldívar teaches at the University of Texas at Austin. His publications include *Figural Language in the Novel: The Flowers of Speech from Cervantes to Joyce*.

Cheryl Herr teaches English at the University of Iowa. She has published articles in the *James Joyce Quarterly* and the *Journal of Modern Literature*. She is the author of *Joyce's Anatomy of Culture*.

Bibliography

Adams, Robert Martin. *Surface and Symbol: The Consistency of James Joyce's* Ulysses. New York: Oxford University Press, 1962.

———. *James Joyce: Common Sense and Beyond.* New York: Random House, 1966.

Attridge, Derek and Daniel Ferrer, eds. *Post Structuralist Joyce: Essays from the French.* Cambridge: Cambridge University Press, 1984.

Bazargan, Susan. " 'Oxen of the Sun': Maternity, Language, and History." *James Joyce Quarterly* 22 (1985): 271–80.

Benstock, Bernard, ed. *The Seventh of Joyce.* Bloomington: Indiana University Press, 1982.

———. *James Joyce.* New York: Frederick Ungar, 1985.

Benstock, Shari. "The Dynamics of Narrative Performance: Stephen Dedalus as Storyteller." *ELH* 49 (1982): 707–38.

———. "The Printed Letters in *Ulysses.*" *James Joyce Quarterly* 19 (1982): 415–27.

———, and Bernard Benstock. "The Joycean Method of Cataloguing." *James Joyce Quarterly* 17 (1979): 49–60.

Blamires, Harry. *The Bloomsday Book: A Guide through Joyce's* Ulysses. London: Methuen, 1966.

Bloom, Harold, ed. *Modern Critical Views: James Joyce.* New Haven: Chelsea House, 1986.

Boone, Joseph Allen. "A New Approach to Bloom as 'Womanly Man': The Mixed Middling's Progress in *Ulysses.*" *James Joyce Quarterly* 20 (1982): 67–85.

Bowen, Zack. *Musical Allusions in the Works of James Joyce.* Albany: SUNY Press, 1974.

———, and James F. Carens. *A Companion to Joyce Studies.* Westport, Conn.: Greenwood, 1984.

Boyle, Robert, S. J. *James Joyce's Pauline Vision: A Catholic Exposition.* Carbondale: Southern Illinois University Press, 1978.

Brown, Richard. *James Joyce and Sexuality.* New York: Cambridge University Press, 1985.

Budgen, Frank. *James Joyce and the Making of* Ulysses. 1934. Reprint. Bloomington: Indiana University Press, 1960.

Burgess, Anthony. *Re Joyce.* New York: Norton, 1965.

———. *Joysprick: An Introduction to the Language of James Joyce.* London: Deutsch, 1973.

153

Chace, William M., ed. *Joyce: A Collection of Critical Essays*. Englewood Cliffs, N.J.: Prentice-Hall, 1974.

Cixous, Helene. *The Exile of James Joyce*. Translated from the French by Sally A. J. Purcell. New York: David Lewis, 1972.

Cope, Jackson I. "Joyce's Waste Land." *Genre* 12 (1979): 505–32.

———. *Joyce's Cities: Archaeologies of the Soul*. Baltimore: Johns Hopkins University Press, 1981.

Curtius, Ernst Robert. "James Joyce and his *Ulysses*." In *Essays on European Literature,* translated by Michael Kowal. Princeton: Princeton University Press, 1973.

Davies, Stan Gebler. *James Joyce: A Portrait of the Artist*. New York: Stein & Day, 1975.

Deming, Robert H. *A Bibliography of James Joyce Studies*. 2d ed. Boston: G. K. Hall, 1977.

Derrida, Jacques. "Ulysse gramophone: l'oui-dire de Joyce." In *Genèse de Babel. Joyce et la création*. Paris: eds du C.N.R.S., 1985.

Devlin, Kimberly. "The Romance Heroine Exposed: 'Nausicaa' and *The Lamplighter*." *James Joyce Quarterly* 22 (1985): 383–96.

Druff, James H., Jr. "History vs. the Word: The Metaphor of Childbirth in Stephen's Aesthetics." *James Joyce Quarterly* 19 (1982): 303–14.

Eddins, Dwight. "*Ulysses:* The Search for the Logos." *ELH* 47 (1980): 804–19.

Ehrlich, Heyward, ed. *Light Rays: James Joyce and Modernism*. New York: New Horizon, 1984.

Ellmann, Richard. *Yeats and Joyce*. Dublin: Dolmen, 1967.

———. *Ulysses on the Liffey*. New York: Oxford University Press, 1972.

———. *The Consciousness of Joyce*. London: Faber, 1977.

———. *James Joyce*. 2d ed. Oxford: Oxford University Press, 1982.

Ford, Jane. "Why is Milly in Mulligar?" *James Joyce Quarterly* 14 (1977): 436–49.

French, Marilyn. *The Book as World: James Joyce's* Ulysses. Cambridge: Harvard University Press, 1976.

Gifford, Don Creighton, and Robert J. Seidman. *Notes for Joyce: An Annotation of James Joyce's* Ulysses. New York: Dutton, 1974.

Gilbert, Stuart. *James Joyce's* Ulysses. 1930. Reprint. New York: Vintage, 1955.

Givens, Seon, ed. *James Joyce: Two Decades of Criticism*. New York: Vanguard, 1948.

Goldberg, Samuel Louis. *Joyce*. New York: Barnes & Noble, 1962.

———. *The Classical Temper: A Study of James Joyce's* Ulysses. London: Chatto & Windus, 1961.

Goldman, Arnold. *The Joyce Paradox: Form and Freedom in his Fiction*. Evanston, Ill.: Northwestern University Press, 1966.

———. *James Joyce*. London: Routledge, 1968.

Gordon, John. *James Joyce's Metamorphosis*. Totowa N.J.: Barnes, 1981.

Gose, Elliot B., Jr. *The Transformation Process in Joyce's* Ulysses. Toronto: University of Toronto Press, 1980.

Gottfried, Roy K. *The Art of Joyce's Syntax in* Ulysses. Athens: University of Georgia Press, 1980.

Groden, Michael. Ulysses *in Progress*. Princeton: Princeton University Press, 1977.

Grose, Kenneth H. *James Joyce*. London: Evans Brothers, 1975.

Gross, John. *James Joyce*. New York: Viking, 1970.

Hannay, John. "Coincidence and Analytic Reduction in the 'Ithaca' Episode in *Ulysses*." *Journal of Narrative Theory* 13 (1983): 141–53.

Harkness, Marguerite. *The Aesthetics of Dedalus and Bloom*. Lewisburg, Pa.: Bucknell University Press, 1984.

Hart, Clive, and David Hayman, eds. *James Joyce's* Ulysses: *Critical Essays*. Berkeley: University of California Press, 1974.

Hayman, David. Ulysses: *The Mechanics of Meaning*. 2d ed. Madison: University of Wisconsin Press, 1982.

Henke, Suzette, and Elaine Unkeless. *Women in Joyce*. Urbana: University of Illinois Press, 1982.

Herr, Cheryl. *Joyce's Anatomy of Culture*. Urbana: University of Illinois Press, 1986.

Hodgart, Matthew J. C. *James Joyce: A Student's Guide*. London: Routledge, 1978.

————, and Mabel P. Worthington. *Song in the Works of James Joyce*. New York: Columbia University Press, 1959.

Jones, W. Powell. *James Joyce and the Common Reader*. Norman: University of Oklahoma Press, 1955.

James Joyce Quarterly, 1963–.

James Joyce Review, 1957–59.

Joyce, James. Ulysses: *A Critical and Synoptic Edition*. Edited by Hans Walter Gabler. 3 vols. New York: Garland, 1984.

————. *The Critical Writings of James Joyce*. Edited by Ellsworth Mason and Richard Ellmann. New York: Viking, 1959.

————. *Letters of James Joyce*. Vol. I, rev. ed. Stuart Gilbert. New York: Viking, 1966. Vols. II and III, ed. Richard Ellmann. New York: Viking, 1966.

————. *Selected Letters of James Joyce*. Edited by Richard Ellmann. New York: Viking, 1975.

Joyce, Stanislaus. *My Brother's Keeper*. Edited by Richard Ellmann. London: Faber, 1959.

Kain, Richard M. *Fabulous Voyager: James Joyce's* Ulysses. Chicago: University of Chicago Press, 1947.

Kenner, Hugh. *Dublin's Joyce*. London: Chatto & Windus, 1955.

————. *Joyce's Voices*. Berkeley: University of California Press, 1978.

————. *Ulysses*. London: Allen, 1980.

Kimball, Jean. "Family Romance and Hero Myth: A Psychoanalytic Context for the Paternity Theme in *Ulysses*." *James Joyce Quarterly* 20 (1983): 161–73.

Lawrence, Karen. *The Odyssey of Style in* Ulysses. Princeton: Princeton University Press, 1981.

Levin, Harry. *James Joyce: A Critical Introduction*. 2d ed. New York: New Directions, 1960.

Litz, A. Walton. *The Art of James Joyce: Method and Design in* Ulysses *and* Finnegans Wake. London: Oxford University Press, 1961.

————. *James Joyce*. New York: Twayne, 1966.

————. "The Genre of *Ulysses*." In *The Theory of the Novel; New Essays* edited by John Halperin. Oxford: Oxford University Press, 1974.

Maddox, James H. *Joyce's* Ulysses *and the Assault Upon Character*. New Brunswick, N.J.: Rutgers University Press, 1978.

Manganiello, Dominic. *Joyce's Politics*. London: Routledge, 1980.

MacCabe, Colin. *James Joyce and the Revolution of the Word*. London: Macmillan, 1978.

———, ed. *James Joyce: New Perspectives*. Bloomington: Indiana University Press, 1982.

McCormack, W. J. and Alistair Stead, eds. *James Joyce and Modern Literature*. London: Routledge, 1982.

Morse, J. Mitchell. *The Sympathetic Alien: James Joyce and Catholicism*. New York: New York University Press, 1959.

Moseley, Virginia D. *Joyce and the Bible*. DeKalb: Northern Illinois University Press, 1967.

Noon, William T., S. J. *Joyce and Aquinas*. New Haven: Yale University Press, 1957.

O'Brien, Darcy. *The Conscience of James Joyce*. Princeton: Princeton University Press, 1968.

O'Shea, Michael J. "Catholic Liturgy in Joyce's *Ulysses*." *James Joyce Quarterly* 21 (1984): 123–35.

Parr, Mary. *James Joyce: The Poetry of Conscience—A Study of* Ulysses. Milwaukee: Inland, 1961.

Parrinder, Patrick. *James Joyce*. Cambridge: Cambridge University Press, 1984.

Peake, Charles H. *James Joyce: The Citizen and the Artist*. Stanford: Stanford University Press, 1977.

Peterson, Rilchard F., Cohn, Alan M., and Epstein, Edmund L., eds. *Joyce Centenary Essays*. Carbondale: Southern Illinois University Press, 1983.

Prescott, Joseph. *Exploring James Joyce*. Carbondale: Southern Illinois University Press, 1964.

Pringle, Mary Beth. "Funfersum: Dialogue as Metafictional Technique in the 'Cyclops' Episode of *Ulysses*." *James Joyce Quarterly* 18 (1981): 397–416.

Rabaté, Jean-Michel. *James Joyce: Portrait de l'auteur en autre lecteur*. Petit-Roeulx: Cistre, 1984.

Rader, Ralph W. "Exodus and Return: Joyce's *Ulysses* and the Fiction of the Actual," *University of Toronto Quarterly* 48 (1978): 149–71.

Raleigh, John Henry. *The Chronicle of Leopold and Molly Bloom:* Ulysses *as Narrative*. Berkeley: University of California Press, 1977.

———. "Bloom as a Modern Epic Hero." *Critical Inquiry* 3 (1977): 583–98.

Reynolds, Mary T. *Joyce and Dante: The Shaping Imagination*. Princeton: Princeton University Press, 1981.

Rice, Thomas Jackson. *James Joyce: A Guide to Research*. New York: Garland, 1983.

Schlossman, Beryl. *Joyce's Catholic Comedy of Language*. Madison: University of Wisconsin Press, 1985.

Schutte, William M. *Joyce and Shakespeare: A Study in the Meaning of* Ulysses. New Haven: Yale University Press, 1957.

Scott, Bonnie Kime. *Joyce and Feminism*. Bloomington: Indiana University Press, 1984.

Seidel, Michael. *Epic Geography: James Joyce's* Ulysses. Princeton: Princeton University Press, 1976.

Senn, Fritz. *Joyce's Dislocutions: Essays on Reading as Translation.* Edited by John Riquelme. Baltimore: The Johns Hopkins University Press, 1984.

Shechner, Mark. *Joyce in Nighttown: A Psychoanalytic Inquiry into* Ulysses. Berkeley: University of California Press, 1974.

Spilka, Mark. "Leopold Bloom as Jewish Pickwick: A Neo-Dickensian Perspective." *Novel, A Forum in Fiction* 13 (1978): 121–45.

Staley, Thomas F., ed. *James Joyce Today: Essays on the Major Works.* Bloomington: Indiana University Press, 1966.

———, ed. Ulysses: *Fifty Years.* Bloomington: Indiana University Press, 1974.

———, and Bernard Benstock, eds. *Approaches to* Ulysses: *Ten Essays.* Pittsburgh: University of Pittsburgh Press, 1970.

Steinberg, Erwin Ray. *The Stream of Consciousness and Beyond in* Ulysses. Pittsburgh: University of Pittsburgh Press, 1973.

———. "Telemachus, Stephen, and the Paradigm of the Initiation Rite." *James Joyce Quarterly* 19 (1982): 289–301.

Steppe, Wolfhard, with Hans Walter Gabler. *A Handlist to James Joyce's* Ulysses: *A Complete Alphabetical Index to the Critical Reading Text.* New York: Garland, 1985.

Storey, Robert. "The Argument of *Ulysses,* Reconsidered." *Modern Language Quarterly* 40 (1979): 175–95.

Sullivan, Kevin. *Joyce among the Jesuits.* New York: Columbia University Press, 1958.

Thornton, Weldon. *Allusions in* Ulysses: *An Annotated List.* Chapel Hill: University of North Carolina Press, 1961.

Thomas, Brook. *James Joyce's* Ulysses: *A Book of Many Happy Returns.* Baton Rouge: Louisiana State University Press, 1982.

Tolomeo, Diane. "The Final Octagon of *Ulysses.*" *James Joyce Quarterly* 10 (1973): 439–54.

Tucker, Lindsey. *Stephen and Bloom at Life's Feast: Alimentary Symbolism and the Creative Process in James Joyce's* Ulysses. Columbus: Ohio State University Press, 1984.

Weinstein, Philip M. "New Haven, New Earth: Joyce and the Art of Reprojection." In *The Semantics of Desire; Changing Models of Identity from Dickens to Joyce.* Princeton: Princeton University Press, 1984.

Acknowledgments

"The Backgrounds of *Ulysses*" by Richard Ellmann from *James Joyce* by Richard Ellmann, © 1959, 1982 by Richard Ellmann. Reprinted by permission.

"Doing Things in Style: An Interpretation of 'The Oxen of the Sun' in James Joyce's *Ulysses*" by Wolfgang Iser from *The Implied Reader: Patterns of Communication in Prose Fiction from Bunyan to Beckett* by Wolfgang Iser, © 1974 by the Johns Hopkins University Press, Baltimore/London. Reprinted by permission of the Johns Hopkins University Press.

"Ithaca" by A. Walton Litz from *James Joyce's* Ulysses: *Critical Essays,* edited by Clive Hart and David Hayman, © 1974 by the Regents of the University of California. Reprinted by permission of the University of California Press.

"The Autonomous Monologue" by Dorrit Cohn from *Transparent Minds: Narrative Modes for Presenting Consciousness in Fiction* by Dorrit Cohn, © 1978 by Princeton University Press. Reprinted by permission of Princeton University Press.

"The Aesthetics of Delay" by Hugh Kenner from *Ulysses* by Hugh Kenner, © 1980 by George Allen & Unwin (Publishers) Ltd. Reprinted by permission.

"Fathers, Dead or Alive, in *Ulysses*" (originally entitled "A Clown's Inquest into Paternity: Fathers, Dead or Alive, in *Ulysses* and *Finnegan's Wake*") by Jean-Michel Rabaté from *The Fictional Father: Lacanian Readings of the Text,* edited by Robert Con Davis, © 1981 by the University of Massachusetts Press, Inc. Reprinted by permission.

"Righting *Ulysses*" by Fritz Senn from *James Joyce: New Perspectives,* edited by Colin MacCabe, © 1982 by the Harvester Press Ltd. Reprinted by permission of the Harvester Press Ltd., Wheatsheaf Books Ltd., and Indiana University Press.

"Bloom's Metaphors and the Language of Flowers" by Ramón Saldívar from *James Joyce Quarterly* 20, no. 4 (Summer 1983), © 1983 by the University of Tulsa. Reprinted by permission of the *James Joyce Quarterly,* University of Tulsa, Tulsa, Oklahoma.

"Nature and Culture in the 'Sirens' Episode of Joyce's *Ulysses*" by Cheryl Herr from *Essays in Literature* 11, no. 1 (Spring 1984), © 1984 by Western Illinois University. Reprinted by permission.

Index

Abraham (*Leah*), 92
Achilles, 11
Adams, Robert M., 54
Addison, Joseph, 35
"Aeolus" episode, 16, 102–3, 115–16;
    setting of, 17–18
Ajax, 11
Alf, 2
Allegory, 32–33, 52, 54; of the
    indeterminacy of meaning, 130; of the
    self-begotten Son, 131
Anastomosis, 128–30
"Anna Livia Plurabelle" (*Finnegans Wake*),
    55
Aristotle, 134
Art of James Joyce, The (Litz), 56
Athena, 89
Athos, 21
Atonement, 82–83, 94, 97. *See also*
    Fatherhood
Aunt Sara. *See* Goulding, Sara
Autonomous interior monologue. *See*
    Interior monologue

Babbitt (*Babbitt*), 12
Ball, Sir Robert, 70, 73
Ballast Office Clock, 69–70, 71, 72, 79
Balmer, 19
Barry, Mrs. Yelverton, 19
Barthes, Roland, 1, 49
Bellingham, Mrs., 19
Benveniste, Emile, 66
Bérard, Victor, 109
Bertha (*Exiles*), 9, 11
Best, Dr. Richard, 14
Betty, Lady, 18
Bible, The, 91, 92
Birth. *See* "Oxen of the Sun, The"
Blake, William, 15, 19, 20, 40, 43, 72
Bloom, Leopold, 16, 123–32; in "Aeolus,"
    102–3; anastomotic view of history of,

128–29; as archetypal figure, 26, 41, 55;
in "Calypso," 73; and the Clown, 83;
completeness of, 1, 3, 6; in "Cyclops"
episode, 2–3, 7–8, 10–11, 19; desire for
knowledge of, 11–12; equanimity of,
127–28, 129; as Everyman, 53–54, 55,
56; and father-son relationship with
Stephen, 84–88, 94, 97; and father's
name, 92–93; and flower metaphors,
12, 74–75, 124–25, 127; in "Hades"
episode, 100–101, 113; and Hamlet, 3,
5, 6, 50, 54; as Henry Flower, 75, 92,
94, 123, 139; as heroic figure, 52–53;
individuality of, 12, 27–28; interior
monologue of, 12–13, 14, 66;
Jewishness of, 1–4; kindness of, 22; and
Martha Clifford, 123–24; memories of,
74–76, 137; mental vs. physical
strength of, 10–11, 18–19, 22, 45; as
Messiah, 4, 6; and metempsychosis, 70,
71, 79, 104, 119, 126, 138; and Molly's
infidelity, 11, 44–45, 54–55, 136, 143;
naming of in "Sirens," 139–40, 141;
narrative progression and thoughts of,
101–2, 104–6; in "Nausicaa," 8, 10,
124–25; in "The Oxen of the Sun," 29,
30, 32, 35; and parallax, 48, 70–71, 72,
73–74, 78, 110; in "Penelope," 57, 61,
65, 67; and the potato, 76–77; quest of
unity of, 130–31; resourcefulness of,
50–51; and Richie Goulding, 86–87;
and "righting" things, 101–4, 108; and
Rudy, 4, 21, 84, 112, 124, 126; as
Sancho Panza, 1, 3, 4–5; and sexual
triangles, 94–95; and Simon Dedalus,
84, 86, 88; Stephen as substitute heir
to, 92–93, 125–27; and Stephen
compared, 3, 9–10, 18–19, 22; and
structure of *Ulysses*, 40; symbolic union
with Stephen of, 51–52, 53; thoughts of
about culture, 134–38, 142–43;
thoughts of about Molly, 138, 142–43;

Bloom, Leopold *(continued)*
    as Ulysses, 2, 9, 27, 54, 84, 117. *See also* "Circe" episode; Fatherhood; "Ithaca" episode
Bloom, Marian, 137
Bloom, Milly, 86, 124, 126
Bloom, Molly, 15–16, 53, 78; as archetype, 55; and Bloom, 102, 104, 124; Bloom's thoughts about, 74–75, 76, 137, 138, 142–43; and Boylan, 58, 64, 67; as emblem of plentitude and self-sufficiency, 125; and family love theme, 21; infidelity of, 11, 44–45, 54–55, 136, 143; in "Ithaca" episode, 46; and metempsychosis, 71, 79, 104, 126, 138; naming of in "Sirens," 140–41; questions of, 63–64; sequence of thoughts of in "Penelope," 58–60; and sexual polarization, 68; and sexual triangles, 94–95; and Stephen, 59, 65, 67, 86, 95; use of language by, 13, 97, 118; "yes" of, 82, 130. *See also* "Penelope"
Bloom, Rudolph, 93–94, 126
Bloom, Rudy, 4, 21, 84, 112, 124, 126
Bloomgatner, 140
Bloomers on the Liffey (Van Caspel), 112
Bloomsday, 1, 57, 61, 73, 94, 121, 123
Book as World; James Joyce's Ulysses (French), 137
Bowen, Zack, 141
Boylan, Blazes, 78, 94, 137, 140, 142; and Bloom, 11, 20, 22, 54, 136; Molly's thoughts of in "Penelope," 58, 64, 67
Broch, H., 31
Budgen, Frank, 2, 39, 45, 58, 117, 133
Bunyan, John, 32–33, 35
Burke, Pisser, 16
Byrne, J. F., 17

Caffrey, Cissey, 78
"Calypso," 73
Carlyle, Thomas, 34
Castration, 82, 90, 93–94, 96
Cato (*Purgatorio*), 52
Cervantes, Miguel de, 4, 5
Chamber Music, 53, 133
Characters: differences in style among, 13–14; models for, 14, 15–16, 18; and . myth, 9, 10–11, 27–28
Chronicle of Leopold and Molly Bloom: Ulysses as Narrative (Raleigh), 119
Circe, 10, 17
"Circe" episode, 14, 16–17, 55, 103–4, 116; Blake's influence on, 20; and Bloom on art, 134; Bloom's visions in, 21–22, 73–74, 93, 94, 103–4, 123; and family

love theme, 20–21; and father-son theme, 18, 84, 93, 94; and kindness to animals theme, 22; language in, 111; masochism in, 20; and repetition in *Ulysses,* 10, 73–74; setting of, 17; and Shakespeare, 5; tableaux in, 50, 51; *Venus im Pelz* influence on, 19–20
Citizen, the, 1, 2, 19, 22
Citron, 10
Clancy, George, 17
Classical Temper, The: A Study of James Joyce's Ulysses, (Goldberg), 28
Clifford, Martha, 78, 123–24, 126
Cloud imagery, 110, 113
Clown, the, 83
Cockshott, Mr. (*Finnegans Wake*), 93–94
Coffey, Father, 91
Cohen, Bella, 18, 20
Commedia (Dante), 5, 52
Conmee, Father, 13
Connolly, Connie, 16
Conroy, Gabriel ("The Dead"), 12
Consubstantiality, 83, 84, 85, 130–31; and names, 138–41
Conventionality, 135–39, 141, 142, 143
Convivio (Dante), 52
Cooper, Becky, 18
Cowley, Father, 135, 137, 139
Cranly, 69
Crawford, Fleury, 18
Crise de vers (Mallarmé), 123
Crissie, 86
"Croppy Boy, The," 133
Crusoe, Robinson, 40–41
Culture, 135, 136–37, 141
Cunningham, Martin, 71, 93, 102
Cunningham, Mr., 13
Cyclops, 10, 22
"Cyclops" episode, 16, 113; rejection of violence in, 2–3, 10–11, 19; narrator of, 7–8

Dante, 1, 3, 5, 9, 10, 11, 52
"Dead, The" (*Dubliners*), 9, 12, 50
Deconstruction, 1, 4
Dedalus, Maurice, 91
Dedalus, Simon, 16, 133–34; Bloom's reaction to singing of, 136, 137, 141–42; and father-son theme, 84, 85–86, 87–88; and Siopold, 138–39, 140
Dedalus, Stephen, 14, 17, 75, 112; anastomotic view of history of, 128–29; on art, 107; and Bloom compared, 3, 9–10, 18–19, 22; as a child, 75–76; and the Church, 90; as clown, 83; eloquence of, 13; on

fatherhood, 90, 96; and father-son relationship with Bloom, 84–88, 94, 97; as flower, 127; and Hamlet, 5–6, 9, 18–19, 50, 83; as heroic figure, 52–53; and his family, 21, 85–86, 95–96; and his mother, 21, 75–76, 82, 84–85; and incest, 85, 86, 89; mental vs. physical strength of, 18–19, 22; and Molly, 58–59, 65, 67, 86, 95; name of, 9, 90–91; in "The Oxen of the Sun," 32, 125–27; and parallax, 48, 69–70, 72–73, 110; in *A Portrait of the Artist*, 7, 8–9, 11, 102; quest for unity of, 130–31; and repetition of incidents in *A Portrait* and *Ulysses*, 9–10; on Shakespeare, 14–15, 18–19, 88–89, 95, 113; and Simon Dedalus, 84, 85–86, 87–88; and structure of *Ulysses*, 40; as substitute heir to Bloom, 92–93, 125–27; and symbolic union with Bloom, 51–52, 53; as Telemachus, 27, 83. *See also* "Circe" episode; Fatherhood; "Ithaca" episode

Deedpoll, 93–94
Defoe, Daniel, 40, 41, 43, 53
de Kock, Paul, 140
Demiurge, 4, 108
Derrida, Jacques, 1, 4
Devin, Tom, 16
Dichten und Erkennen (Broch), 31
Dickens, Charles, 33
Dignam, Paddy, 13–14, 22, 74, 91
Dillon, Atty, 75
Dillon, Floey, 74, 75, 78
Dillon, Mat, 74, 75, 76, 78
Dillon, Tiny, 75
Dlugacz, Moses, 73–74
d'Oblong (*Finnegans Wake*), 18
Dodd, Reuben J., 16
Dollard, Ben, 133, 137, 139, 141, 142
Don Giovanni, 109
Donizetti, Gaetano, 141
Don Quixote (Cervantes), 4
Douce, Lydia, 137, 138, 139, 140
Dranly (*A Portrait of the Artist*), 11
Dublin, 9, 10, 15, 29, 107, 112; and Bloom, 123; culture in, 134; and setting for "Circe" episode, 17–18; sexual customs in, 137; "street furniture" of, 69–70, 71; and violence of *Ulysses*, 45
Dubliners, 8. *See also specific stories*
Duff, Pisser, 16
Dujardin, Edouard-Emile-Louis, 61
Dynasts (Hardy), 48

Egan, Kevin, 84
Earwicker (*Finnegans Wake*), 6

Eden, 74, 75, 76
Eglinton, John, 88, 95
Eliot, T. S., 8, 25, 44, 53
Ellmann, Richard, 1–2, 5, 67
Elpenor, 54
Eneas (*Finnegans Wake*), 7
Esau, 91, 92
"Eumaeus," 8, 45, 103, 120
Evening Telegraph, 17
Exiles, 8, 9, 11

Falstaff, 1, 3, 88
Fanning, Long John, 113
Farrell, "Endymion," 15
Fatherhood, 81–97, 131; and atonement, 82–83, 94, 97; and the clown, 83; and creation, 88–89, 94; and flower images, 125, 127; as a function, 82; and *Hamlet*, 5–6, 18–19, 83, 90; and language, 89–90; and law, 82, 86, 87; meaning of, 81–82; and Name, 82, 90–94; and Oedipal complex, 85–87; and physical resemblance, 84, 91, 96; and physical shame, 96; and power of mother, 84–86, 88, 89; and real vs. symbolic father, 84, 87; uncertainty of, 86, 87–88, 89. *See also* Bloom, Leopold; Castration; Consubstantiality; Dedalus, Simon; Dedalus, Stephen; Incest
Faust Walpurgisnacht (Goethe), 76
Figatner, Aaron, 139
Figbloom, 140
"Final Octagon of Ulysses, The" (Tolomes), 58
Finnegans Wake, 4, 6, 7, 14, 15; artist's voice in, 90; deedpoll in, 93–94; Dublin as d'Oblong in, 18; fatherhood theme in, 82, 83, 97; influence of Blake on, 20; and incest, 86, 95; and Jacob and Esau, 91–92; language in, 107, 113, 121, 133; and metaphor, 132; as a rewriting, 108; as self-righting literary work, 107–8; urination as creativity in, 53
Flaubert, Gustave, 3
Flower, Henry, 75, 92, 94, 123, 139. *See also* Bloom, Leopold
Flower images, 12, 74–75, 123–25, 127
For a New Novel: Essays on Fiction (Robbe-Grillet), 48–49
Fraulein Else (Schnitzler), 61
French, Marilyn, 137
Freud, Sigmund, 4, 6, 8, 82, 95
"Frontiers of Criticism, The" (Eliot), 44

Gae-Tellus, 55, 97
Gamble, Major, 113

Gardiner, Alan, 62
Garryowen, 16, 22
Gertrude (*Hamlet*), 5
Gifford, Don, 87, 115
Gilbert, Stuart, 10, 31
Giltrap, Grandpa, 16
Gnosticism, 4
Goethe, Johann Wolfgang von, 76
Gogarty, Oliver, 17, 112
Goldberg, S. L., 28, 29, 31, 37
Goldman, Arnold, 39, 48
Goulding, Richie, 85, 86–87, 135, 136, 142
Goulding, Sara, 85, 86
"Grace" (*Dubliners*), 9
Graves, Robert, 46
Great Expectations (Dickens), 78
Groden, Michael, 107
Gunn, Michael, 137

"Hades" episode, 46, 110; language in, 100–101; and metaphors of death, 101, 113
Haines, 83
Hamlet (*Hamlet*), 6, 90; Bloom as, 3, 50, 54; Stephen as, 9, 18–19, 50
Hamlet (Shakespeare), 5–6, 83, 109
"Hamlet" (Eliot), 25
Hand, Robert (*Exiles*), 9, 11
Hardy, Thomas, 48
Hart, Michael, 16
Hathaway, Anne, 5, 14
Hayes, Mrs., 18
Historical and Miscellaneous Questions (Mangnall), 46–47
Homer, 3, 45, 116; division of works of, 119; physical vs. mental abilities of heroes of, 11. *See also* Myth; *Odyssey, The*; Ulysses
Horatio (*Hamlet*), 3
Horne, Dr., 30, 32
Howth Head, 66
Humphrey, Robert, 66
Huxley, Aldous, 12

Icarus, 9, 91
Incest, 82, 85, 88, 96; and "knowing," 86–87, 89; and language, 89–90; and sexual triangles, 94–95
Inferno (Dante), 5, 11, 52
Ingarden, Roman, 37
Interior monologue, 8, 39, 57–68, 106; avoidance of narrative in, 64–66; combined with narration, 39, 106; exclamatory syntax in, 63–64; lack of exposition in, 60–61; linguistic texture of, 61–68; physical activities during,

61, 64; tenses and moods in, 65–66; time dimension in, 58–60; use of pronouns in, 66–68. *See also* Language; Style
In the Track of the Sun, 115
Isaac, 92
"Ithaca" episode, 22–23, 39–56; and Bloom's response to Molly's infidelity, 54–55, 136; catechistical form of, 45, 46–50; and the clown, 83; as comedy, 53; details in, 41–43, 116; as ending and beginning, 55; exodus image in, 51–53; and father-son theme, 127; form as substance in, 40; movement from microcosm to macrocosm in, 50; myth and fact in, 45; vs. nouveau roman, 48–49; parlor scene in, 53–54; recapitulations in, 10, 76, 103, 110; relationship between objects and personality in, 49–50; as satire, 44; street scene in, 50–51; stylistic extremes of, 39; symbolism vs. realism in, 39, 43–44, 54–55; urination scene in, 53, 117–20; water in, 41–43

Jacob, 91, 92
James, Henry, 8, 44
James Joyce: A Critical Introduction (Levin), 27
James Joyce and the Making of "Ulysses" (Budgen), 133
J.J., 93
Joyce, James: and accomplishment of *Ulysses,* 56; and affirmation of human spirit, 23; anastomosis in writings of, 128–30; Bloom as image of, 2–3; on Defoe and Blake, 40, 43; development of interior monologue by, 8–9; and different versions of events, 72–73; and fatherhood theme, 82, 84, 90; and identification of micturition with creativity, 43, 53; influence on French literature of, 4; influences on 1, 4–5, 8, 19–20; on "Ithaca," 39, 40, 58, 117; interpretations of works of as rewriting, 108; on limits of style, 30; and metaphor, 123, 124, 130–32; as mimic vs. creator, 14; and music, 133–34, 141, 143; obsessiveness of, 43–44, 107; and *The Odyssey* as model for *Ulysses,* 9, 10–11, 12, 26, 27; and ordinary life as myth, 55; on "Penelope," 40, 56, 58, 59, 60; preparation of to write *Ulysses,* 7, 10; and relationship between objects and personality, 49–50; revisions of *Ulysses* by, 40, 100, 107; and Shakespeare, 5–6,

14–15; and sources for *Ulysses* in Dublin life, 15; and structure of *Ulysses,* 40, 107; and style of "The Oxen of the Sun," 34–38; and technique of delayed recognition, 115; tenderness of, 21–22; and uniqueness of individual, 12; and writing of "Ithaca" episode, 45–48
Joyce, Stanislaus, 28
Joyce Paradox, The (Goldman), 39
Jung, Carl, 82

Kearney, Kathleen, 15
Kearns, Anne, 112
Kennedy, Miss, 141
Kennedy, Olive, 15
Kenner, Hugh, 1
King Lear (Shakespeare), 14
Kreuder, Ernst, 27

Lacan, Jacques, 1, 4, 89, 90, 97; on fiction and the Unconscious, 81, 82
Landor, Walter Savage, 33
Language: and fatherhood, 89–90; relationship of to object, 31; and significance of letter Y, 118–19, 120; universal, search for, 130–32; and use of Greek works, 110; use of in "Ithaca" urination scene, 118–19. *See also* Interior monologue; Style
Larbaud, Valery, 45
Laredo, Lunita, 78
Launcelot, 86
Lawless, Mrs., 18
Leah, 92
Lenehan, 12, 16, 87–88, 137
Les Lauriers (Dujardin), 61, 64
Letter to Can Grande (Dante), 52
Levin, Harry, 27
Lewis, Sinclair, 12
Library episode, 18, 54
Lidwell, George, 137, 139
Linati scheme, 83, 87
Litany of the Daughters of Erin, 77
"Literary Work of Art, The" (Ingarden), 37
Livia, Anna (*Finnegans Wake*), 115
Loré, Prosper, 140
"Lotus Eaters" episode, 123
Love, 2; and limitations of style, 34, 35, 36, 37; and music, 136, 142–43; and parody of literary styles, 29, 31, 32, 33, 34
Lowes, J. Livingston, 44
Lucifer, 9
Lynch (*A Portrait of the Artist*), 9, 47, 72

MacCabe, Florence, 112
MacDowell, Gerty, 10, 16, 78, 124–25
MacHugh, Professor, 116
Mack, Mrs., 18
Magee, 88
Maginni, Professor, 15
Mallarmé, Stéphane, 123
Malory, Sir Thomas, 32, 35
Mangnall, Richmal, 46–47
Mastiansky, 10
Menton, John Henry, 74, 102
Merchant of Venice, The (Shakespeare), 86
Messiah, 4, 6, 93
Metaphor: and bird images, 138–39, 141–42; and cloud images, 110, 113; and flower images, 74–75, 123–25, 127; need for, 131–32; and potato image, 76–77; and search for universal language, 130–31
Metaphorical parallax. *See* Parallax
Metempsychosis, 104, 119, 126, 138; and parallax, 70, 71, 79
M'Guinnes, Mrs, 15
Milly, 86, 124, 126
Mina, 139
M'Intosh, 102
Molly. *See* Bloom, Molly
"Monto," 17
Moonstone, The, 78
Moore, George, 8
Mount Jerome, 113
Mulligan, Buck, 16–17, 110, 112, 113, 115; and Bloom, 88; on *Hamlet,* 5, 83; and Stephen, 22
Mulvey, 66, 67
Murray, Aunt Josephine, 16
Murry, John Middleton, 34
Music, 133–43; and bird metaphor, 138–39, 141–42; conventionality of, 135–39, 142; effects of, 138–39, 141, 143; Joyce's reverence for, 133–34; and love, 136, 142–43; as a mode of knowledge, 134–35, 143; and sex, 131, 135, 137. *See also* "Sirens" episode
Musical Allusions in the Works of James Joyce: Early Poetry Through "Ulysses" (Bowen), 141
Myth, 54; and *The Odyssey* as model for *Ulysses,* 10–12, 25–28, 119; and fact, 9, 39, 45; and Judeo-Christian imagery in *Ulysses,* 51–53; ordinary life as, 55

Nagle, Joseph, 14
Names: and consubstantiality, 138–41; and fatherhood, 82, 90–94. *See also individual characters*
Nathan (*Leah*), 92

"Nausicaa," 8, 10, 46, 124–25
"Nestor," 46, 51
Newman, John Henry, 34
Nietzsche, Friedrich, 131
"Nighttown," 17, 78, 96
"Nostos," 40, 120
Notes for Joyce: An Annotation of James Joyce's Ulysses (Gifford and Seidman), 87, 112, 115

Oblong, May, 18
Odysseus. *See* Ulysses
Odyssey, The (Homer), 22, 89, 108, 109; as model for *Ulysses*, 10–12, 25–28, 119. *See also* Homer; Ulysses
Oedipal complex, 85–87, 89–90, 95
Oedipus Rex (Sophocles), 78
"On Truth and Falsehood in Their Extra-Moral Sense" (Nietzsche), 131
O'Rourke, Larry, 13, 103
"Oxen of the Sun, The," 14, 25–38; codified introduction of, 29–30, 31; description of maternity hospital in, 30–31, 32–33; and father-son theme, 125–26; function of style in, 28–29, 34–38; grammar and syntax in, 35; imitation of styles in, 31–34, 35–36, 110–11; as Joyce's commentary on *Ulysses*, 37; and role of myth in *Ulysses*, 25–28; and sin, 37–38

Parallax, 48, 112; and the Ballast Office clock, 69–71, 72; and the cloud, 72–73, 110; and metempsychosis, 79; and repetition of incidents, 73–74, 78
Pater, Walter, 133
Penelope, 11, 44, 119
"Penelope," 45, 57–68; activity in, 61, 64; avoidance of narrative in, 64–66; and cyclic renewal, 56; exclamatory syntax in, 63–64; lack of exposition in, 60–61; lack of punctuation in, 59–60, 111; linguistic texture of, 61–68; missing facts supplied in, 76; Molly's "yes" in, 82, 130; sentence structure in, 62; and structure of *Ulysses*, 10, 40, 57–58, 82; tenses and moods in, 65–66; time dimension in, 58–60; use of pronouns in, 66–68. *See also* Bloom, Molly
Pepys, Samuel, 33
Portrait of the Artist, A, 72, 99, 102; character development in, 8, 9; and catechistical form, 46, 47; conclusion of, 26, 36, 44; interpretation of, 108; and mythic universal language, 130–31; and narrowmindedness, 18; sources of,

15; and Stephen's relationship to family, 88, 95–96; style of, 7, 8–9, 39; and *Ulysses*, 10, 116
"Post-structural Joyce," 1, 4
Potato image, 76–77
Pound, Ezra, 11–12, 29
"Problem of Style, The" (Murray), 34
Problems in General Linguistics (Benveniste), 66
Procreation. *See* "Oxen of the Sun, The"
"Proteus," 110
Proust, Marcel, 6
Psychoanalysis, 81, 88–89
Purefoy, Dr. R. Damon, 14
Purefoy, Mrs., 14, 29
Purgatorio (Dante), 52
Pythagoras, 119

Quinn, John, 40
Quixote, Don, 4

Raleigh, John Henry, 119
Rank, Otto, 82
Rebekah, 92
Richard III (Shakespeare), 14
Ricketts, Kitty, 18
Road to Xanadu (Lowe), 44
Robbe-Grillet, Alain, 48–49
Roberts, Mrs., 18
Rosenbach Manuscript, 100
Rosenbloom, 12
Rowan, Richard (*Exiles*), 9, 11
Ruby, Pride of the Ring, 79
Rudy, 4, 21, 84, 112, 124, 126
Ruggiero, Paul, 133
Ruskin, John, 34
Russell, Mr. Geo ("AE"), 71–72, 73

Sacher-Masoch, Leopold von, 9, 19, 20
Sacred Fount, The (James), 44
Santayana, George, 532
Sargent, Cyril, 91
Schnitzler, Arthur, 61
Schutte, W. M., 5
"Scylla and Charybdis," 40
"Sechseläuten," 115
Seidman, Robert J., 87, 115
Severin (*Venus im Pelz*), 19–20
Sex, 86, 94; conventionality of, 137; and music, 131, 135, 137
Shakespeare, William, 54, 91, 109, 113; language of characters of, 13; influence on Joyce of, 1, 5–6; Stephen as, 9; and life and art, 14–15, 18–19, 88, 90

Shelley, Percy Bysshe, 1
Shem the Penman (*Finnegans Wake*), 15, 90
Sinbad the Sailor, 55
Siopold, 138–39, 140
"Sirens" episode, 40, 87, 112, 116, 133–43;
    musical techniques of, 39, 106, 111,
    143; naming in, 139–41; and power of
    music, 133–34, 138–39; and power of
    the conventional, 135–39, 141–43; use
    of word "move" in, 134, 136, 138. *See
    also* Music
"Sisters, The" (*Dubliners*), 108, 119
Stephen Hero, 69
Stephen. *See* Dedalus, Stephen
Sterne, Laurence, 53
Stevens, Wallace, 12
Storm, The (Defoe), 41
Story of the Heavens, The (Ball), 70
Stream of Consciousness in the Modern Novel
    (Humphrey), 66
Structure and Motif in Finnegans Wake, 53
Style: and accumulation of details in
    "Ithaca," 41–43; and ambiguous
    language, 113; as "anti-style," 8; and
    apparent redundancy, 100–101; of
    Bloom chapters, 99–100; and
    catechistical form of "Ithaca," 45,
    46–50; changes in, 39–40, 99–100, 101,
    116; and combination of monologue
    and narration, 39, 106; and deceptive
    identity of appearance, 101; differences
    in among characters, 13–14; and
    differentiation among thought,
    language and action, 99, 105–6, 111,
    112, 117; function of, 28–34, 37; and
    grammar and syntax, 35; and ideology,
    33; and imitation in "The Oxen of the
    Sun," 31–36; limitations of, 30, 34–38;
    and musical techniques of "Sirens," 39,
    106, 111, 143; and narrative
    progression, 104–6; and realism vs.
    symbolism in "Ithaca," 39, 43–44,
    53–55; and rerighting, 111; as shaped
    by historical factors, 36–37; and
    undependable narrator device, 7–8; and
    verb conjugations, 120–21. *See also*
    Interior monologue; "Ithaca" episode;
    Language; "Penelope"; "Sirens"
    episode
*Surface and Symbol: The Consistency of James
    Joyce's* Ulysses (Adams), 54
Swan, Brother, 13

Talbot, Florry, 18
Talboys, Mrs. Mervyn, 19
Telemachiad, 110
Telemachus, 27, 83, 89, 91, 116

"Telemachus," 73
Tennyson, Alfred Lord, 3
Theory of Speech and Language, The
    (Gardiner), 62
Thomas, St., 89, 96
Thoth, 94, 130
Three Essays on the Theory of Sexuality
    (Freud), 4
Tindall, W. Y., 53
Tolomes, Diane, 58
Tolstoy, Leo, 8
"Tradition and the Individual Talent"
    (Eliot), 53
Trojan Horse, 10
"Two Gallants" (*Dubliners*), 16

Ulysses, 2, 3, 54, 83, 93; as archetype for
    humanity, 26; and Bloom's
    individuality, 12, 27–28; as Dubliner, 9;
    and Penelope, 119; and the suitors, 11,
    44–45, 117; as symbolic father, 84. *See
    also* Odyssey, The
Ulysses (*Inferno*), 10, 11
Ulysses: active interpretation of, 108–9,
    113–14; blurred margin in, 16–17;
    coincidences in, 76; corrections in, 104;
    Dublin as setting of, 17–18, 69–70, 71;
    as epic and irony, 27, 44–45; errors in,
    109; family love theme in, 21–22; and
    illusion, 141; and Joyce's influence on
    French literature, 4; lack of physical
    violence in, 11; literary allusions in,
    25–28, 31–34; misreadings of, 112, 113,
    115; models for characters in, 14,
    15–16, 18; and novel form, 39, 44,
    48–49, 56, 101; and quest for unity,
    130–31; revisions of, 40, 100, 107;
    scheme of value of, 22–23; source of
    title of, 9; theme of everyday human
    life in, 37, 55; time in, 59, 60, 114–15;
    translations of, 101, 102, 112–13;
    unanswered questions in, 78;
    verisimilitude in, 14; women in, 32.
    See also Fatherhood; Interior
    monologue; Language; Metaphor;
    Music; Myth; Odyssey, The, Parallax;
    Structure; Style *and specific characters and
    episodes*
Ulysses in Progress (Groden), 107
Ulysses on the Liffey (Ellman), 67
"Ulysses, Order and Myth" (Eliot), 25
Ulysses, structure of: and aesthetic of delay,
    69–79, 115–16; as anastomotic, 129–30;
    and body and time as frameworks, 10;
    and different versions of events, 72–73;
    in individual chapters, 30; and Joyce's
    Schema, 107; and narrative

Ulysses, structure of *(continued)*
  progression, 104–6; and order of
  presentation, 77–78, 110; and placement
  of "Ithaca" and "Penelope," 40, 55,
  57–58; and repetition, 9–10, 73–74,
  103; and style changes, 39–40, 99–100,
  116. *See also* Parallax; Style: *Ulysses*
Unanswerable (Krendler), 27
Uncle Richie. *See* Goulding, Richie
Università Popolare of Trieste, 40

Van Caspel, Paul P. J., 112
Venus and Adonis (Shakespeare), 14
Venus im Pelz (Sacher-Masoch), 19
Virag, Leopold, 94
Virag, Rudolph. *See* Bloom, Rudolph
Virgil (*Commedia*), 5, 52

Walter, 85
Wanda (*Venus im Pelz*), 19–20
"Wandering Rocks" eposide, 13, 29, 40,
  112
Waste Land, The (Eliot), 55
Weaver, Miss Harriet, 10, 143
Wedding of the Trees, 75
"Welt-Alltag," 25, 28
Whitman, Walt, 43
Word, the, 128, 130, 131
Wordsworth, 1, 48
Wyse, John, 2

Yahweh, 4
Yeats, William Butler, 43